As BRITISH as the KING

As BRITISH as the KING

Lunenburg County *During the* First World War

GERALD HALLOWELL

NIMBUS
PUBLISHING
— NIMBUS.CA —

Nimbus Publishing Limited
3660 Strawberry Hill Street, Halifax, NS, B3K 5A9
(902) 455-4286 nimbus.ca

Printed and bound in Canada

NB1422

Cover artwork: *Victims of the German U-boat*, by Jay Langford.
Design: John van der Woude, JVDW Designs
Editor: Paula Sarson

Library and Archives Canada Cataloguing in Publication

Title: As British as the king : Lunenburg County during the First World War
    / Gerald Hallowell.
Names: Hallowell, Gerald, author.
Description: Includes bibliographical references and index.
Identifiers: Canadiana (print) 20190143053 | Canadiana (ebook)
    20190143088 | ISBN 9781771087728
    (softcover) | ISBN 9781771087742 (HTML)
Subjects: LCSH: World War, 1914-1918—Nova Scotia—Lunenburg (County)
Classification: LCC FC2345.L86 H35 2019 | DDC 971.6/23—dc23

Canada

Nimbus Publishing acknowledges the financial support for its publishing
activities from the Government of Canada, the Canada Council for the Arts,
and from the Province of Nova Scotia. We are pleased to work in partnership
with the Province of Nova Scotia to develop and promote our creative
industries for the benefit of all Nova Scotians.

CONTENTS

The journey to Nova Scotia had been a long one. Having made their way to Rotterdam, they crossed the turbulent North Atlantic on weeks'-long voyages crowded in small vessels with names like Ann, Betty, Pearl, *and* Speedwell. *Although there were Swiss and French among them, they had come mainly from various German states that would eventually join together, a hundred years later, to form a united Germany. They waited impatiently for several months in Halifax, but finally boats brought them to a large, tree-lined bay with a splendid harbour at a place then called Merligueche.*

The 1,453 newcomers who came ashore at Rous's Brook that June day in 1753—the founders of Lunenburg—would become known as the "foreign Protestants." The town and the county they eventually inhabited were named by the British after the royal house of Braunschweig-Lunëburg. In the early days, some fortifications were necessary because of the presence of the Mi'kmaw inhabitants. The British had conquered what became mainland Nova Scotia from the French in 1710, had established the capital at Halifax in 1749, and fortified it to counter the influence of the formidable French fortress of Louisbourg on Île Royale, now Cape Breton Island. They were concerned about the loyalty of the large French and Catholic Acadian population scattered about the colony, and so they looked for solid Protestant stock in central Europe. Any threats from the French were removed when, in 1755, some ten thousand Acadians were deported from Nova Scotia in the infamous grand dérangement.

Colonel Charles Lawrence, a military man, liked order, and he complained that the new arrivals under his supervision were "inconceivably turbulent, I might have said mutinous, and are only to be managed like a great ship, in a violent storm, with infinite care, vigilance & attention." He felt they needed a tight hand to begin with, and he would continue to complain of "ye Sloth of these Germans, & their unwillingness to do any part of what they call ye King's work." They expected to be paid for their labour in public works, he grumbled, and they even ran off with boards needed for building the blockhouses for their own protection.

Although by far the largest proportion of the newcomers gave their occupation as farmers, they took to the sea, and within a couple of generations they had become successful sailors, shipbuilders, and especially fishermen. Indeed, in time Lunenburg would become the major deep-sea fishing port on Canada's east coast.

Over the generations, the Germans of Lunenburg County retained pride in their roots, though naturally they adapted to the Anglo-Saxon world around them. To some they came to be known as "Dutchmen," mainly because of the English mispronunciation of the word "Deutsch." For many years they worshipped in German, mainly in the Lutheran church. They maintained and developed their own special foods, notably Lunenburg pudding and sausage, house bankin (a mixture of dry cod, potatoes, and salt pork, also sometimes known as Dutch Mess), and sauerkraut: "Put the cabbage in the bar'l, / Stamp it with your feet, / When the juice begins to rise, / The kraut is fit to eat." When the Ladies Auxiliary of Fishermen's Memorial Hospital put out what became a very successful cookbook in 1953, they called it Dutch Oven, *a "Cook Book of coveted traditional recipes from the kitchens of Lunenburg."*

But most notably, over the years, as the descendants of the German settlers became anglicized, they used their native language less and less, though in speaking English certain German expressions and syntax were retained and a distinct accent developed. Surnames, too, were transformed as time passed. Some of them, uniquely Lunenburg County names like Wentzell, Berringer, Hebb, Bachman, Spindler, Beck, and Zwicker, remained the same. Others were anglicized: Schmidt, for instance, became Smith; Born became Burns; Reichert became Richard; Koch became Cook; Kraus became Crouse. The spelling Whynacht is still widely used, but so is Whynot. Some spellings changed over time and appear less German: Gertzen became Getson, for example; Speidel became Spidle; Schauffelberger became Schaffelburg; Rehfuß became Rafuse. The surname Knickel became Knickle, with the initial K pronounced hard to this day.

It's difficult to know just how "German" Lunenburg remained in the early twentieth century. Some of the people were no doubt closer to their roots than others. An item in the Progress-Enterprise *of Lunenburg in 1908 told of an elderly German couple, Jacob Zinck and his wife, aged ninety-five and ninety-three respectively, who had lived together happily for sixty-two years. Mrs. Zinck still attended to her domestic duties "with a degree of activity and preciseness worthy of emulation by many of the younger generation." The couple conversed together in German; Mrs. Zinck in fact was unable to speak English. They had been confirmed and married by Reverend Father Cossmann and were blessed with a family of five children. Devout adherents of the Lutheran church, rain or shine on the Sabbath day this venerable couple could be seen "wending their way to the House of Prayer, a worthy example of true piety and faith, and shining examples too of the good old German stock, which has brought so much lustre and renown to this fair county of Lunenburg."**

One hundred and sixty-one years after their ancestors arrived on Nova Scotia's South Shore, the descendants of the Germans who founded Lunenburg County would find themselves at war with Germany.

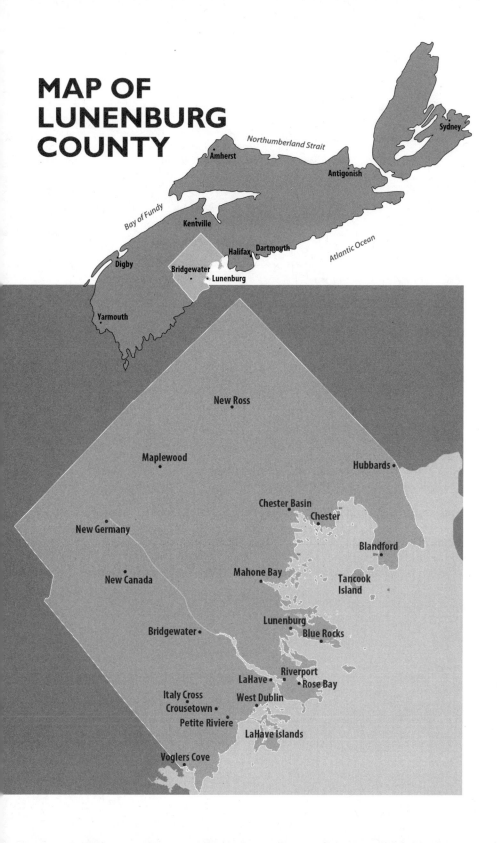

MAP OF
LUNENBURG
COUNTY

Northumberland Strait

Amherst

Antigonish

Sydney

Bay of Fundy

Kentville

Halifax Dartmouth

Atlantic Ocean

Digby

Bridgewater

Lunenburg

Yarmouth

New Ross

Maplewood

Hubbards

Chester Basin

Chester

New Germany

Blandford

New Canada

Mahone Bay

Tancook
Island

Lunenburg

Bridgewater

Blue Rocks

Riverport

LaHave

Rose Bay

Italy Cross

West Dublin

Crousetown

Petite Riviere

LaHave Islands

Voglers Cove

LUNENBURG SONG

I've come from German Lunenburg
    Where they live on herring and cod,
Where the Rudolphs speak with the
Zwickers
    But the Zwickers speak only with
God.

Where the Kaulbacks ape the English,
    And the Smits aspire for place,
Where the Shupes ignore the Arenburgs,
    Tho' they're all from the German
race.

Where the Hirtles and the Morashes
    Change churches with the moon,
And the newly rich in sealskin sacks,
    Parade the streets at noon.

What's bred to the bone, will show in
the flesh,
    They're German and proudly they
show it.
They're proud of their town, proud of
their race,
    And they want the world to know it.

They'll smile in your face, and stab you
in the back,
    They're alike be they Rudolphs or
Zwickers,
Their God is the cod, their religion
themselves,
    And at everything modern they're
kickers.

Schaffelburg and Arenburg,
    Rudolph, Feener, Kaizer,
      Falkenham, Slaughenwhite,
      Fink, and Zinck, and Schmeizer,
Himmelman and Eisenhauer,
    Garhardt, Zwicker, Herman,
    Rodenhizer, Spindler,
    All proud because they're German.

By a Lunenburger not of
German descent…†

Chapter One

"THE GREAT BROIL ACROSS THE SEA"

"The Peace of the World Disturbed," proclaimed the headline in the *Progress-Enterprise* of Lunenburg on August 5, 1914. According to the editorial, Germany was massing men to strike at neutral countries. The *Niobe*, one of the ships of the newly created Naval Service of Canada, was being prepared for active service, and Halifax had "its war face on." Reports were conflicting; it was next to impossible to learn the true state of affairs. If the headline was an understatement, the editor's final comment was perceptive: "Fears for a long European war are very great and the consequence will be so disastrous to the world at large that it will pass all human understanding."

When Gavrilo Princip assassinated Archduke Franz Ferdinand, heir to the Austrian throne, and his wife in the faraway Bosnian city of Sarajevo on June 28, 1914, most Nova Scotians likely paid little attention. Within weeks, however, Europe had descended into madness. The Great Powers—Austria-Hungary and Germany, Russia, and France—were at war. As Sir Edward Grey, Britain's foreign secretary, famously remarked, "The lamps are going out all over Europe; we shall not see them lit again in our lifetime." Closer to home, Halifax's *Morning Chronicle* on August 3 concluded, "The German Emperor has made war....In the shadow of these fateful happenings and tragic possibilities, all is doubt and uncertainty. But all the omens spell War on a mighty scale." Bound to honour a long-standing treaty to protect Belgian neutrality, Britain declared war on Germany on August 4. Canada, as a member of the British Empire, was at war.

A week later, on August 11, the town of Lunenburg, greatly excited, was said to be "filled with the military spirit that seems to be almost in the air." People thronged the street in front of Kinley's drugstore, where the latest bulletins were displayed. That evening a crowd enthusiastically applauded the band of the 75th Lunenburg Regiment, which performed patriotic airs on the bandstand, opening with "Rule Britannia." When the old favourite "Soldiers of the King" was played, the clapping began even before the last bar had closed.

The next day, August 12, the *Progress-Enterprise* observed there was no doubt that war was on in earnest:

> *You can see it in your neighbor's face. You can gather it from the tense, drawn appearance of small groups on the streets. Every corner has its small contingent discussing the news with an animation that approaches hysteria. The uncertainty of it all just catches your breath....Here in Lunenburg we are thousands of miles from the actual zone of battle yet the atmosphere is charged as though a terrific conflict were being waged within eye distance....You wonder how long it is going to last and where you can get your food for the approaching winter. Out of your window you see team after team laden with flour slowly wending homewards. The cautious ones are preparing for a siege. The cowards who joined the militia to have a lark at Aldershot are quaking and trembling in their shoes. Occasionally one more knowing than his neighbors stoutly asserts it makes no difference to Canada, that we won't be affected. But the average man is placing his reliance and his trust in God and the*

British navy and calmly awaits the full development of the crisis.... Yes, war is on and we know and feel it.

A fairly typical reaction to the outbreak of the war, not just in Lunenburg but across the country, was expressed by G. E. Romkey of West Dublin, a small community in Lunenburg County on the west side of the LaHave River. Romkey was owner of a general store that specialized in buying and selling fish and lumber; later he would become the owner of the G. E. Romkey & Company fish plant in West Dublin. In his memoirs, published in the *Progress-Enterprise* in the mid-1970s, he wrote:

> *1914 will always be remembered as the start of the first Great War. No one seemed to take it seriously at first and somehow we expected the British Navy and the great French Army to clean up the German forces in a few weeks. We were very much shocked and disappointed when the Germans rushed through Belgium, and France not able to stop them. Canada began to wake up and start enlisting men and many who signed up expected the war would be all over before they were trained and would not see England. Events were to show how badly all were wrong and Canada had to pay the price that all our Allies shared.*[1]

On August 14, only ten days after Britain declared war, three young men from the town of Lunenburg volunteered to serve the Empire overseas. Two of them were natives of the town: Ned Coldwell, son of A. B. Coldwell, collector of customs, who was of English descent; and Charlie Cossmann, whose grandfather had come to the town as a Lutheran missionary in 1835. The third man was a Norwegian, Emil Olsen, who had lived in Lunenburg for almost ten years. These men enlisted at the military camp at Valcartier, near Quebec City, in September 1914, and after some training there in October they embarked on the ss *Ruthenia* bound for England.

As Lieutenant Colonel Charles A. Andrews of Mahone Bay insisted on August 20, just before the Maritime Express pulled out for

Valcartier with the first Nova Scotia volunteers on board: "If you want to find a staunch and solid son of the Empire, look down Lunenburg way. We know the value of British liberty. We are prepared to fight for it and that is the best test." The LaHave Chapter of the Imperial Order Daughters of the Empire (IODE), organized in Bridgewater that September, sent thirty "housewives" (portable sewing kits) to the Lunenburg contingent at Valcartier, and Colonel Andrews had sent a telegram saying they were deeply grateful for the kind gift.

The recruitment officer in Lunenburg was Lieutenant Colonel Titus A. Mulock of the 75th Regiment, called "the War Lord of Lunenburg County" by the *Progress-Enterprise* on September 9. Through him and his officers the connection of the county with the battlegrounds of the Empire would be honourably maintained. Already a noble little band had gone forward, observed the paper. Not all the men were connected with the militia, but they had gone nevertheless. The 75th used to play an important part at camp drill when there was only mimic warfare; now that the real thing had come, "surely there would be no shirking."

Sam Hughes, minister of defence in Sir Robert Borden's Conservative government at Ottawa, had set up the camp at Valcartier in August 1914, having scrapped all pre-war mobilization plans. Preferring citizen volunteers to professional soldiers, he encouraged militia from all over the country, including members of Lunenburg's 75th Regiment, to assemble there. Volunteers crowded in, many fearing they might not get overseas before the war was over. The *Bridgewater Bulletin*, the newspaper in Lunenburg County's largest town, on September 26, 1916, would have some kind words for "fighting Sir Sam," calling him "Canada's War Lord": his "wonderful success in enlistment will entitle him to the designation of 'the Kitchener of Canada.'" In his early sixties, the paper remarked, he had closely cropped white hair, but "the vigor of perfect manhood is manifest in every action…of striking appearance and personality he is every inch a soldier; especially is this noticeable on the occasion of a review, when he sits his charger like a centaur." Not everyone was so enthusiastic about Sir Sam, who was ultimately removed from his post in December 1916 because of his erratic behaviour.

The First Contingent of the Canadian Expeditionary Force (CEF), Canada's wartime army overseas, sailed from Quebec to Plymouth in October in a great armada of transport vessels, with more than thirty thousand men and about seven thousand horses. The majority of the men on board had been born in the United Kingdom.[2] After many miserable months in southern England, in the rain and mud on Salisbury Plain, the troops crossed to Belgium in February 1915. There, they would face their baptism of fire in the Second Battle of Ypres, in which the Germans first used poison gas against the Allied lines.

Shortly after the First Contingent left for England, the Canadian government authorized the recruiting of a second division. Unlike the gathering at Valcartier, this time the men were trained at various locations across the country. They sailed to England in the spring of 1915 and completed their training at Shorncliffe on the coast of Kent. In September they joined the First Division in France to form the Canadian Corps.

The 25th Battalion, Nova Scotia Rifles, in the Second Division, was the first of the battalions to be raised entirely in Nova Scotia during the war. Mobilized at Halifax in the final months of 1914 and housed in the armoury and in tents on the Common, the battalion sailed to Plymouth on the *Saxonia* in May 1915 and crossed the channel to Boulogne in September. The necessary thousand men had come forward readily, and among them were volunteers from Lunenburg County. The *Bulletin* reported in its Lunenburg column on November 17, 1914, that the new soldiers had been conveyed to the station, behind the 75th Regiment band, in automobiles draped with flags. On their arrival there, Mayor J. Frank Hall and Rev. F. C. Ward-Whate of St. John's Anglican Church addressed them. The "feminine portion of the assemblage wept unrestrainedly, realizing the horrors of war and the fear that harm might befall the bright faces which on that occasion were smiling so uncon-cernedly." As a young soldier put it in Frances Itani's novel *Tell*, "We went off to war like children who'd been blindfolded for the occasion."

Pressure to enlist continued in the following months and it came from all sides and in many forms. In the *Bridgewater Bulletin* of May

18, 1915, a poem appeared, written for the paper by "a Bridgewater young lady":

> Come, take a stand for your native land,
>   Come, with determined will;
> Join with a genial sturdy band,
>   And drill, my boys, and drill.
> O take a stand for your country now,
>   'Tis the time she needs you most,
> Although you work with pen or plough
>   Come, join the patriot host.

One of many patriotic evenings "in aid of the soldiers and sailors" had been held at the small community of Rose Bay in February 1915, according to the *Progress-Enterprise* on the seventeenth. The dramatic talent of nearby Riverport put on a farcical comedy in five acts called "Punkin Ridge." The Welsh singer Madame Lily Hambly-Hobbs, resident in Riverport at the time, sang the stirring war song "Land of Hope and Glory" in a way "to touch each British heart." Kenneth Creaser gave a splendid rendition of "King and Country" and everyone welcomed Hector MacGregor in "The Call of the Motherland." The "quiet unassuming postmaster" of Riverport, Daniel Myra, startled his fellow townsmen by his remarkable ability as a comedian. The concert was so successful that it played for three

Young recruits larking about.

evenings to crowded houses. Indeed, patriotic concerts took place all over the county, including one in March at the Foresters Hall in Petite Riviere featuring talent from Dublin Shore; the star piece of the evening, six-year-old Lois Bell's rendering of the verses of "Tipperary," assisted by the full chorus in the refrain, "literally brought the house down."

Even the advertisers of the day got caught up in the spirit of the times. The Hubley Company of Bridgewater, in the *Progress-Enterprise* on August 12, 1914, announced a "Great War on Prices" in a "Special White Wear Sale for Ladies": "These be war times, when prices need watching. Every opportunity to save a dollar is now more than ever necessary." "Don't Let the War Scare You," declared Bridgewater's P. G. Corbin store on September 9; because the Rayner International Fur Company owned their foxes, there would be no wartime shortage. "THE BATTLE of prices is still on," maintained H. S. Hall of Bridgewater the same day; they had "flour, feeds, hay, etc., and always coal." And the pharmacy in Lunenburg assured everyone: "*The War* will increase the cost of Drugs and Medicines, but KINLEY's Drug Stores are fully equipped with large stocks on hand, and prices will be kept down to the very lowest." "These Are Hard-War(e) Times," said the Bates-Freeman Hardware Company of Bridgewater. And William A. Banks, eyesight specialist, claimed that you would need good glasses to be able "to read the War News and keep posted....We are certainly lucky to have the British fleet to protect us, otherwise it would only be a question of time when we would be used like the Belgians have been used." Throughout the war there were ads and posters for various wartime fundraising purposes, but these commercial advertisements based on military themes generally

Progress-Enterprise, *Lunenburg, June 7, 1916.*

disappeared once it became apparent how awful the war was going to be.[3]

And so began what the Springfield columnist in the *Progress-Enterprise* of September 2, 1914, had referred to as "the great broil across the sea." Many men from Lunenburg County would perish in one of the deadliest conflicts in human history. Many others would return home wounded in body and spirit. Lives around the world would be changed forever.

"Our Soldiers Gone," lamented the *Bridgewater Bulletin* on May 18, 1915. The whole town had turned out to give "their soldier boys," members of the Bridgewater detachment of the 40th Battalion, a rousing send-off. The men had been drilling there for the past six weeks or so and had become familiar figures on the streets. The town was dull without them. On Sundays, they had attended as a body each church in turn. A tremendous crowd gathered at the station to see the detachment entrain for Halifax en route for the training camp at Aldershot, near Kentville. One special treat had been a ride in an automobile provided by some of the town's better-off citizens. The soldiers had gone to the theatre and afterwards had been served ice cream by the girls of the Baptist Sunday school. As they paraded to the station, mingled feelings of pride and sorrow took possession of the onlookers, "pride because of the courage of the lads and sorrow to think that such promising and physically fit young men should be exposed to the bullets of an unscrupulous enemy."

Lunenburg County, then, shared the national "jubilation," the sense of euphoria that swept the country in the early days of the war. And yet, there was also apparently a quiet resistance, a reluctance to participate fully in the war effort, or at least a hesitation to join the ranks. There was a suspicion, especially among the press, that some were not as loyal as they ought to be and that others were not doing their bit as they should.

The editor of the *Bulletin*, on August 11, 1914, maintained he had heard that certain persons about town had been indulging in pro-German talk, sympathizing with the Germans and against the British. He warned that such talk would not be tolerated, and, if persisted in, "summary steps would be taken to prevent a recurrence." On October 6, in its Lunenburg column, the *Bulletin* commented on strange rumours of treasonable remarks uttered by one of Lunenburg's fishing skippers. Unless he changed the tenor of his conversation, the customs officials could refuse to clear him, "as he has showered the most abusive remarks on the British flag, one which he would be the first to run up were danger to threaten him....A much needed lesson will be taught to this and other persons by those of the old town who are loyal to king and country." A "citizen" in Mahone Bay on October 28 was incensed because a man "though born in little Mahone" had the nerve to "fly the stars and stripes as well as the French flag without our Union Jack at the top of the pole."

On November 17, the *Bulletin* claimed to have heard that there were some school teachers in the county who were pronounced German sympathizers. Any teacher not thoroughly patriotic and not inculcating the principles of British patriotism and British loyalty in their students should be "weeded out of this British country." A disloyal teacher could do harm to the nation by sowing seeds of sedition in the rising generation. "German sympathizers must get it into their heads that the British Empire, of which we are a component part, is at war with Germany because Germany FORCED the war on us, by violating Belgian neutrality. We have the uttermost contempt for those who were born and live under the British flag and who air pro-German sentiments, slyly or otherwise."

A man who hid his identity by signing himself "John Bull" wrote to the editor of the *Progress-Enterprise* on November 20, noting that there were a great many "heroes in disguise" in Lunenburg; with their "martial bearing and apparent esprit de corps" they should be falling over one another to enlist. A number of officers, "regular bluchers on dress parade," were happy to remain in the back seats when it came time for active service. One of the officers was "a pronounced German, who rejoices in any misfortunes that overtake the old flag on land or sea"; the authorities "should empound him among other species of cattle that are running at large." Another veteran who was shooting the kaiser with his mouth, charged the correspondent, was Captain Owen G. Dauphinee of the 112th Battalion, a practical illustration of "afraid to go" (Dauphinee did in fact go, and was killed in action in France in August 1917). One of the teachers in town was "strong on German Kulture." John Bull's main point was that there were quite a number of young men who should enlist for the country's good, "but what can you expect from fellows who have no occupation except playing pool in the barber shops. In Yarmouth this class of men are named 'Feather Bed Brigade,' in Moncton 'Sidewalk Heroes,' and here in Lunenburg the 'Apron String Brigade' and they're fit only to play the mouth organ for the Red Cross Brigade."

The *Yarmouth Times* alleged that town did indeed have candidates for the "White Feather," traditionally handed out, usually by women, to men who were perceived to be cowards. "This hen extract is presented to young men who are in a position both from a physical and worldly standpoint to go and fight but who are so convinced that the foundation of the post office building is weakening, that they must remain at home and hold it up every night and bedeck the sidewalk with molasses flavouring." Lunenburg also had a few of these "featherbed heroes," complained the *Progress-Enterprise* on November 23. "Fair weather soldiers. They took all that was coming when there was no trouble in sight but now when the Empire needs their services they sulk in their tents."

On December 2, the *Progress-Enterprise* claimed to have heard that Colonel Sam Hughes was coming to the Maritimes on a tour of inspection. The newspaper hoped, for the sake of Lunenburg's good name, that he would keep away from this county, for then he would not see how little the officers of the 75th Regiment—"this gallant band of bedroom heroes"—were doing with the money spent on them. One reason the rank and file was slow to enlist was that the officers seemed "horribly reluctant to do anything." Only two of them had gone to the front. Others were lagging behind, and not even encouraging enlistment. Thousands of dollars had been poured upon these officers in transportation, training, schools, rifle ranges, military school camps, and other expenses. "Remember Kitchener wants men and more men. Don't permit the world to say that Lunenburg's militia belonged to the Feather Bed brigade."

The *Bulletin* on November 3, 1914, called for a home guard to protect the homeland against possible invasions from the neutral United States. The small community of Parks Creek (now East LaHave), near Riverport, was also concerned about security. A number of citizens unable to go to the front themselves thought they should train to handle a rifle in order to defend their own place, in case the need arose, for there was "no telling what might happen." The Lunenburg paper scoffed: "Why organize for home defence? Have we not sleeping soldiers in Lunenburg? What enemy dare disturb their slumbers! Remember the adage: 'Wake not a sleeping lion.'"

At least the war was not without a humorous side early on. The *Progress-Enterprise* on September 30, 1914, commented that when the Russians finally took the city of Przemyśl in Poland, the site of the longest siege in the war so far, they "should shoot a few vowels into its midst." Writer Lucy Maud Montgomery, in her journals on December 7, claimed that the war was at least extending her knowledge of geography. Among several new names to her was Przemyśl: "At the last mentioned the newspaper wits have been poking fun since the siege of it began. Nobody seems to know how it is pronounced. I daresay the Austrians would think that Saskatchewan and Musquodoboit were about as bad."

Apart from encouraging the recruitment of men to swell the ranks of the army, there was plenty to be done on the home front. With so many men going overseas, the people necessarily left behind wondered how they might best contribute to the war effort. One matter of great importance was the raising of money for all kinds of useful purposes.

If the soldiers in the trenches were willing to sacrifice so much, then surely the people at home must do all in their power to help. As the *Bridgewater Bulletin* put it on May 18, 1915, "the publication of the casualty list made its shadow of grief upon the land." Every man and every woman must do what they could to support the men at the front and take some personal share of the burden. They must do something "to really justify British citizenship."

One tangible contribution to the war effort was made on the very day that war was declared. Judge Samuel Ansley Chesley, grand master, Maritime provinces, sent a telegram to the militia department in Ottawa announcing that the "Oddfellows of Lunenburg County, largely of German descent," wished to present a machine gun to the CEF; sufficient funds had been guaranteed by the different lodges in the county. Would it be accepted? A cheque for $1,000 was eventually sent, to purchase a Lewis machine gun. A small silver plate with an inscription giving the names and numbers of the contributing lodges was sent to be attached to the gun. It was hoped that one of the lodge members, who held a commission in the militia and had been taking a machine gun course, could man the gun with a crew composed of Lunenburg County Oddfellows. They were told politely but firmly in September, by the minister of militia himself, Sam Hughes, that such a request would not be possible to meet.

The long-expected acknowledgement of the machine gun finally came to Judge Chesley in a letter dated July 20, 1916, from the commander of the 40th Reserve Battalion in Shorncliffe. He thanked the Oddfellows for their kindness and generosity: "So useful and valuable a gift will always be remembered as a sincere compliment to a Battalion of Nova Scotians, which has furnished most enthusiastic and valuable additions to the forces of Canada in the Field." As historians Desmond Morton and Glenn Wright note in *Winning the Second Battle*, the national mood early in the war was one of fervid patriotism, and the machine gun fund was popular. Schoolchildren, businessmen, and service clubs were caught up in the crusade to provide guns at a cost of $1,000 each. But the machine gun scheme was ended when the government decided more effort should be spent instead on wounded and returned soldiers.

Another early charity was the Canadian Women's Hospital Ship Fund. The women of Lunenburg County contributed to this cause, for instance, at a convention held in Lunenburg's Methodist church in September 1914. At a patriotic concert given by the women of Petite Riviere the same month, the combined choirs of the Anglican and Methodist churches rendered Kipling's "Recessional." Rev. J. S. Coffin's lecture on "The Union Jack" was "brimful of lessons and facts on justice, sincerity, democracy and loyalty which are so fully availed of by the people over whom the glorious flag of England waves." Rev. A. Lund spoke happily of his privilege of being a Britisher. The hospital ship fund was soon closed because the sum of $214,034.71 had been reached, over twice the amount originally called for. Forwarded to the British Admiralty through Her Royal Highness the Duchess of Connaught, wife of the Governor General of Canada, the money was used to help build the Canada Block at the Royal Naval Hospital at Haslar, near Portsmouth.

In late September 1914, various newspapers published an open letter "To the People of Nova Scotia" from Premier George Henry Murray. It was a plea to come to the aid of the Belgians, who were facing "appalling suffering and destruction, almost unparalleled in the history of warfare....Their lands have been laid waste, their towns sacked, their homes wrecked, their women and children outraged, their famous churches and cathedrals pillaged, their priceless art treasures destroyed—everywhere across the Belgian country is the invader's ruthless trail of ruin and blood." There was scarcely a home in the province, Murray suggested, that could not afford to give a bushel of vegetables, a sack of potatoes, or some articles of clothing. "Let our response be prompt, generous and worthy of Nova Scotia." On September 29, the *Bulletin* called for help for Belgium, "this most gallant of little countries, ground, because of sheer loyalty, under an iron heel...this most innocent of sufferers from God's Own Armageddon....The Belgians have won immortal glory....They have borne so much that anything we can do for them is too little."

Such sentiments in several countries led to the formation of one of the foremost international relief organizations of the First World War. The Belgians were in fact starving. Heavily urbanized, the country produced little food on its own; at seven million people, its population was only slightly less than Canada's. After the invasion, the Germans requisitioned much of what food there was to feed their army. Additionally, the British had set up an economic blockade, fearing the Germans would take anything that was sent in. The Commission for Relief in Belgium—generally known as Belgian Relief—was established in October 1914, largely through the efforts of Herbert C. Hoover, who became the commission's director. Its purpose was to supply food, obtained abroad and shipped to Belgium through neutral Rotterdam, to the millions of people in German-occupied Belgium and northern France. Because this imported food remained the property of the American ambassador it could be distributed to the needy by the commissioners without having to obey the orders of the German soldiers.

Belgian Relief was one of the first causes taken up by the people of Lunenburg County. A garden party in aid of the Belgians, reported the *Progress-Enterprise* of October 14, 1914, was held in Lunenburg on the grounds of George Zwicker's property, raising the "goodly sum" of $100. On October 9, entertainment "for the benefit of the homeless Belgians"—a play, readings, vocal selections, and music by the Rose Bay orchestra—was also provided in the basement of the Presbyterian church in Riverport. The people of Petite Riviere and Moshers Island prepared boxes full of clothes and foodstuffs and collected money. At LaHave, a patriotic meeting was held in the Templars Hall, and the principal speaker was Reverend Coffin of Petite Riviere, "known throughout the province as a scholarly and eloquent speaker." His subject was "Our Flag and What It Stands For." The sum of twenty dollars was collected.

After reading Premier Murray's appeal, Owen G. Dauphinee suggested that at the close of the annual provincial exhibition the farmers of the county should offer their exhibits of fruit and vegetables to the Belgian Relief committee in Halifax. He would be pleased to add twenty-five bushels of potatoes and two barrels of apples. A correspondent from Lunenburg urged that, whether by direct contribution of the town's merchants or by action of the town council, Lunenburg should send a hundred or more quintals of good dry fish. This would be the only food contribution the town could make, but some of the local farmers might contribute potatoes, rye, or barley.

That November the secretary of the Belgian Relief committee in Halifax received a note from a Belgian refugee in Holland saying that he had seen on a wharf at Breskens, a little Dutch village at the mouth of the Scheldt, an unusual quantity of cases and trunks of all shapes and sizes. He was overcome with emotion when he noticed on one of these the inscription: "Pour les Belges nos braves allies avec l'amiration et la sympathie des habitants de la province de la Nouvelle-Ecosse." The many families of poor Belgian workmen who were starving, he maintained, would heartily wish their gratitude conveyed to the people of Nova Scotia for the things sent, and how needed the articles of clothing and bedding would be in the complete destitution in which they found themselves, with winter so near.

Feelings against the Germans and in favour of helping the Belgians were kindled by accounts of "German atrocities," such as one that appeared in the *Bulletin* of October 20, 1914. A baker was forced for three days to bake bread for the Germans, and then he was thrust into his oven to burn alive while his wife watched. Little children were reported massacred, and a youth had had his tongue cut out. A woman was forced to stand and see the hands of her two small boys cut off so they would never be able to hold a gun, and afterwards she was tortured in a way the reporter "did not care to explain." A wounded British soldier reported seeing a baby stuck on a bayonet at the end of a German rifle. There were dozens of stories of the murderous licentiousness of the German soldiers as they quartered in Belgian towns and villages. Verified or not, such propaganda aroused abundant sympathy for the plight of the Belgians living under cruel occupation.

Especially in the early years of the war, patriotic concerts were held around the county to raise funds for various causes. A concert in Lunenburg on November 11, 1914, to raise money for the Red Cross, deserves to be covered in some detail because it was typical, if grander, than most but also because of the delightfully entertaining, and unrelenting, critique offered by the reporter from the *Progress-Enterprise*. Clearly this reporter was not overly impressed. Held in the crowded Opera House, it was alleged that the concert revealed the patriotic spirit of the inhabitants of Lunenburg. The entertainment had been arranged by the teachers of the Academy, the local high school.

The opening number was Gounod's "Soldiers' Chorus," rendered by a choir of picked voices and conducted by W. A. Whynacht, choirmaster of the Methodist church. It "would have been faultless if the base had been heavier," commented the reporter dryly. Arthur Hirtle's solo "For King and Country" was splendid for the occasion, "but it did not seem to suit Mr. Hirtle, or else the singer was not in good form." Next was a tableau with the subject "Home from the War," with Miss Eva Rafuse in the role of the mother reading a letter from her son, who came in the door in the person of C. E. Miller, to loud applause. A duet for cornet and euphonium followed; the selection was "very pleasing but it would have been better if proper accompaniment had been present." Miss Isabel MacGregor's recitation "Under Two Flags" was decidedly well done and was an appropriate number, but, "a little more animation would have added considerable to the latter part of the reading, which lends itself admirably to the elocutionist's art."

During the intermission, the orchestra "played their worst, in fact in places during the March they didn't play at all, whether by accident or intent we know not. Why Mr. Penn Spicer chose the one piece they couldn't play for such an important place as the 'Interval' will remain a mystery." After the intermission came the drill, "The Allied Nations": this number was "practically perfect...one of the prettiest intricate performances ever offered the Lunenburg theatre-going public," but, the reporter remarked, never passing up a chance to damn with faint praise, "had the chorus work been attacked with greater surety it would have ranked as a masterpiece." The drill was followed by an extravaganza called "A Sailor's Life," performed by Penn Spicer, the only humorous number in the program so there was much applause; with his free and easy stage manner, Mr. Spicer was "always a favourite with a Lunenburg audience." Another tableau followed, and then Mrs. Hobbs, "an artiste of the first water," received a great reception for her "Angus MacDonald."

Regrettably, and not surprisingly, the concluding vocal number, a quartet entitled "Sweet and Low," was "not a success, as the balance was not good, the soprano being overpowered and the pitch kept falling, which cannot be tolerated in Quartette work with any good result." "Britannia" was the title of the last tableau, with the leading figure supported by men representing the navy and the army. The colonies and Allied nations were grouped about the pedestal at the feet of Britannia, representing Canada, Australia, India, South Africa, Ireland, Scotland, France, Belgium, Japan, and Russia. The sum of $159 for the Red Cross was realized at the door, thanks to the kind patriotic efforts of the Academy teachers and their friends.

The Canadian Red Cross was one of the most important of the charitable organizations during the war. The *Bulletin* reported on September 15, 1914, that the Opera House in Lunenburg had been packed the previous evening in response to a call by Mayor Hall for a public meeting to establish a branch of the Red Cross relief work in the town. There were stirring addresses and music furnished by the regimental band. Ada Powers, a leading light in the Woman's Christian Temperance Union, offered the use of the union's room as a meeting place for the organization.

Every village and hamlet in the county eventually had Red Cross workers who contributed a steady stream of supplies. The Halifax Red Cross served as headquarters for the four hundred affiliated units in the province and also as a depot for the national organization in shipping medical and other supplies overseas. As early as the first Christmas of the war, the Lunenburg Red Cross was busy preparing boxes of gifts for the town's "boys at the front." Many inexpensive trifles, the *Bulletin*

of December 1 advised, could be sent: "small packages of smoker's articles, candy, shaving and toilet soap, indelible pencils, leather bootlaces,
chewing gum, boracic acid, and carbolated Vaseline would be most
acceptable." Among the more unusual items the Red Cross dispatched
overseas, according to a list in the *Progress-Enterprise* of January 20,
1915, were cholera belts, nightingales (a shoulder shawl worn in hospital), housewives, and court plasters.

A major task, of course, was the raising of funds to support the
Red Cross's work. One such event, reported in the *Progress-Enterprise*
of June 16, 1915, took place in the open air on a "real June day." The
"picture presented by the huge gaily dressed audience, the many teams
and autos in waiting, the imposing band stand, with its uniformed
occupants will be stamped in the minds of every citizen present." The
75th Regiment band, under musical director John T. Arenburg, was
out in full strength, playing the national anthems of Belgium, France,
Russia, and Italy. Speakers confined their remarks to the subject of
the Red Cross work and the war in general. A collection taken up by
young women from the different churches came up with the handsome sum of $150 to swell the Red Cross coffers.

A month later, Lunenburg's Boscawen Chapter of the IODE hosted
a lawn party to raise money to help their sister society, the Red Cross.
The sum of $55 was collected "to carry on their splendid and self-sac-
rificing work." The event took place on the St. John's rectory grounds
in Lunenburg, tastefully decorated with flags, and with tables selling
ice cream, cake, and candy. The 75th Regiment band provided music.
(On the same page the newspaper noted that a musical comedy,
"The Richest Coon in Georgia," with plantations and cotton fields,
and introducing two great "coloured comedians," had opened at the
Music Hall.)

Smaller places, too, raised funds. A concert was held on August
6, 1915, for the benefit of the Red Cross at Mulberry Beach on
Heckmans Island under the auspices of Mrs. R. C. S. Kaulbach and
family, assisted by Misses Mary Heisler and Hazel Heckman, and Mrs.
Ellison Corkum. An admission fee of ten cents was asked and the sum

of $6.35 was realized. There were songs, recitations, and "acts." Lettie Knickle sang "Sailor Boy," and the last number on the program was "A darky chorus."

The New Germany column in the *Progress-Enterprise* of May 3, 1916, reported that many items had been shipped to Red Cross headquarters in Halifax. Mrs. Willie Feindel had knit upwards of 40 pairs of socks since the organization had started there. Mrs. Feindel was surpassed in her efforts, however, by Mrs. Edward Zwicker, an aged lady also from New Germany, who had "passed her seventy-ninth milestone on life's journey...[and had] done her bit for the boys in the trenches by knitting 210 pairs of socks all forwarded to them through the proper channels." "In the eyes of the all-wise Creator and in the hearts of the nation," suggested the *Bulletin* on March 26, 1918, Mrs. Zwicker "should take no second place to Lady Borden and Lady Foster," wives of the prime minister and of one of his prominent cabinet ministers. According to historians Sarah Glassford and Amy Shaw, in *A Sisterhood of Suffering and Service*, "the knitting woman, especially the knitting mother, exemplified a societally approved means of fulfilling a female citizen's wartime obligations" and became "a powerful and enduring icon of an engaged home front."

On December 20, 1916, a rather unkind little poem, supposedly written by one of the soldiers on active service, appeared in the *Progress-Enterprise*:

Received your Sox "Lady,"
    Some fit!
Used one for a hammock,
    One for a mit;
Like to meet you Lady
    When I've done my "bit"
In the meantime Lady,
    Where in H---
Did you learn to knit?

An item in the Lunenburg paper of January 19, 1916, gives a good sense of the Red Cross's work. The Mahone Bay Red Cross Auxiliary reported sending yet another box to the headquarters in Halifax, in which was included "22 hospital shirts, 3 field shirts, 13 pyjama suits, 168 handkerchiefs, 160 prs. socks, 1 Balaclava cap, 52 fomentation wringers, 51 pillow cases, 6 towels, 1 pr. wristlets, 468 bandages, 7 cakes soap, 2 boxes stationery, and magazines." Earlier they had sent Christmas boxes containing "candy, nuts, cake, tobacco, stationery, etc., to the soldiers in the trenches...to be given to boys from Lunenburg County who had no one at home to send gifts to them."

Letters of thanks came back from the front, one man declaring that he was "writing this letter with the hopes that you will give my address to some nice young lady that wants to write to a lonely soldier at the front." Requests for amorous connections also came in the other direction. According to the *Progress-Enterprise* of July 11, 1917, letters came by the bushel from Canada and elsewhere to the Canadian Red Cross and similar institutions asking if they might correspond with a lonesome soldier, but these organizations were forbidden to put the men in contact with unknown correspondents. One writer boldly stipulated that her letter should be sent to some soldier "who must be good looking."

The work of the Red Cross went on throughout the war, of course, and long after. The *Halifax Herald* on June 18, 1918, promoting Nova Scotia's Red Cross Week, July 8 to 15, said that the organization was the greatest instrument of mercy the world had ever seen. "The Red

Red Cross recruitment campaign, July 27, 1918.

Cross is, we may say, the arms of the mothers of the world reached out to their sons to bind up their wounds and comfort them. The Red Cross is an army without a gun that wages war only upon suffering and heart-ache. Where our flag goes the banner of the Red Cross must fly beside it. We watch our boys go forth to war with a spirit of hopefulness because we know that this great agency of humanity presses close behind them." The plan was to raise $250,000 throughout the province during the week. Arrangements were made so the fishermen of Lunenburg, who might be off to the banks before the start of the campaign, could sub-scribe before they left. In the end, Lunenburg deposited over $5,600 to the credit of the Red Cross in this campaign.

Bridgewater also continued to be generous to the Red Cross. The LaHave Chapter of the IODE initiated a garden party there on June 24, 1918. The account in the *Halifax Herald* declared it to be "without ques-tion the most successful affair of its kind ever held in the town." A parade led by Corporal Harry Fawson Sorette, a returned soldier, formed up at Clark's Hotel and proceeded through the town to Queen Park. Despite the uncertainty of the weather, the decorations of the various cars were said to be "superb, beyond praise." The main feature of the evening was the presentation of a service flag with four maple leaves by Mrs. A. W. Olive, regent of the LaHave Chapter, to Freeman Veinot, honouring a family that had four sons who were on active service or had been. The event raised the magnificent sum of $920 for the provincial Red Cross.

One novel approach to raising funds was described in the *Progress-Enterprise* on April 25, 1917. A steel helmet as worn by British and Canadian soldiers, complete with a hole caused by shrapnel, had been secured by Captain John James Ower of the medical staff, "somewhere in France." Ower sent it to his wife in Lunenburg, who decided to dispose of it, with all the money devoted to the Junior Red Cross. A draw took place for "this interesting trophy," on display in Kinley's drugstore, following the sale of one hundred tickets issued at twenty-five cents each.

Apart from raising money and sending parcels to the troops, the Red Cross performed many other valuable functions. The women visited wounded Canadian soldiers at convalescent hospitals in England, providing each soldier with items such as toiletries, cigarettes, and writing paper, and they also contributed funds to the British organization. They met hospital ships when they arrived in Halifax, and they helped look after the soldiers' wives and children. One important task was the sending of parcels, largely through the postal services of neutral nations, to the men in German prisoner-of-war camps.

The Imperial Order Daughters of the Empire did much work similar to the Red Cross. The Lunenburg column in the *Bulletin* of November 17, 1914, claimed that the ten-cent tea given by the IODE in the room formerly occupied by Miller's restaurant was an unqualified success, raising almost thirty dollars. Candles had been set out in pretty holders, their shades decorated with Canadian holly, with English, French, and Belgian flags. Streamers of red, white, and blue crepe paper ran from the electrolier to the corners of the centre table. A number of gentlemen patronized the affair. The reporter remarked that Lunenburg was very busy these days, everybody being engaged in raising money for patriotic work of some description.

"Help Fill Field Comfort Boxes for Soldier Boys," declared a headline in the *Bulletin* of February 1, 1916. The troops were clamouring for warm socks and cigarettes. The Princess Louise Chapter of the IODE was responsible for the large boxes that appeared in many of the town's stores labelled "Field Comforts." An opening at the top was big enough to drop in a contribution. Each week the boxes were opened, sorted, and sent to the men at the front. Suggestions for contributions were "socks, khaki handkerchiefs, mufflers, wristlets, safety pins, automatic bachelor buttons, linen thread, soap, face cloths, small towels, tooth brushes, foot powder, draught-board, handkerchiefs with a set of counters for playing the game (a distinct novelty), chocolates, chewing gum, cigarettes—or give money if you prefer." (Automatic bachelor buttons were buttons secured by sticking the stud into a key, thus needing no thread.)

The *Malagash News* of Lunenburg, on March 4, 1917, observed that the town's Boscawen Chapter of the IODE had been organized for patriotic work in the autumn of 1914 with twenty-four members. Now there were sixty-six. They had made shipments of clothing for Belgian Relief, had sent "field comforts" parcels to Halifax to be shipped overseas, and they had supported a prisoner of war in Germany during the year by each member paying a small contribution monthly. On May 8, 1918, the IODE made a special plea in the *Progress-Enterprise*: "Attention, Women of Lunenburg." The article carried on, "Our soldiers need socks and yet more socks. The IODE has purchased a very large quantity of splendid wool and are busily engaged in knitting socks. Every woman who can knit and will knit may procure wool for socks by applying to Mrs. G. A. Polley, regent of the chapter, who will give all information on the subject. Hundreds of socks are asked for. Will you knit your bit?" The women of the IODE certainly did more than knit socks and roll bandages. Historian Joan Sangster points out that in 1914 alone, countrywide, the IODE "helped fund a naval ship, a hospital wing, and many ambulances."[4]

An item in the *Progress-Enterprise* of November 6, 1918, explained how the members of the Boscawen Chapter prepared Christmas boxes for the men overseas that year. "First gay little tartan bags must be made to hold loaf sugar, candy and raisins. A lovely cake was then put in the box, then a good thick warm pair of socks, then a trench candle, wax candle, milk chocolate, chewing gum, letter pad and envelopes, lead pencil, shoe laces, soap, can of coffee, cigarettes, tobacco and lastly a card with a special message to each boy." The 107 boxes were soon packed, tied, pinned in a good towel, and wrapped in heavy paper. Each box contained articles valued at three dollars.

One letter from France to the secretary of the IODE was particularly moving. U. W. Tanner wrote that it was a pleasure to get the first parcel he had ever received from any society. He was the only Lunenburg boy in his battalion, and had no friend at home to send him a parcel. He had lost his mother when he was eight years old and had no home, "like some chaps who are over here and get parcels from home." He had two sisters in Lunenburg, but he very seldom heard from them. The *Progress-Enterprise* of February 6, 1918, commented that surely some of the Lunenburg citizens could well send this lonely soldier "out there fighting our battles" some little remembrance, a letter, paper, or some little gift. Urban Wilbert Tanner, a fisherman, son of Captain John Edmund Tanner, had been born in Tanners Settlement in 1895.

Printed in the *Progress-Enterprise* of April 10, 1918, was a "charming letter" of February 18 to "Dear Sec. of Daughters of the Empire," to say, "I received your parcel sent for Xmas, last night, and cannot tell you how glad I was to get it, as I was real hungry after walking 14 miles, on a Sunday afternoon. Please thank all the ladies that made it up. I guess you will think this is kind of a funny letter, but I'm not much good at a letter of this kind. Thanking you very much. I remain Pte N. J. Crouse."

As if the work of the Red Cross and the IODE were not enough, "An Appeal to Young Women of Lunenburg" appeared in the *Progress-Enterprise* of November 1, 1916. "The costliest war in the history of the world, both in treasure and human lives, has drawn into the deadly vortex the flower of the manhood of Canada." The casualties in the great offensive on the Somme had been staggering. Although much had been done to alleviate the sufferings of the sick and wounded and to procure comforts for the convalescents, there was much more to be done. There was an assumption that there must be scores of young women in Lunenburg who did not belong to either of these organizations, and yet would be willing to "do her bit." Ada Powers, a Lunenburg woman "always ready to stand forth to aid any good cause," kindly offered the Red Cross room for the convenience of any who volunteered to help meet the urgent call for hospital supplies. So many "brave young lads from the old town" had answered the call of king and country. It was time for the young ladies of Lunenburg to lend a hand.

Yet another worthy group was the Women's Institute, organized locally in November 1914 by Superintendent Miss Jennie Fraser, according to the *Progress-Enterprise* of February 23, 1916. The WI did not take up patriotic work because an excellent Red Cross auxiliary already existed, and the IODE was ably looking after Belgian Relief work. Nearly all the members also belonged to one of these flourishing organizations. There was, however, need for an anti-tuberculosis campaign, and they decided to give it their particular attention. They also collected jam for soldiers, and supplied indigent children with clothes. As well, schoolgirls met in the WI's rooms and rolled countless bandages to be sent overseas, the roller having been kindly donated by J. J. Kinley, former mayor of the town. The social side of the WI, entertaining soldiers for instance, was "always a charming feature" but "necessarily to be neglected now owing to the National calamity which forbids unnecessary expenditure."

The Women's Institute of Bridgewater, according to the *Progress-Enterprise* of May 9, 1917, had another concern. They had drawn up a resolution having to do with the regrettable lack of respect shown by adults and children during the singing of the national anthem, "God Save the King," in schools, places of amusement, and even in churches. It was suggested that clergymen, teachers, and managers of theatres lay the matter before their audiences and "request that the position of 'attention' enforced in the Army and Navy of our Empire" be used in the future by the general public. And all who can, must join in the singing, "remembering that it is our National Prayer, urgently needed at this time."

There were many other worthy causes to which one could make a contribution. James D. McGregor, lieutenant-governor of Nova Scotia, made a plea to the people of the province in the *Progress-Enterprise* of June 16, 1915, for a hearty response to the Overseas Club. The sum of $12,000 was needed to purchase a "100 H.P. Gnome Vickers Gun Biplane" for the Royal Flying Corps, to strengthen the aircraft fleet of the British army. The biplane would be named Nova Scotia.

The *Bulletin* of December 12, 1916, reported that the Nova Scotia Auxiliary of the Canadian Bible Society, affiliated with the British and Foreign Bible Society, had received funds from the Bridgewater branch: $40 from Emma Gow, down to $1.15 from Blanche Dolliver,

and $1.15 from the sale of Bibles. "The society is doing a most patri-
otic work," the newspaper maintained, "in supplying millions of our
soldiers with the Word of God to take with them into the trenches."

Loyalty to the Empire was a sentiment commonly expressed in
Lunenburg County. On February 17, 1915, a Masonic banquet, Unity
Lodge no. 4, was held at the new Alexandria Hall in Lunenburg.
Augustus J. Wolff, past grand master, and a former mayor of Lunenburg,
took advantage of the occasion to declare himself emphatically, though
born in Prussia, a true British subject. His statement was greeted with
an enthusiastic round of applause. A display of loyalty to the crown
and king also took place on June 3 that year. The town was gaily decorated with flags, and the chimes of St. John's Anglican Church played
the national anthem and other patriotic tunes to commemorate King
George v's fiftieth birthday. "Long may he live!"

Nova Scotians, like other Maritimers, were certain of their place
within the British Empire, and ready to support it. At a "combined
patriotic and prayer service" in Bridgewater in January 1915, Arthur
Roberts, KC, pointed out "the real root from which grows our ever warm
attachment for the motherland, the real foundation of our enlightened
loyalty…our allegiance not to the king personally but to him as the
symbolic head of the Empire and the representative of all the Empire
stands for." And what did the Empire stand for? "British institutions
and British traditions, British courts and justice, British freedom—serf
to no man and slave to no system." Freedom was not the product of
this continent, Roberts maintained, it had its birth in England. All this
must be fought for.

But Nova Scotians were members of the British Empire with a dis-
tinct Canadian cast. A selection of poetry (obviously borrowed from
E. Pauline Johnson's "Canadian Born"), published in the *Progress-
Enterprise* on May 23, 1917, catches something of the dual nature of
Canadian sentiment back then:

No title and no coronet
Is half so proudly worn
As that which we inherited
As men Canadian born.
We count no man more noble
Than he who makes the brag
That he was born in Canada
Beneath the British flag.

Empire Day was naturally celebrated in Nova Scotia at this time. At a gathering in the assembly hall of the Lunenburg Academy, also in May 1917, the room was crowded with the teachers and more than five hundred pupils of the public schools, who met to carry out the exercises authorized and prescribed by the Council of Public Instruction for Empire Day. The usual patriotic songs were sung: "O Canada," "We'll Never Let the Old Flag Fall," "Rule Britannia," and "God Save the King." One can imagine the emotions aroused by Cuthbert Holder's recitation, "What can a little chap do?" Miss Doris Mahoney, for her encore, sang "There's a Girl at the Front among the Soldiers"; a popular song during the war, the girl depicted wears a red cross on her sleeve. Principal McKittrick gave a fifteen-minute address on the meaning of Empire Day, particularly upon the necessity of increased food production in order to win the war and save the Empire. Ada Powers showed the children how they could "help the nation by personal thrift and economy in little things."

Some, if not most, of the Germans of Lunenburg County seem to have shared in these benign views of the Empire. Thanks to the diary of millwright John Will Crouse, as revealed in Robert M. Mennel's book *Testimonies and Secrets*, we know more about the thinking of at least one man and his attitude toward the British connection. As Mennel points out, because of the influence of publications in English—from the Bible to books, newspapers, magazines, and missionary publications—the local German culture had been declining for years. Most of the German families in the area had emigrated many years before and had long since adopted the English tongue and English-Canadian institutions. John Will Crouse spent his entire life within a twenty-mile radius of Crousetown, a community in the western part of the county. His diary entries, as well as the periodicals and pictures hanging around the house, portrayed "an unabashed anglophile." He affirmed that his greatest attachment was to the British Empire and the crown. Enthusiastic about the Boer War, he observed Empire Day and the queen's birthday, and there were pictures of the royal family in the front rooms. "Crousetown families with German origins," Mennel observes, "were proud of their ancestry, which they saw as rooted in the culture of the eighteenth-century Palatinate," and they rejected suggestions that they were somehow linked to "Kaiserism" and "the twisted course of modern German history." John Will "exemplified this loyalty to the representative democracy of the Dominion, to the symbolism of the Crown, and to the patriotic values of empire."

In mid-August 1915, a year after the outbreak of the war, a "Great Patriotic Meeting" took place in Lunenburg. Mayor Hall had called it to express support for Great Britain's stand in the war and for the purpose of securing recruits for overseas service. Rev. Harvey Eisenhauer, one of Lunenburg's young men who was said to be making a mark as a minister in the Methodist church, led the gathering in prayer. The ubiquitous 75th Regiment band began with "Rule Britannia" and during the evening played the anthems of the various Allies and other patriotic songs. The resolution put forward by the mayor stated: "That on the anniversary of the declaration of a righteous war, this meeting of citizens of Lunenburg record its inflexible determination to continue to a victorious end the struggle in maintenance of those ideals of Liberty and Justice which are the sacred cause of the Allies." D. J. Rudolph and A. R. Morash moved and seconded the resolution.

Following the Russian anthem, William Duff, who would soon become mayor of the town, addressed the meeting, opening his remarks by expressing regret that the audience was chiefly composed of ladies, but he gave as the reason that the men were away on the fishing banks, earning bread and butter for the people who stayed at home. He paid a high compliment to the men of the fishing fleet in Lunenburg County, claiming a finer class of men did not exist in Canada or any part of the Empire. Among other speakers, Mr. Hirtle, who was acting pastor for the Lutheran congregation, explained that the Allies were fighting a righteous war and he was confident of victory. Reverend Eisenhauer impressed upon the audience the necessity for men to go forth and fight the battles of the Empire. The audience passed Mayor Hall's motion by rising to their feet, and this "most enthusiastic meeting" closed with the singing of "God Save the King."

The highlight of the program, however, was Judge S. A. Chesley's brief history of the people of Lunenburg County. Entitled "Lunenburg Germans Hereditary Subjects of King George," the *Progress-Enterprise* of August 11, 1915, claimed the speech helped to explain the "universal loyalty of the people of Lunenburg County." Chesley began by noting that the census of 1911 credited the county with 22,837 inhabitants of German descent, and, with hardly an

Judge S.A. Chesley.

exception, these were people whose ancestors always owed allegiance to the ancestors of George v, king of Great Britain and her dependencies. The German settlers who landed at Rous's Brook on June 8, 1753, were the subjects of George II, king of Great Britain and elector, that is, the hereditary ruler, of Hanover.

In other words, when George II invited to Nova Scotia the people who came to Lunenburg in 1753, he invited and secured the emigration of his own Hanoverian subjects, the great-great-grandfathers and great-great-grandmothers of the men and women of German origin who still inhabited Lunenburg town and county. King George v was the lineal descendant of George ii, who was ruler of the emigrants from Lunëburg and other parts of Hanover in the 1750s. (George v was in fact sensitive about his German ancestry and put himself forward as a patriot-king. When H. G. Wells criticized his "alien and uninspiring court," George declared, "I may be uninspiring, but I'll be damned if I'm an alien.") George ii, iii, and iv, and William iv were kings of Great Britain and Hanover. Under Salic law, Queen Victoria, as a woman, was not allowed to succeed to the Hanoverian throne; otherwise, Hanover, including the province of Lunëburg, would probably still be a part of the British Empire. The independent kingdom of Hanover was overrun by the Prussians in 1866 and, said Chesley, its people were treated much as Belgians had been treated during the last twelve months.

Judge Chesley's history may be a bit fuzzy. Apparently few if any of the settlers had come from Hanover,[5] but his basic point is clear enough. If George v could be British despite his German lineage, so could the German people of Lunenburg County. They were, indeed, as British as the king.

Chapter Two

MANLY MEN AND FORMIDABLE WOMEN

With the men of the 25th Nova Scotia Battalion fighting like "seasoned vets" overseas, the *Progress-Enterprise* observed on October 20, 1915, that the previous Monday had been yet another historic day for the town of Lunenburg. Hundreds of people had lined the streets from the drill hall to the railway station to bid farewell and Godspeed to the men who had volunteered for active service with the 85th Battalion. Businesses and private dwellings had been handsomely decorated for the occasion. The 75th Regiment band headed the parade of volunteers to the station, and during the intermissions in the ceremony played patriotic airs. Several ministers made speeches, filled with good advice not only in connection with the enemy but also for the soldiers' spiritual welfare. The women of the IODE then handed each of the recruits a lunch that would "satisfy the cravings of the inner man" until their arrival in Halifax: a box, tied with a ribbon, containing confectionery, cigarettes, sandwiches, and cake, all addressed to "A Soldier of the King." During this "interesting proceeding," Mrs.

Polley stood "on the left flank of the platoon gracefully waving the good old British flag over the boys, thus indicating that they were an active part of that great institution, the British Empire."

Enlistments continued around the county, as did recruiting efforts, in smaller communities as well as in the bigger towns. At a patriotic meeting in Blue Rocks, according to the Lunenburg paper of October 20, Lieutenant S. G. Micklewright gave a clear presentation about why the British Empire was at war. The recruiting officer claimed he had never had a more appreciative and attentive audience, and he felt convinced that the men of Blue Rocks would not be found wanting in their loyalty to king and country. Some had already stated their intention to enlist. Another recruiting meeting was held at the Foresters Hall in Petite Riviere, with clergymen making a stirring appeal to the men there to line up with the rest of Nova Scotia and Canada.

The *Bridgewater Bulletin* of September 7, 1915, described a typical recruiting meeting at Wentzells Lake, a picnic area about fourteen kilometres up the LaHave River from Bridgewater. In a Scottish Highlander uniform, Captain W. H. Allen, late of the 17th Battalion, who had been to the front, spoke at the Lutheran reunion at the lake. He showed scenes on lantern slides of the First Contingent at Valcartier, of the troops crossing the ocean, on Salisbury Plain, and in the trenches, and he made a strong appeal for volunteers. Life in the trenches, he maintained, was not as bad as was supposed; food was good and regularly served except at times of severe fighting. "The men who go and fight for our common country," he predicted, "will return bigger men in every way and will in future have a prominent part in directing the affairs of the land that they helped to save from German tyranny."

On October 26 the *Bulletin* provided some practical information, highlighting several facts that enlisting men would want to know. How long would they be expected to serve? Until the end of the war, and six months after if required. Pay? As a private, one dollar a day and ten cents field allowance; besides this they would be clothed, equipped, and subsisted by the government. What would the soldier's wife receive during his absence? A monthly separation allowance of twenty dollars;

if this was not enough the Canadian Patriotic Fund would further assist. If the soldier was wounded or sick he would be cared for by the government and his pay would be continued until discharged. If permanently disabled, allowance would be paid, varying according to the extent of the injury or disability. And what would be done for a wife and children if the soldier died? The government would provide an adequate pension until the children were old enough to look after themselves. The widowed mother of a single man, if the son were her sole support, would be treated the same as a wife. It's hard to know if the average prospective soldier would find these terms tempting, the reporter acknowledged, but at least they would know.

Apparently, some thought the recruiting on Nova Scotia's South Shore was not going as well as the authorities would have liked. An article about enlistment in Lunenburg County appeared in the *Halifax Herald* on November 6, 1915. The *Bulletin*, which reprinted the item on the ninth, claimed that the *Herald* correspondent had had unique opportunities to witness the efforts of the recruiting officers along the county's coast, and he was "convinced absolutely that it would take a man with the wisdom of Socrates, the eloquence of Cicero, the persuasiveness of Premier Borden and the oratorical outspoken sledge hammer blows of Sergeant Knight, all rolled into one, to call a large percentage of the young men living in the remote hamlets and villages along these shores to realize their solemn obligations to king and country." They were "strapping young fellows, clean limbed, bronzed, possessing lion courage to face the vigors of an angry sea while following their avocation." They crowded the recruiting meetings held at Mill Cove, Chester Basin, Gold River, Martins River, and Chester, yet the speakers' most potent arguments seemed to fall on deaf ears. They listened most attentively and respectfully when personally approached by the recruiting officer, then turned their backs and went home. Lieutenant Micklewright's enthusiasm in Blue Rocks was perhaps misplaced.

The *Herald* reporter went on to speculate that these young men, through their boyhood, attended schools where the national anthem was never sung, the Union Jack never displayed. Then they followed their avocation as fishermen, having "perhaps some local weekly journal as their only mental pabulum; they enjoyed three square meals a day and slept comfortably at night, having 'never learnt the power and might of the British Empire with its principles of Justice, Liberty and Brotherhood.'" How would you expect to teach such men "patriotism" in one evening? "They have no more conception of the value of love of country than a baby has of the value of a diamond necklace." It's not their fault that they are "indifferent to the call of the blood." And here, perhaps, opined the *Bulletin*, was the crux of the *Herald*'s argument, what the newspaper was really getting at. These men were not British enough, perhaps too tied to their German ancestry? They should not be condemned because they could not see "the difference between living under the good old Union Jack and the muddy German flag with its horrible bars sinister." The *Herald* correspondent did concede that some three hundred men had in fact enlisted in the county, in spite of the disadvantages in never having been taught patriotism and loyalty in childhood. "The men of Lunenburg county will 'make good,' depend upon it, if persistent hammering away is maintained."

On January 12, 1916, an appeal for recruits appeared in the province's newspapers made by David MacKeen, lieutenant-governor, on behalf of the Nova Scotia Recruiting Association. The "young men of this noble little Province of ours" should enlist so that Nova Scotia would "take second place to no other part of the King's Dominions." On November 8, the *Progress-Enterprise* carried an even more earnest appeal from MacKeen, urging Nova Scotians to be "a worthy link in the golden British chain." The feelings of parents were natural, he argued, but "private feelings in times of dire national stress, must always yield to public necessity.…Let Mothers, who are preventing their sons from enrolling, consider how those sons will remember them, when they have to tell their children, in years to come, that they failed in their plain duty to our great British Brotherhood because 'Mother Forbade.'"

Another high-powered appeal came from Sir Frederick Fraser, acting chairman of the recruiting association, in a letter in the *Bulletin*, February 22, 1916. Among the many products of Nova Scotia, he wrote, there were "none of which she may be more justly proud than her splendid manhood....There are glens in Scotland without a man, shall it be so in New Scotland? Never has cause been more honorable; never has peril been so deadly. Life, love and liberty are at stake; the ruin of Belgium and Serbia must be averted. Therefore, 'For all we have and are / For all our children's fate / Stand up and meet the war / The Hun is at the gate.'"

Recruiting was encouraged in many ways. Writing shortly after the war, M.S. Hunt in *Nova Scotia's Part in the Great War* points out that soldiers, especially those of the popular 85th, the Nova Scotia Highlanders, were given leave to recruit other men. In the first few weeks of 1916, he explained, a far-reaching publicity campaign was organized. Pulpits, the press, and even schoolrooms were commandeered. At religious services, moral issues of the war were brought home forcibly to the congregants. Military uniforms appeared in the pulpits and martial strains could be heard in sacred precincts. The Union Jack was widely displayed in public schools, and children were drilled in patriotic songs. Prominent citizens delivered addresses "until to the impressionable mind of the little children it was incredible that anyone should stay at home." Thus a child was converted into "an irrepressible recruiting agent among his big brothers at home."

Schoolchildren were indeed drawn into the recruiting campaign. Teachers at the Parks Creek School, including the principal, Carrie E. Himmelman, celebrated "Recruiting Day" in March 1916. The schoolroom was "beautifully decorated with drawings, mottoes, and flags, suitable for the occasion." The titles of the various songs and recitations reveal the kind of information that was being forced into susceptible young heads. Songs reportedly included "The Maple Leaf," "Tipperary," "Men of the North," "The Soldiers of the King," "Boys in Khaki," "Rule Britannia," and "The British Grenadiers." Among the recitations were "Ye Mariners of England," "The Flag Goes By," "Your King and Country Need You," "The Little Wet Home in the Trench," "Tommy the Recruiting Officer," "England My England," and "The Charge of the Light Brigade." It's not clear if there were potential soldiers in the large audience that attended this event, but the little ones would have fathers and big brothers at home.[1] No doubt, German children were equally exposed to such pressure.

Several of Canada's military historians have pointed out that a high level of voluntary recruitment was sustained through 1915 and the first half of 1916, but thereafter the level fell. The increasing number of casualties meant that more and more volunteers were needed, hence the extensive recruiting efforts. As well, the Borden government raised the number of soldiers required to maintain the army's strength at the front. In the summer of 1915, the government had determined that 150,000 volunteers were required. That fall, however, after the prime minister returned from visiting England and France in July and August, the enlistment target was boosted to 250,000 men. Then in January 1916, the number was doubled to 500,000. Prime Minister Borden announced this goal in his New Year's address, "in token of Canada's unflinchable resolve to crown the justice of our cause with victory and with an abiding peace."[2]

In *The Greatest Victory*, J. L. Granatstein observes that the large number of casualties during the battle at Ypres in the late spring of 1915 had shocked Canadians and led them to question who among them were failing to play their part. It was easy to blame Quebec, for the province—outside of the English-speaking minority—was clearly a less enthusiastic supporter of the war effort. "What few of the Anglo critics of French Canada admitted even to themselves," however, Granatstein remarks, "was that enlistments from English Canada were very light among the Canadian-born." In fact, British-born immigrants made up a large proportion of the volunteers. "The reality was that, through 1915, most native-born Canadians evidently had little desire to volunteer to fight for king and Empire."

The appalling cost of the Somme offensive that began in July 1916 brought an end to large-scale, enthusiastic voluntary recruiting. Canadians joined the battle there late in the year, and, like their allies, sustained enormous casualties for trivial gains. According to Desmond Morton in *When Your Number's Up*, by the fall of 1916 voluntary enlistment in the infantry had dried up across the country. There were plenty of complaints that French Canada was not doing its share, but Morton alleges that rural Ontario or the Maritimes could also have been criticized.

Men were becoming reluctant to volunteer, in part because they had expected to serve together overseas but on arriving in England battalions were very often broken up to reinforce existing units. The 112th Battalion, for instance, according to Brian Douglas Tennyson in *Nova Scotia at War*, was authorized in December 1915, went to England in July 1916, and was used to supply reinforcements until January 1917, when it was absorbed by the 26th Reserve Battalion. The Nova Scotia Highland Brigade, made up of four battalions, was disbanded by January 1917 to provide reinforcements for existing battalions. Only the 85th Battalion survived to become, along with the 25th, the second Nova Scotia battalion.

There were also, inevitably, questions about the quality of the recruits. On May 30, 1916, the *Bulletin* complained that the *Progress-Enterprise* had reported almost 50 per cent of the soldiers sent from Lunenburg and Bridgewater had been returned as incompetent and unfit. This was "not only a libel on our soldiers," exclaimed the editor of the *Bulletin*, but also a falsehood, "since only about 5 per cent had been returned unfit." Desmond Morton remarks in *Fight or Pay*, however, "One shocking fact about this country in 1914 is that less than half of its keenest volunteers could meet the modest physical standards of its army." Tim Cook points out in *At the Sharp End* that the more stringent medical regulations were increasingly relaxed, so by 1916 "the malformed, maladjusted, and miniscule were routinely embraced by a man-hungry military."

Given the increasing number of casualties and the slowing of voluntary enlistment, recruiting efforts were intensified. A "great mass recruiting meeting" took place in Bridgewater in 1916, according to an enthusiastic reporter in the *Bulletin* of March 7, under the bold headline "The Breed of Manly Men." Lieutenant Colonel A. H. Borden of the 85th Battalion had arrived by train from Halifax to a huge crowd and streets lined with cadets. That evening the local band and the band of the 85th led the parade to the drill hall where, unfortunately, the doors had not been closed and the "seating capacity was almost taxed to its limits by ladies" and many men could not be accommodated. Borden, who had gone to school in Bridgewater, delivered with "impassioned and fervid oratory" for over an hour one of "his best and most spirited addresses." There should have been fifty recruits, the *Bulletin* lamented, rather than only sixteen. A likely highlight of the evening before Borden spoke was the patriotic song sung by Rev. Charles R. Cumming, the words and music composed by "a lady of this town":

From out the realms of Nova Scotia,
    Fair Province down by the sea,
They go to fight for England's right;
    For JUSTICE, TRUTH and LIBERTY;
To swell the ranks of Allied Nations;
    To vanquish a brutal foe;
To quell the tyrant's proclamations:
    So cheer them as they go.

England expects of every brave man
    To quickly rally to her call;
The FLAG of PEACE must tumult cease
    Unfurled it will the foe appal.
And you, true sons of Britain glorious,
    Will carry the flag we love
O'er fields of death until victorious;
    In triumph it floats above.

Chorus:
Cheers to you, lads of Nova Scotia,
    Stalwart, courageous, brave and true,
Each gallant lad in KHAKI CLAD,
    Forward! His willing bit to do!

Cheers to you, lads of Nova Scotia;
And this will be our plea:
GOD RETURN THEE IN VICTORY
TO THE HOMES BESIDE THE SEA!

After a similar meeting in Mahone Bay, fourteen more "gallant men enlisted for the Kilties." One man there, so moved by the colonel's "compelling convincing" speech, cried out from the audience that, although he had a good business, he was ready to sacrifice all in order to enlist. He hurried up the aisle, followed to the platform by his five-year-old daughter, shook hands with the colonel, and enrolled on the spot—a splendid example, it was said, to the other men in the audience.

An unusual form of recruiting took place in late 1916. The *Bulletin* on December 12 announced that the band of No. 2 Construction Battalion, travelling in a special car, would be giving a series of concerts all along the South Shore in the interests of recruiting. The battalion was the first and only "colored" unit ever raised in Canada, the paper noted, and wished "good luck to the boys" and hoped that "capacity houses will show the colored lads that we are behind them as behind all 'Soldiers of the King.'" No appeal had been made to the public for assistance to this unit, and to date they had not received the generous help from the public that had been accorded other overseas units.

Many of the troops who volunteered from the South Shore took their initial training at Camp Aldershot, near Kentville in the Annapolis Valley. On August 25, 1916, the Halifax & Southwestern Railway ran an excursion to the camp, advertised as the "last opportunity for mothers, sisters, wives, brothers, and sweethearts of the soldiers in the Nova Scotia Highland Brigade to see them carrying out their work as they will in Flanders." Aldershot, the largest military camp in the Maritime provinces, was now on a warlike basis, with barbed-wire entanglements, lines of trenches, dugouts, and bomb-proof shelters, and "in every way a miniature Flanders without the danger experienced in that shell-stricken territory."[3] A trip on this train would be "both instructive, pleasant and cheap," the *Progress-Enterprise* ventured ungrammatically on August 23. At the camp, a crowd of five thousand watched "with thrilled hearts, and faces alight with pride, the Nova Scotia Highland Brigade swing past them in military manoeuvres….A great miracle has been worked in Nova Scotia; the fishermen, the lumbermen, the farmer, the clerk, the student of a year ago, was moving along that parade ground a part of a great human machine vibrant with determination surging with the manly blood of wholesome, keen eye, clear cut, clean limbed, sunburned manhood of the bluenose stock."

———————

At the beginning of the war, on August 12, 1914, the *Progress-Enterprise* had called for an end to political squabbles. This was not the time for party divisions, debate, or party struggles. "Nothing should be done to arouse political strife at a time when there is a need for united action in the Dominion and throughout the British Empire, facing a war of defence forced upon Britain and her dominions by the German emperor." This accommodating stance was not to last.

The provincial election of June 1916 is of little consequence in the grand scheme of things. The Liberals had been in power in Nova Scotia since Confederation, apart from one short break of three years, between 1878 and 1882. George Henry Murray, premier since 1896, would remain so throughout the war and until 1923. Regrettably, however, from the government's standpoint, the sitting members from Lunenburg County were Conservatives. The incumbents in the 1916 election were Joseph Willis Margeson and A. Clairmonte (Monte) Zwicker, while John J. Kinley and O. G. Donovan ran for the Liberals. Margeson, Donovan, and Kinley were all officers in the 75th Regiment. Dr. Donovan, from New Germany, having been turned down by the Canadian Army Medical Corps (CAMC), had been accepted by the British medical corps and was serving in France at the time of the election. The results on June 20 were split, with Kinley and Margeson chosen to represent their respective parties in Halifax. A much more important election would take place the following year.

Despite the *Progress-Enterprise*'s plea for unity at the outbreak of the war, consideration of the 1916 election reveals the fierce, and often hilarious, partisanship that existed among newspapers at the time. The Lunenburg paper, strongly in support of the Liberals, had already contended back in April 1914 that the people of the province were unlikely to trust the destinies of Nova Scotia to "such an aggregation of pinheads and pea-nutters as now constitute the opposition." The county should be where it belongs, "under the great free banner of Liberalism." The "Tory opposition obstructionists at Halifax" were accused of making "inane and silly speeches, empty and groundless chatter, cowardly and snakelike charges, insinuation and innuendoes," similar to the suffragettes in England. The *Bridgewater Bulletin*, a strong supporter of the Tory obstructionists, claimed in July 1914 that the *Progress-Enterprise*'s editorials were written by a "nincompoop," and later the paper retaliated by calling attention to the "baseness, vindictiveness and devilishness" of the "Lunenburg grit organ." In response, the grit organ called the Tories "'crib biters' and 'wind suckers.'"

There was plenty of sniping at the candidates of the opposing party. Joseph W. Margeson was a member of the Bridgewater Lodge of the Loyal Order of Moose, a fraternal and service organization. On his leaving Bridgewater in March 1915 to become paymaster of the 25th Battalion overseas, the *Halifax Herald*, a Conservative paper, maintained in all seriousness that it would be "a loss for the Moose men but may it be the empire's gain on the battlefields of Europe." The *Progress-Enterprise*, not convinced that Margeson's presence overseas would greatly aid the

J. W. Margeson, May 1915.

path to victory, commented on May 24, 1916, that "handing out cheques to soldiers is not of itself extremely hazardous." Margeson, a "featherbed soldier," was also accused of charging soldiers in his regiment to draft their wills at $2.50 a shot, an accusation he denied. On his return home from England with some ill soldiers, the editor of the Lunenburg paper harrumphed that Margeson went to Ottawa, and "like the process of caterpillar to butterfly overnight he became a major."

A minor tempest had broken out a year earlier, in April 1915, when a card that "circulated around the smoking car" on a trip from Mahone Bay to Bridgewater "caused a sensation." It read: "If you want to fight, go to Europe / If you want to talk war, go to Hell / I'm for business." It was signed by Nathan Veinot, a well-known Bridgewater businessman. The ensuing scandal arose from the fact that the reverse side of the card read: "Vote for Duff, Donovan, and Kinley." (William Duff, who would be elected mayor of Lunenburg over J. Frank Hall in February 1916, had also recently been nominated to run for the Liberals in Ottawa.) There was "no thought for the flower of the land that is being sacrificed in this horrible war," fumed "Disgusted Spectator" in the *Bulletin* of April 27, "no thought for the rivers of blood, and the agonies of the wounded, no thought for anything but a brutal selfishness that is expressed in a manner amounting almost to blasphemy." There was no need to censure the Germans "when a thing like that can exist in the midst of our fair county of Lunenburg." The *Bulletin* charged that the cards were printed at the *Progress-Enterprise* offices; and the same card had been "issued by a wholesale grocery (AND LIQUOR) firm of Halifax," but without the advice on how to vote. As someone claiming to be a "Life Long Liberal" asserted in the *Halifax Herald* of May 18, the notion that anyone who talked war should go to hell was enough to make a decent Christian man's blood run cold. This, and other incidents, would later allow the Conservatives to charge that William Duff did not support the war effort.

A great fuss had also arisen in the local press in May 1915, when the *Bulletin* raised the hackles of those at the Lunenburg paper by referring to it as "alien." This charge led to a torrent of patriotic fervour in the *Progress-Enterprise* on May 12. Alien means "Foreign; of a different nature," according to the dictionary, exclaimed the latter. "Were we possessed of the same nature as the editor of the *Bulletin* we would invite a speedy death." Everyone connected with "this great family Journal" is a Canadian and true loyal Britisher.

> *In these great days of national peril the natives of India, the blacks of South Africa, and the Indians of the Plains are giving of their life's blood for the Empire's Cause, along with the sons of Canada, of New Zealand, of Australia, of Newfoundland and of every other British Colony. Their mangled forms are piled together in one horrible bleeding mass; shot down in the performance of their sacred duty of protecting the British Empire.... They are brothers in arms and comrades even in death. No one is alien to the other. Wherever the Union Flag flies under God's blue sky, whether in Labrador or Ceylon, all British subjects are welded together by a common bond. Only in the pin head of the pigmy editor of the Bridgewater Bulletin Organette can any other thought be found.*

The sourness lingered, and after years of squabbling in October 1917 the fight became particularly personal between the managers of the two papers. Charles J. Cragg of the *Bulletin*, apparently under the impression that a new manager had been appointed at the *Progress-Enterprise*, remarked that such a person would "have an easy job elevating the standard of that paper's journalistic ethics which were certainly at a low ebb for some years past." J. H. Hall replied in his paper on October 31 that he was in fact still very much the manager. "Every individual that opposes your arrogant opinions," he told Cragg, "is sure to get an odorous dose from your depraved mind…in this perilous time of war, and the constant demand for munitions, it would seem like treason to load a cannon to shoot a skunk. Your measure has been taken years ago and if your status is no larger than your mind, principle and everything pertaining to manhood, you could easily kiss a rat's hind legs without bending your knees." Fortunately, it was no longer common to settle disputes with firearms in a duel.

When Agnes McGuire eventually took over as editor and manager of the *Progress-Enterprise* in January 1918, the *Bulletin* commented that she was eminently qualified and the "elimination of distasteful personalities and other unjournalistic proclivities may be confidently expected."

In the meantime, women continued their hard work on behalf of worthy causes. The Woman's Christian Temperance Union was one of the most important of the women's organizations in Lunenburg during the war. A branch had been established in the town on January 1, 1890, according to the Lunenburg Academy's newsletter *The Seagull* in 1971. As it happened, two of the most powerful women in the provincial organization at the time were from Lunenburg. Ada Louise Powers, born in the town in 1859, was actively involved in many of the social causes of the day. Her principal role, however, was as long-time president of the Nova Scotia WCTU. She was a widow; her husband, Frank, owner of a successful hardware store and plumbing business, had died in 1911. Equally prominent in the local and provincial WCTU was Mary Russell Chesley, superintendent of the Department of Franchise. Born in Dartmouth in 1847, Chesley and her husband, Judge S. A. Chesley, lived in Lunenburg and had three children. The two eldest were tragically killed in their late teens in 1895, the result of a boating accident in the harbour. As well as supporting temperance, Mary Chesley argued persuasively on behalf of women's suffrage over the years, and she was also a formidable advocate for peace.

Ada Powers was fond of writing letters to the local newspapers. In the *Progress-Enterprise* she informed readers that Temperance Sunday in 1914 would be held on August 9. The lesson was to be entitled "The Barren Fig Tree and the Defiled Temple," based on passages from St. Mark and St. Matthew. The general topic would be the curse of intemperance and how to remove it. "Surely the liquor traffic is a tree barren of good fruit and should be cursed unto its death. The Temple which is a symbol of a people, a nation or a person in which God dwells, is defiled by strong drink and should be cleansed as was the temple of old." The children in the Sunday schools should have a vital part in this cleansing. On May 18, 1915, readers were told about an appeal from the Nova Scotia Temperance Alliance to print pledges that would be circulated in churches and schools to be signed by those willing to forgo the use of intoxicating beverages. Such people would be following the example of King George v himself, who supported a temperance campaign in Great Britain by promising that no

Ada Powers.

alcohol would be consumed in the royal household until the war was over.

At a WCTU provincial convention held in Truro in September 1917, the Lunenburg branch was said to be the largest in the province, followed by Halifax and Wolfville. The first resolution passed, not surprisingly, was that "we of the Nova Scotia WCTU urge that men and women everywhere practise and encourage total abstinence from alcoholic drinks." Other resolutions concerned the need to report violations of the Lord's Day Act, the prohibition of the use of foodstuffs for brewing and distilling, and opposition to raising money by raffles or other methods suggestive of gambling. One speaker deplored the fact that so many girls from refined and respectable homes talked to and wrote to soldiers absolutely unknown to them. It was shocking that their mothers not only allowed this but encouraged it. Better class girls should set an example for those not so protected: "No nation ever rises above its women." The *Halifax Herald* on September 28 reported that provincial president Ada Powers "thanked all who helped to make our stay in Truro so delightful."

In a letter to the *Morning Chronicle* of Halifax on March 17, 1917, Ada Powers had argued that liquor sellers everywhere opposed women's suffrage, because they knew that women would use the vote to overthrow the liquor traffic. "It is doubtful," she wrote, "whether prohibition will ever prohibit with only men as executive power behind it." The home represented the top of civilization, the saloon the bottom. There must be mothers in government as well as fathers. According to local lore, Ada Powers also organized a group called the Loyal Temperance Legion, which rolled bandages during the war and put on musicals to raise money for the Red Cross. Always busy, she also arranged for competitions in elocution and singing.

Among the good works of the Lunenburg WCTU was a comfortable building in Canso, at the eastern end of mainland Nova Scotia, built in 1893 for the use of mariners. Called Sailors' Rest, there was reading material, checkers and other games, and an organ. "Here the Lunenburg County men, with the heart-whole enthusiasm for music which they inherit as part of their German ancestry, love to gather and wake the echoes with their hearty singing of the old songs and hymns." The fisherman often had long waits for bait at Canso, and "enforced

Fishermen's Picnic parade, Lunenburg, 1917. The sign reads "LESS BEER MORE BOOTS – DRINK: A Destructive Evil & a Curse."

idleness hung heavily on their hands." The *Progress-Enterprise* on July 8, 1914, noted that the WCTU also sent clothing and quilts to the poor fishermen and their families in Labrador. Anyone with items to send was to phone Mrs. Powers.

A lasting gift to the town of Lunenburg from the WCTU had been made before the war. According to *The Seagull*, Ada Powers had organized in 1900 the Young Woman's Christian Temperance Union, known as the "Y." It had been noticed that oxen and horses drawing heavy loads of wood and produce into town often stood for hours at the market with no water to quench their thirst. As well, the national WCTU had declared that every union should erect "a fountain of pure water symbolizing the sort of drink that Womanhood approves of." On Thanksgiving Day, October 30, 1911, Mayor J. J. Kinley presided over the ceremony known as the "Presentation of the Fountain." The 75th Regiment band "enlivened the proceedings with sweet music," and Ada Powers spoke on behalf of the Y, presenting the drinking fountain for use by man and beast.

The young people, teenage girls and boys, had raised the money for the gift through various projects, such as sales of food and candy, musical teas, bazaars, and finally a canvass of the leading citizens of the town. The *Progress-Enterprise*, on November 1, noted that in fact the basins on the fountain were too small to water a yoke of oxen. Nevertheless, "we hope it will stand here for many years, a beacon light for temperance, and be well taken care of so that all who pass by weary and thirsty, may be refreshed by partaking of the pure sparkling water, one of God's best gifts to man." The fountain remains, at the intersection of Falkland and Lincoln Streets, but, appropriately perhaps, given its origins in the temperance movement, it is now dry.

A shocking event occurred in the town of Windsor, in the neighbouring county of Hants, in 1918, a "very sad incident," according to the account in the *Bridgewater Bulletin* of September 24. A casket, "presumably containing the remains of a dear, departed friend of somebody," arrived at the railway station in a hearse. It was remarked, however, that the people accompanying the casket "presented a jubilant rather than a sad appearance." Mixing with the usual station crowd was the local liquor inspector, and he, instead of the "mourners," took charge of the "remains." Upon opening, the casket was found to contain many bottles of booze. "Prohibition, even war-time prohibition, may not be an unqualified success and stop all drinking of intoxicating liquors," commented the *Bulletin*, "but when dealers in booze must resort to shipping their wares in coffins and moving it about in a hearse, the traffic must be pretty nearly dead and prepared for burial."

Bridgewater was in no position to cast aspersions. Letters to the editor on August 7 and 21, 1917, complained about "drunkenness on our streets." It was very noticeable on Saturday nights, "and quite offensive to ladies." One J. F. Ronand of Halifax wrote that he was "amazed at this state of things in a prohibition country. Your town is a very pretty one and it is a shame that it is getting a reputation for booze joints and drunken men on the streets. What is the matter with your town officials?" A columnist in the *Bulletin's* Town and Country News column grumbled about the "drunks and disorderlies" who were "kicking up shindy in town on Saturday night." It was a disgraceful business. "Is this a prohibition town or a refuge for BOOZORIUMS?"

Matters were apparently even worse in Lunenburg. Back on June 23, 1915, an irate ratepayer had written to the *Progress-Enterprise* fulminating about crime in the town. For a long time there had been "common street talk" about the criminal acts of a group of boys and young men. There was thievery, burglary, and other forms of lawlessness. "Assaults and drunken brawls and riots and breaches of the peace are so common that after the striking and the cursing have passed by the affair is forgotten. Lawlessness seems to thrive, in fact to be encouraged." The impression was that there must be something wrong with the police and the administration of justice in the town. The correspondent's list of all the places broken into and the goods stolen provided a "startling record of unpunished crime." It was "only a short step from thieving and house-breaking to murder and shooting and arson and all the crimes in the calendar." Although he does not actually say so, many would assume that "drink" was behind all these troubles.

Certainly, progressive reformers considered alcohol to be at the root of many of society's problems. A taste for rum in particular had developed through long-time trade with the West Indian colonies. One Nova Scotian claimed, according to historian Craig Heron in *Booze*, that spirits "were almost universally regarded as little less necessary to

Whiskey and the Open Saloon. The Dealer: The only man it ever benefited. Halifax Herald, *October 20, 1917.*

man's healthful existence than flesh and bread. Alcohol, it was thought, kept out heat in summer and cold in winter, supplied strength to labour, helped digestion, warded off disease, and did many other marvellous things." Following on a long tradition of fighting the liquor traffic in the nineteenth century with some success, real progress was made in 1910 when a Nova Scotia prohibition law was enacted in the legislature, despite the reluctance of Premier Murray's Liberal government. This law prohibited the sale of alcohol for beverage purposes, though it was allowed for medicinal, sacramental, and manufacturing use.

Bootleggers had been operating in Lunenburg County before prohibition, and their activities would not cease. At a patriotic meeting in the Opera House in September 1914, it was alleged that no one would doubt the sympathy of Lunenburg people for the wounded on the battlefield, "but what about protection for the men of our town, who even on a Sunday are enticed by the bootleggers to throw away not only their money but their manhood....If you have not the interest of your weaker brethren at heart be sure that the women who have to bear the disgrace can and will soon do something." The extent of resistance to the law around the county can be seen in a single item in the *Progress-Enterprise* of February 3, 1915. Francis Holloway, liquor inspector for the municipality, with the assistance of a constable, visited Petite Riviere, Italy Cross, Upper Branch, Bakers Settlement, New Germany, and Oakland. At The Narrows forty-three bottles of ale were confiscated; at Maitland one barrel containing twelve bottles of ale; at Mahone Bay one barrel of Budweiser Lager beer in bottles; and at New Germany a barrel containing Scotch whisky and rum in bottles, also one gallon jug containing rum. All was destroyed.

Nine convictions were secured, one case was lost, and one of the accused skipped out to the States. Abdoo Younis of Martins River was convicted for selling liquor. William Hiltz of The Narrows was similarly convicted and jailed. Noble Crouse of Bridgewater and Snyder Slauenwhite of Mahone Bay were charged with bringing liquor into the municipality. Valentine Jodrey was convicted for selling, but got off because the forms were not properly filled out. Covering such a large area cost a lot, declared the exasperated inspector, and the traffic now largely took place in outlying districts not easily reached. And he must deal with far too many idle rumours of suspected illicit liquor violations. He justifiably asked for a raise.

There was, regrettably to some, an enormous loophole in the law, for the capital city, Halifax, was excluded. The slow progress forward, argued the *Bulletin* of March 28, 1916, was "owing to the obstruction of government members and the untiring opposition of Halifax brewers and saloon-keepers." But as the war raged on, it was increasingly thought to be self-indulgent and unpatriotic to drink when men were risking their lives at the front. As well, many considered spending money on alcohol as a beverage to be wasteful. As historian C. Mark Davis notes, a "wet Halifax undermined the effectiveness and intent of the law." In the words of Ian McKay, Halifax was a "wet blot on an otherwise well-regulated moral landscape."[4]

Prohibition was extended to the entire province in March. Conservative A. C. Zwicker, from Lunenburg, remarked in the debates in the legislature that "it was only a matter of right and wrong." Only three members from Halifax had voted against the new law, which went into effect on July 11, 1916. The federal government in Ottawa, which maintained control of the importation and manufacturing of alcohol, also eventually brought in new laws: from December 1917 intoxicating beverages could not be imported into Canada, and after March 1918, alcohol for beverage purposes could not be manufactured or sold in Canada for the duration of the war and for one year after. Total prohibition had come to the Maritimes.

As E. R. Forbes explains in "Prohibition and the Social Gospel in Nova Scotia," the prohibitionists wanted to create a new society in which crime, disease, and social injustice would be virtually eliminated. Not only was alcoholism a serious social problem in itself, but also it was thought to be an important contributory cause to a host of other ills, including poverty, disease, the disintegration of the family, and traffic and industrial accidents. "Prohibition thus became an integral part of a sweeping programme for social reform." It was understandable that the problem of intemperance would be tackled by the churches, by women's groups, by social reformers, and by organizations such as the Independent Order of Good Templars and the Nova Scotia Temperance Alliance. In Lunenburg, for instance, according to the local paper on February 7, 1917, the Lunenburg Rock Division, No. 539, Sons of Temperance, was reorganized to "escape the guilt of prolonging this war by either implicitly or explicitly consenting to the drinking customs that, as a monster cancer are eating the vitals of the Empire."

With alcoholic beverages about to be unavailable, at least legally, J. J. Kinley came to the rescue of thirsty Lunenburgers by installing in his drugstore an "up-to-date and sanitary soda fountain of the latest design." The *Progress-Enterprise* maintained on July 5, 1916, that more soda water drinks were said to be consumed in the larger cities of Canada and the United States than any other beverage, "the reason being that pure fruit syrups combined with good carbonated water makes the best of temperance beverages." Kinley's was also the first to install a modern soda fountain in Halifax, "a great attraction" with "a reputation for cleanliness, good service, and the quality of the goods dispensed." It's hard to know if the soda fountain would compensate for the loss of the city's many taverns.

The *Bulletin* commented on August 15, 1916, that after being forced to go "Dry as a Bone" in July by the passage of the prohibition bill in March, Halifax had had to bid farewell to its forty-six barrooms. "Hats off to Water Street! Think of it! There she was, dry, orderly and quiet." Dazed policemen looked as if they were lost or had been sent to the wrong beat. Restaurants and lunch rooms were filled with sober and jolly sailors, soldiers, and civilians. Children were playing in the street. Women chatted on their doorsteps. On the whole, a rather idealized portrait of the port city.

Not just men at home must be saved from "demon rum," but the soldiers overseas as well. General Edwin A. H. Alderson caused a storm of protest late in 1914 when he gave his permission for the use of intoxicating beverages by Canadian troops in training on Salisbury Plain. The Women's Foreign Missionary Society of the Presbyterian church in Lunenburg sent a letter to Prime Minister Borden, according to the *Progress-Enterprise* of November 18, expressing "deep regret": "in the name of Canadian mothers whose sons have offered themselves for their country's service, we express our utter disapproval of their unnecessary exposure while in course of training, to the temptation of strong drink." At the same time, Alderson's action was earnestly protested by the Women's Missionary Society of Lunenburg's Methodist church: "in the name of Canadian mothers who have given their sons to serve in this terrible crisis we protest against this needless addition to the dangers they are called to face." Temperance women, supported by the Christian sentiment of the people, had exerted their influence to have drink removed from military camps, and now they had learned "with dismay and alarm" that this temptation was being deliberately placed before the soldiers in England. A union meeting of the town's Sunday schools forwarded resolutions to the prime minister protesting against General Alderson's wet canteens, as did Riverport's WCTU. In the words of historian Michael Bliss, "Many Canadian Methodists came to believe that sex and liquor in England were worse threats to Canadian manhood than the guns in France."[5]

Some individuals and temperance associations were even against the rum ration in the trenches, and they insisted that soldiers were compelled to take it. The fact is, explained the *Bulletin* of March 6, 1917, rum was "issued to the troops only at the discretion of the General Officer Commanding and individual soldiers who have any objection to the spirit may be supplied with cocoa or chocolate in lieu thereof." In *At the Sharp End*, Tim Cook tells of one commanding officer, Victor Odlum, a strict teetotaller, who gave his men lime juice and pea soup instead of the rum ration; mutinous feelings became so strong that his superior officer overruled him.

There was concern also for the thousands of soldiers and sailors who passed through Halifax, especially the returned wounded soldiers who were being supplied with "vile and poisonous concoctions." The *Halifax Herald* was not above using the issue of race to make a point. In an item on October 29, 1917, decrying the many "Blind Piggers" and "Bootleggers" operating in the city, the headline read: "Battle Scarred Heroes Doped with Poison and Then Entertained with a 'Skirt Dance' by a 250 Pound Colored Woman." In an accompanying sketch, the woman was trying to "torpedo a jack tar with cigarette smoke" while they "cavorted about the room and stumbled over the legs of the guests around the tables...'Lady' HELPERS were engaged to serve the drinks." It was "not a very edifying sight....What would you think if your boy was entertained this way when he reached London or some other city in England?"

Those opposed to the liquor traffic were also often against tobacco and smoking. Some months before the outbreak of war, on April 29, the *Progress-Enterprise* announced that May 3, 1914, was to be known as Anti-Cigarette Sunday, because, as the ever-present Ada Powers declared on behalf of the South Shore Temperance Society, "the evil of cigarette smoking would be the chief topic of discussion." She provided a helpful pamphlet called "The Cigarette Smoking Boy" and urged that pledges be taken against the habit. Also, as temperance secretary for the Lunenburg County Sunday School Association, Mrs. Powers asked in September that year that a list of members who had pledged against liquor, tobacco, and profanity be sent to her—at once.

The *Progress-Enterprise* of October 27, 1915, reported that Jennie Waters of Hamilton, Ontario, Dominion superintendent of anti-narcotics for the WCTU, had written to the Duchess of Connaught at Rideau Hall. Waters had heard that Her Royal Highness intended "to present each of our first contingent of Canadian soldiers with a gift of maple sugar...just such a choice our late beloved Queen Victoria would have made," for it not only represented a Canadian industry but was also a harmless and enjoyable luxury. It was "lamentable to see so many of our cultured women contributing cigarettes through the patriotic societies…a mistaken kindness responsible for many fatalities at the camps with the very articles that unfits them for their very strenuous and hazardous life."

At a Methodist conference in Toronto that year a resolution was passed condemning the sending of tobacco to soldiers at the front and expressing disapproval of the men smoking. However, a letter in the Lunenburg paper on July 7 criticized this view as narrow-minded, bigoted, and unpatriotic, and "a surprising stance for such an enlightened body": "To expect soldiers who have been under severe shell fire for days, often without food or water, facing death at all times and subjected to the most nerve racking and exhausting experience that a man could possibly endure to go without a smoke is the height of folly. Surely a man who goes out and risks his life in order that we might breathe the air of freedom should at least be given the opportunity to have a quiet smoke after he has returned from the trenches."

Contrary to the Lunenburg WCTU's unanimous April 1916 vote against sending cigarettes to the troops, apparently a feeling prevailed among many, including women, that the soldiers deserved and needed their smokes. Both the IODE and the Red Cross included tobacco and cigarettes in some of the parcels they sent overseas. In May 1916 the Masons of Lunenburg "tendered the soldier boys a Smoker in the Empire," with "speech-making, moving pictures, music, ice-cream, cigars, etc.—'no dull moments were experienced.'" Many people gave to the Overseas Tobacco Fund: contributions collected by the postmaster in Upper Kingsburg in December 1915, mainly from Moshers and Mossmans, amounted to $8.50, and in February 1916 sixteen people from Parks Creek and Dublin Shore donated $0.25 each to the fund.

In the summer of 1916, Mrs. W. D. Haughn of Pentz received a letter, reprinted in the *Progress-Enterprise* of July 19, from her son Grover who, among other things, wrote about the importance of tobacco while in the trenches.

We certainly had a hot time of it this time in.…You talk about chewing and smoking but I certainly did some of it while in the Trenches.

We were not allowed to smoke during the night, only through the day. The way my jaws were going during the night was no way slow. I chewed all the Tobacco sent me. At least I chewed two figs while we were in, and that was only five days. You will no doubt think I am getting to be, or rather am a regular tobacco fiend but you know we have to do something during such times. When not in the trenches I very seldom use it, so you see I am not too bad after all.

Grover survived the war but, sadly, drowned along with his father, captain of the tern *Maid of Scotland*, off Saint John in February 1924.

In efforts to ease a dark time, the home front did not lack for entertainment during the war. According to an ad in the *Malagash News* of March 4, 1917, for twenty-five cents (fifteen for children), one could go to the IOOF Music Hall in Lunenburg for a cabaret and two reels of motion pictures, changing every night. Coming in May were Frank E. Walsh and his Musical Comedy Company, introducing high-class vaudeville, with catchy music, pretty girls, and clever comedians. The same paper announced the showing of two serials at the Alexandra Theatre for ten cents (five for children). Back in the music hall a few days later, one could see the first of fifteen chapters of the great railroad film novel, *The Girl and the Game*, featuring "The Fearless Film Star," Helen Holmes; a bonus was the appearance of Lunenburg's famous quartet. As the war progressed, many of the shows became war-related, such as *The Kaiser, the Beast of Berlin* at the Empire Theatre in Bridgewater, billed in the *Bulletin* of February 11, 1919, as "THE SENSATION OF THE AGE."

Both the larger towns in the county had well-attended exhibitions. The first Lunenburg County Exhibition was held at Bridgewater in the Drill Hall in 1891. Known today as the Big Ex, it became the region's first major agricultural exhibition. The *Progress-Enterprise* on October 4, 1916, reported the event that year took place in perfect weather, with thousands in attendance. The grounds of the annual event had been much improved with the addition of new cattle sheds, extending nearly the whole length of the property. The main building was filled with exhibits of fruit, vegetables, and grains, providing evidence that "our farmers are forging ahead to front positions in the farming world." The second floor was occupied by manufactures such as exhibits of pianos and furs, though the principal attraction was an exhibit of munitions, "very educative and gave to the onlooker a very accurate idea of the destruction wrought in Europe when missiles of that sort were sent flying through the air." No finer showing of swine was ever put on exhibition in the province, according to the reporter, and the poultry house was equally fine. Highlights were the horse races; "the fakirs barked long and loud and, we are told, acted quite modest in their callings." The ox and horse pulling contests, as always, drew large and enthusiastic crowds. The farmers' wives, too, displayed their wares.

An occasion of note took place in Lunenburg that year, for the first fishermen's picnic was held, starting a tradition that would extend into the twenty-first century. As for the Bridgewater exhibition the weather was fine, and on a late September day thousands of people turned up. The town was dressed in "real holiday attire," with bunting and other decorations freely displayed. The fishermen and their friends came from every part of the county. The reunion, the *Progress-Enterprise* hoped on October 4, 1916, would have a tendency to

Fishermen's Picnic parade, Lincoln Street, Lunenburg, 1916.

create a bond of sympathy between the hardy toilers of the deep and "afford a free exchange of opinions on matters pertaining to our chief industry—fishing."

After praising the "hard and insistent toil" of the fishermen—"No pluckier men can be found in all Canada than our hardy fishermen"—the paper described the first fishermen's picnic parade. Six hundred school-children marching from the Academy were joined at the post office by floats representing nearly all the industries of the town, notably the Lunenburg Foundry, with a big display of their manufactures, motor engines in operation, mechanics at work; W. C. Smith & Company, with a full-rigged fishing schooner with dories on deck, fishing kegs, and trawl gear; Robin, Jones & Whitman, with a complete line of their boneless codfish; and Powers & Company with their mechanical and plumbing gear. The first settlers were represented by "Captain and Mrs. Rouche," garbed as they had landed in 1753. Politicians were present, of course, and gave short addresses, though the first speaker was a lieu-tenant from Halifax who made an earnest appeal for recruits. Sports on land and on the water followed, with various races held, including dory and pleasure boat races, a tug of war between fishermen and shore men, shot-putting, and the fat man's race. Fireworks and band concerts in the evening wound up "one of the most interesting celebrations ever held in the town." For a while, the war could be forgotten.

———

War, it was said, according to Robert S. Prince in "The Mythology of War," was a manly undertaking. Women could support, care, and mourn, but the combat experience defined the very essence of man-hood. There could be no doubt that women made a major contribution to the war effort, but it was men who paid the supreme sacrifice.

One of the first men from Lunenburg to die in the war was Leo Zinck. Born on September 30, 1883, likely at home on Second Peninsula, he was thirty-one when he enlisted at Valcartier on September 26, 1914. A small man, only 162 cm tall, he claimed to be a cook before the war.

He sailed from Quebec City on the ss *Scotian* on October 4, 1914, and eight months later he was dead. Following the Second Battle of Ypres in Belgium, April and May 1915, the Allies went on the offensive farther south in France. Zinck, a private in the 13th Battalion Royal Highlanders of Canada, was killed during the advance on Festubert some time between May 20 and 23, 1915. His grave unknown, his name is engraved on the ramparts of the Canadian memorial at Vimy

Leo Zinck.

Ridge, along with eleven thousand other Canadian soldiers.

Another early casualty of the war was announced in the Mahone Bay column of the *Progress-Enterprise* on April 12, 1916. Corporal Charles Slauenwhite, age twenty-four, was killed fighting for king and country in Flanders on March 31, leaving behind four brothers, three of whom were "in Khaki," and a sister. Later, in July, a schoolgirl in Blockhouse published a very long poem in his honour, which begins:

It was just a month or two ago
When lo! there came the words of woe
To mother, father, family all,
Hearing that their boy did fall.

This lad was born in Mader's Cove,
A hamlet by the sea.
Although 'twas home he longed to rove,
And soon a soldier boy was he.

Gerald Edwin Cragg.

When first he left he thought
'twas fun,
Crossing old England's foam,
But when he heard the
awful gun,
He longed to be at home.

On June 13, 1916, the *Bulletin* noted that Lieutenant Gerald Edwin Cragg had been killed in action on June 3 at Ypres (likely the Battle of Mont Sorrel). He was "one of our own towns-fellows, a lad on the threshold of life, inexperienced and untried in thought and action." Cragg was the son of Charles J. Cragg, who had founded the *Bulletin* in 1888, and he had learned to be a printer and publisher in his father's office. Wounded and back in Bridgewater on sick leave, the junior Cragg could have stayed at home, but he felt it his duty to return overseas. Back at the front by late March, serving with the 3rd Toronto Battalion, he was killed while leading his platoon forward, struck by shrapnel from shellfire on his way to the trenches. Gerald Cragg was buried at Poperinghe, Belgium, at No. 10 Casualty Clearing Station Cemetery. "'And what may quiet us in a death so noble,' *Samson Agonistes*." A plaque in his honour is on display at the Royal Canadian Legion in Bridgewater.

One Lunenburg family made considerable contributions to the war effort by way of family members. Arthur J. Hebb, who ran a sail-making business in town, and his wife Grace, had five sons, all of whom were born in Lunenburg. Four of them went off to war, and the fifth tried to go. The eldest son, Charles Arthur, was born in 1890. He was a fisher-man, married to Alice, and they had four children. Twenty-six when he crossed the ocean on the *Olympic* in October 1916, he served with the 85th Battalion in Belgium and France. After recovering from a severe abscess in his throat, he asked that his tonsils not be removed because he wanted to return as soon as possible to his unit at the front. Struck by shrapnel, he was wounded badly in his buttock and thigh, but survived the war and returned to Canada on the ss *Cassandra* in May 1919. From the army's personnel records we rarely discover what battles the soldiers actually fought in, but here we are told that Charles Hebb was at both Vimy Ridge in April 1917 and in October at what historian Donald Creighton called the "macabre horror of Passchendaele."

Brothers Joseph Malcolm and Dalton Comingo Hebb also survived the war. Joseph, a clerk before the war, was the first to enlist, at Amherst, in March 1915. Apart from a bout of mumps at Valcartier, he seems to have been healthy throughout the war, serving with the 5th Canadian Mounted Rifles. Joe Hebb wrote a letter home to his mother in February 1918, printed in the *Progress-Enterprise* on March 27, in which he described in some detail his leave in Paris, which he preferred to London.

Now about the people, you meet all kinds from bums up to counts and the people sure do know how to dress. Well, I guess you say that they should know, because the world gets all the latest fashions from there. I never saw so many girls in all my life as I did down there. Well I will tell you, without exaggerating a bit that they wear such high heeled boots, should they happen to lose one heel they would have to limp like a man with a wooden leg...they paint and powder something awful, you can't kiss a "jeane" without getting your lips red (Ha! Ha!). So much for the people.

Dalton, a sergeant in the 75th Regiment and a musician, enlisted with the Royal Canadian Regiment in August 1915. All the Hebb boys were a good height, around 173 cm, but lanky Dalton weighed a mere 50 kg when he went to war. Though he spent at least ten months in the trenches, his main task was to play in the regiment's band, at one point being promoted to French horn soloist. He also apparently enjoyed playing for the soldiers at the Young Men's Christian Association huts and gained a reputation as "a cracker-jack at the piano." The RCR was a permanent, regular army infantry regiment and therefore made up of professional soldiers, unlike Sam Hughes's "citizen-soldiers." Rather oddly, the regiment spent a whole year in Bermuda before joining the Canadian Expeditionary Force in France from November 1915 until the end of the war.

John Bruno Hebb, the youngest of the men, did not survive the war. A telegrapher, only eighteen when he enlisted at Sussex, New Brunswick, in September 1915, he fought with the 26th Battalion. He crossed the Atlantic from Halifax on the ss *Adriatic* in March 1916, and six months later he was dead. After a bout of tonsillitis, Bruno had rejoined his unit on September 11, 1916, and was killed while taking part in an attack at the Battle of Courcelette on the Somme four days later. "He was a game kid and died as a hero," wrote his brother Dalton from France. The fifth son, Ellard Hebb of Saskatoon, was also anxious to enlist, but he was unable to pass the medical examination.

It was, indeed, a time of manly men and formidable women! Men were dying overseas. And more would be needed to maintain the ranks. Women at home, especially middle-class women, were perhaps working harder than ever before, and they were instrumental in achieving what, to many of them, was the greatest victory of all, the prohibition of liquor. Women espoused worthy endeavours of many kinds, and though far from the battles at the front, they were doing their best to support the war effort. What could they not achieve if only they had the vote?

Chapter Three

SERVING AT HOME
AND OVERSEAS

I n the early fall of 1917, the loyal men of Lunenburg County heard sincere and sundry patriotic sentiments at a great reunion of Lutherans held at Wentzells Lake, several kilometres upriver from Bridgewater. Several thousand people assembled for the picnic under the noble pine trees that overlooked the waters of the lake. According to the *Halifax Herald* of September 7, apart from a flourishing congregation in Halifax, all of the four thousand or so adherents of the Lutheran Evangelical church in Nova Scotia were found in the "historic county" of Lunenburg.

Along with Lutheran ministers, military men were present in the interests of recruiting. Lieutenant Governor MacCallum Grant declared that this splendid gathering was surely an indication that there was "some good in this old world yet. Our thoughts go out to our brave lads who are across the ocean fighting for you and for me in the cause of justice, right and humanity." Every young man who had reached military age and was physically fit should ask where his duty lay, and "answer the call of his courageous brothers by joining the ranks and preparing to fight under the banner of Old England and her allies, not only thinking but knowing that God will defend his action as he has promised for all who do the right. We can all join as did the old saints in singing that old hymn 'Ein feste Berg ist unser Gott.'" In loyally following our "Great Leader," the lieutenant governor concluded, "we can all the more truly follow our earthly leaders who are fighting that the old flag may never fall." Dean John Plummer Derwent Llwyd of the Anglican Cathedral Church of All Saints in Halifax also addressed the multitude and asked what Luther would do if he were living now. "He would stand side by side with the allies in their battle for liberty for the oppressed and freedom for the small nations. People in whom the spirit of Luther lives must do their part for the principles for which the allies fight." Clearly, the Lutheran God was meant to be on the side of the British Empire.

Fervid patriotism supported by militant religion, along with calls for more and more recruits, remained a staple of gatherings at home. But what about the men in the trenches? It is not possible, of course, to know what individual soldiers were thinking about their predicament: dodging bursting shells and snipers' bullets, crawling with lice, and surrounded by rats, the mud and general filth, the smells of dirty men and decaying bodies. Tim Cook, in *At the Sharp End*, observes that the "demonization of the enemy by the home-front propagandists and editors often sat uneasily with the troops." The soldiers knew that the men in the trenches on the other side were just as badly off. Erich Maria Remarque's protagonist in *All Quiet on the Western Front* evoked similar feelings among the men in the German trenches: "Why do they never tell us that you are poor devils like us, that your mothers are just as anxious as ours, and that we have the same fear of death, and the same dying and the same agony....If we threw away these rifles and this uniform, you could be my brother."

In *The Secret History of Soldiers*, Tim Cook remarks that the men at the front may have become jaded and worn out in the trenches, but most of them continued to see the war as a necessary struggle. This practical perspective, however, was not the same as the flag-waving patriotism at home. As Modris Eksteins says in *Rites of Spring*, "the home front did not understand the nature of the soldier's *via dolorosa*. The only reality that could support the soldier was 'the comradeship of the trenches.'"

An interesting letter, from "somewhere in France," was printed in the *Bridgewater Bulletin* of February 6, 1917. Private R. H. Whynacht of Voglers Cove wrote to his father on December 26, 1916. He had "enjoyed [Christmas] as well as I ever did but in a very funny way." This, he said, was how his fellow soldiers had celebrated the day: "About ten in the morning they looked out of the trench and saw the Germans standing on top of their parapet, the top of the trench which is built of sandbags forming a wall, waving their hands for us to come over. We got on top of our trench and waved for them to come over to us. They would not come so we started walking towards them and then they started towards us. They came right up and shook hands. We could see our boys and them shaking hands about a mile along the line. An officer and some of the men came right over to our trench, they had cigars and cigarettes. An officer and some of the men spoke good English. They gave us a German paper saying war would be over by the middle of January."

It is well known that a widespread but unofficial ceasefire, the famous Christmas truce, took place between the British and German troops along the front in December 1914. The guns went silent and the sound of carols drifted across no man's land. Hands were shaken, small gifts of food and tobacco and souvenirs were exchanged. There were reports of shared religious services and football matches. Something similar, but on a much smaller scale, occurred at Christmas 1915, despite strict orders from the high commands on both sides that fraternization was not allowed. Canadian soldiers, too, met up with the enemy. According to the *Bulletin* of December 28, 1915, a soldier from Saint John, New Brunswick, had reported from the firing line that "when things are quiet our boys and the Germans talk to one another." One morning the Canadians threw over a tin of bully beef. In return, a German hailed one of the 26th Battalion trenches and struck up a conversation in good English, inviting the soldiers there to come over for a drink. After reassurances, the German walked halfway between the trenches and had a drink, and eventually he was joined by six others. The German soldiers warned the Canadians that they would start bombarding at noon.

Private Whynacht's letter above is somewhat surprising, for the war had become more and more bitter by Christmas 1916 because of the terrible losses of human life, and fraternization with the enemy was surely much less common. "The enemy became increasingly an abstraction as the nature of the war changed," Eksteins remarks.

There was a softer side to the war, seldom seen. People at home sometimes received unexpected gifts from the men at the front. A letter home from R. W. Bradbury, "somewhere in France," in the *Bulletin* of May 11, 1915, had included some pressed flowers from the trenches that he had promised to send. The German machine guns had opened fire but fortunately he already had the flowers. He had to roll into a shell hole until the firing ceased. "I know you will like them as a souvenir of the place where the Canadians are doing their little bit.... [T]hey will be a novelty such as I don't suppose any other person in Nova Scotia will have."

Gordon Maurice Hebb also sent flowers home to his mother. The son of Lydia and Levi Hebb of Bridgewater, Hebb went overseas on the *Olympic* with the 112th Battalion in July 1916, then served with the 78th Battalion, the Winnipeg Grenadiers. He had been a bookkeeper before the war, apparently with the LaHave Creamery Company. In his letter of September 27, 1916, Lieutenant Hebb commented that France was a pretty country, much finer than what he had seen of Belgium, and the people were also cleaner and more modern. He enclosed a few flowers from Belgian soil that he had picked along the trench on his way out. "They are very ragged as I had to snatch them and stick them in my note book, but they are souvenirs. I will also enclose a spray of French heather." He enclosed as well "a small bit of Fritz's shell that he sent to us." About to have his twenty-ninth birthday, he hoped he would see many more. He was concerned that his mother would not be alarmed by his letter, for conditions in the trenches were not nearly as bad as she pictured, he assured her, or as bad as he had imagined. He found the rats, "as large as half grown cats," the most disagreeable, and he had had to kill several with a stick and sometimes stamp on them. But at times, "all guns cease and the silence, coupled with the scene of men working at the trenches, the birds flying around serenely, and the flowers blooming, you would not think that such a terrible war was raging." "Be cheerful," he told his mother, "have patience, faith and hope, and all will be well." The *Progress-Enterprise* on October 15 noted that Lieutenant Hebb had since been reported missing. He had in fact been killed in action on October 14, 1916, just a couple of weeks after writing to his mother.

On the home front, women made major contributions to the war effort by raising money and supplies for charities and voluntary organizations; they aided enlistment, promoted food programs, and sold war bonds. As Prime Minister Robert Borden observed, "In a thousand missions of aid and mercy," they were "unwearying in their infinite labour of love."[1] Women also replaced men in munitions factories and in other industries, on railways, and in offices. Lunenburg County was predominantly rural, of course, and munitions factories, for instance, were located mainly in central Canada. As historian Amy Shaw points out, most historical writing about women during the war concerned their roles as nurses or factory workers, but traditional labour was also important. The "non-combatant, voluntary, charitable, stay-at-home roles comprised the bulk of Canadian women's contributions" to the war effort. "Celebrated at the time as a glowing testament to the worth and splendid patriotism of the women and girls who performed them, the humble tasks of knitting, bandage-rolling, and raising funds have not fared well in our cultural memory of the war."[2]

Just as healthy-looking men were pressured into enlisting, women were sometimes shamed into participating in volunteer war work. As

Sarah Glassford and Amy Shaw note in *A Sisterhood of Suffering and Service*, newspapers, for example, would print lists of contributions by volunteers and donors, thus encouraging others to give; classrooms, voluntary groups, and communities competed to raise the most money or produce the most comforts; and "wagging tongues of observant friends and neighbours worked to provide an informal network of community surveillance."

Perhaps the hardest role of all for women was to wait and worry, to wait for news, to wait for the war to be over, to wait for the men to come home. The interminable homeland vigil. In her war novel *Rilla of Ingleside*, set in Prince Edward Island, L. M. Montgomery has her main character cry out with passion when her beloved brother enlists: "*Our* sacrifice is greater than *his*. Our boys give only *themselves*. *We* give them." Later in the novel, the narrator remarks: "There were moments when waiting at home, in safety and comfort, seemed an unendurable thing."³ Montgomery's anguish is revealed in many pages of her *Journals*, written at her home at The Manse, in Leaskdale, Ontario. On June 10, 1916, she wrote, "This war is slowly killing me. I am bleeding to death as France is being bled in the shambles of Verdun."⁴

The *Halifax Herald* on June 21, 1918, paid tribute to "The War Mothers of Nova Scotia." The piece described the sacrificial burden involved by surrendering their men "to the Empire's call and humanity's cause, their patriotism beyond all praise." They must watch and wait with a yearning heart, knowing the postman might arrive any morning as a herald of terrible news. "But still these Nova Scotian mothers lift no voices loud in lamentation, give utterance to no bitter murmurings, but calmly, sweetly and sanely perform their daily tasks with a quiet courage that thrills the hearts of all observers. Not theirs the throbbing excitement, the stir and movement of the battlefield, feel the exhilaration of a charge or the glory of a victory won, but in their own sphere here at home, and in the grandeur of their sublime behaviour, the poet's words are true—'They also serve—who only stand and wait.'"

The First World War, observe Glassford and Shaw, is "generally accepted as being the first 'total war' in which all the resources of the state were directed towards its prosecution....The coining of the term 'home front' to describe the role of non-combatants in such a war reveals the belief that broad, unified participation was necessary to win the war." Women's voluntary, unpaid labour through war charities and voluntary organizations constituted an integral part of the wartime economy. "For four long years women worked, wept, and waited, served, suffered, and sacrificed."

Grace Morris Craig, who wrote her memoirs of the First World War at the age of ninety, recalled being at a recruiting meeting in her hometown of Pembroke, Ontario, and wondering how hundreds of men in "civies" could sit quietly and listen. "It made me almost want to disappear under the stage," she wrote her brother Basil overseas, "just because I was not a man in khaki." Many young women wanted to play a more active role in the war, but there were few ways for women to go overseas. Some women served in non-combat roles as drivers, cooks, or clerks, but the main way to get closer to the front lines was through nursing.

As historian Shawna Quinn puts it, nursing was the only accepted female contribution offering anything close to the front line experience. Nursing gave women an opportunity to stand on the same ground as the men, and a chance to restore them with comfort and healing. Their designated maternal role was reinforced by referring to the wounded soldiers as "lads" or "boys." Most of the wounds the nurses had to deal with were caused by shellfire and machine guns, though there were many respiratory diseases as well. Clare Gass of Shubenacadie, Nova Scotia, served as a lieutenant nursing sister in the CAMC from 1915 to 1919. In her war diary she wrote: "The nurses brought lads back from the brink of madness and accompanied them to the edge of death."[5]

Many nurses sailed overseas with the First Contingent. Indeed, the No. 1 Canadian General Hospital deployed to France in October 1914—well before other units of the CEF—and began receiving patients on October 21. Debbie Marshall in *Firing Lines* observes that the huge medical compound at Étaples became known as the "great white city of healing." Three Canadian army nurses were killed there on May 19, 1918, in a German bombing raid. By 1918 the nurses were serving in dozens of field ambulance units, four casualty clearing stations, in a variety of hospitals, and on hospital ships. Canadian nursing sisters were unique in that they were actual members of the Canadian military, holding the rank of lieutenant in the CAMC nursing service. Qualified military nurses alone were eligible to serve in an official capacity overseas. Casually trained, unpaid, Voluntary Aid Detachment nurses were usually assigned to local military convalescent hospitals at home.[6]

The continued smooth operation of the hospitals overseas was due at least in part to strong moral and material support from home. Women oversaw much of the fundraising through local and provincial branches of the Red Cross, which organized the collection and sending of not only money but supplies, such as bandages, pillow slips, comfort bags, and bales of socks. According to the *Progress-Enterprise* of October 6, 1915, Lieutenant Colonel A. T. Shillington, at No. 2 Canadian Stationary Hospital, Le Touquet-Paris-Plage near Étaples, wrote to Rev. Charles R. Cumming in Bridgewater thanking him for his letter of June 22, which had a cheque for twenty pounds enclosed. The money would be used for the purpose of supporting two beds in the hospital, and would be "known as the town of Bridgewater, Nova Scotia, Donation." One night after a fierce battle, Shillington said, they had over seven hundred patients.

A unique medical project involved Lunenburg County and other communities along the South Shore. Dr. J. Bonsall Porter of McGill University initiated a program of collection of sphagnum moss in Nova Scotia. There was a shortage of absorbent cotton, and the moss could be used as surgical dressings. Gathered by volunteers, particularly children and youth, Girl Guides, Boy Scouts, YMCA groups, and school classes with their teachers, at over twenty sites, the moss was then sorted and prepared by local women. The finished dressings were then turned out in Halifax at a Dalhousie University laboratory, and elsewhere. Almost 15,000 dressings were sent overseas and 476 bed-pads were made and supplied to hospital ships and trains. Some believed the moss dressings were far superior to cotton in hastening the healing of persistent sores.[7]

One notable person who sailed to England from Valcartier with the First Contingent in October 1914 was Nursing Sister Addie Allen (Adruenna) Tupper, from Bridgewater, widow of the late William S. Tupper. Born in Yarmouth in 1870, Addie Tupper enlisted at Quebec in September 1914, in her mid-forties. Standing at 163 cm, she was fairly short, and she weighed only 56 kg. Having volunteered for service with the CAMC, she was stationed first at Salisbury Plain and was then sent to France in April 1915, serving at No. 2 Canadian General Hospital at Le Tréport, where she had charge of 160 beds.

The *Bulletin* on August 3, 1915, reported that a cheque had been sent from Bridgewater to procure extra comforts for the wounded men at the hospital in Le Tréport. Nurse Tupper claimed that she "nearly obliterated the lettering of the letter with grateful tears." She was in England on medical leave, she wrote, and would find out from the nurses what the men wanted and would send a box from Harrods: a few books, some games, toothbrushes, etc. She would subscribe to *Khaki*, a magazine for the soldiers, and everything would be marked, "From the brave boys' friends in Bridgewater, Nova Scotia." On November 9, the *Bulletin* informed its readers that Addie Tupper "signs herself Nursing Sister 'Tupperary'" ("It's a Long Way to Tipperary" being a popular wartime song). She was anxious to get in touch with the Bridgewater soldiers and asked for names, numbers, and battalion. "We have learned to love and admire the British Tommies but in the sanctum sanctorum of our hearts we have a place for our own, and this home money, from home friends, goes to them."

The strain of heavy work, plus exposure to wet and cold, caused Nurse Tupper's health to fail and she was invalided to England, remaining for some time in the Convalescent Home for Canadian Nurses. Eventually, in November 1915, she was sent to Canada on the *Metagama* with other nurses in charge of eight hundred wounded soldiers. After some time at home in Bridgewater, where she spoke to the

Red Cross about her experiences at the front, she returned to France in February 1916. In June, on the King's birthday, at Buckingham Palace, she was awarded the Royal Red Cross, a military decoration recognizing exceptional service in medical nursing, for her self-sacrificing work of over twelve months in France. After the investiture, Queen Alexandra summoned her to Marlborough House where she received congratulations and a photograph of the queen.

Nurse Tupper died of pneumonia in England on December 9, 1916, at the Canadian Convalescent Hospital, Hillingdon House, Uxbridge, "worn out in heart and body," according to the *Bulletin*. She was buried with full military honours. At her funeral on December 12, she received "Royal Tributes to her valorous service in the Imperial Army of the Defenders of Humanity....[T]o the measured march of soldiers, with their rifles reversed, and the beat of muffled drums and the stately Dirge in Saul was borne the body of the heroic woman to the grave made in the 'mighty heart' of England for her." Among the floral offerings at her funeral was a large red cross from Queen Alexandra.

———

Voting would "interfere with the true functions of women," argued Nova Scotia's Attorney General James Wilberforce Longley, opposing an 1895 bill to enact provincial enfranchisement of women. His notions of what those functions entailed reveal contemporaneous thinking that was objectionable even at the time: "First, the bearing and bringing up of children, and this is the highest. Second, the creating of home and the beautifying of home life....Third, to charm men and make the world pleasant, sweet and agreeable to live in. Fourth, to be kindly and loving, to be sweet and to be cherished, to be weak and confiding, to be protected and to be the object of man's devotion." No doubt, the women in the legislature's gallery were not amused. Described by a member of his own party as "conceited, unlovable and unbearable," Longley was Attorney General for almost twenty years, a staunch opponent of women's suffrage.[8]

Despite Longley's opposition, there was considerable support in Nova Scotia for women having the right to vote, for the bill was only narrowly defeated. Women continued to work hard for the social causes they believed in, but without the vote they could not do much except write letters to the newspapers, give public speeches, sign petitions, issue pamphlets, and lobby the powers that be—all men. The National Council of Women played an important role, which "gradually helped women understand that politics was the only effective route to reform and only voters counted in politics." Historian Cheryl Krasnick Warsh maintains that the "temperance crusades served as the catalyst for the women's movement," and that was perhaps particularly true in Nova Scotia.⁹ Catherine L. Cleverdon, in *The Woman Suffrage Movement in Canada*, claims that the support of the Nova Scotia wctu, with Ada Powers as provincial president and Mary Chesley as chair of the standing committee on franchise, was crucial. Both women were ardent feminists.

Beginning in 1894, Mary Chesley regularly petitioned the provincial legislature concerning votes for women. She belonged to the Methodist church, "but in the matter of belief holds herself free," believing that "'righteousness exalteth a nation'" but that "no nation or state has its foundations in righteousness which excludes the best half of its citizens" from a voice in its government. As Sharon MacDonald writes, Mary Chesley, from the small town of Lunenburg and an active leader in the wctu, contradicted earlier historians' assumptions that urban women led the struggle and that those working through such organizations as the wctu tended to be conservative in their politics. Late in life, after the war, Chesley would devote her time to promoting peace and encouraging women to take part in the electoral process. It was because of her that Lunenburg had the first, if short-lived, Canadian Chapter of the Women's International League for Peace and Freedom.¹⁰

At the annual meeting of the National Council of Women, a national umbrella organization, held in Halifax in 1910, a resolution was passed endorsing the principle of enfranchisement of women. This resolution was reaffirmed by the Halifax Local Council of Women in

1917 and passed with a unanimous standing vote. On February 22, the LCW, representing forty-one women's organizations, voted unanimously to ask the legislature to extend the parliamentary franchise to all duly qualified adults, regardless of sex. The officers of the WCTU, headed by Ada Powers as president, sent a supporting resolution to the council and to the assembly.

An important development that year was that Halifax's *Morning Chronicle* began to champion the women's cause, having been won over by the part women had played in the war. When the war began, the paper asserted, "certain noisy, not to say nasty, 'females of the species,' known as 'suffragettes,' had almost succeeded in bringing their sex into contempt among good women as well as among manly men." But the outbreak of war saved the situation. The "suffragette scum," which had "boiled to the top," was "blown off by the first blast of war from the pure underlying sweets of true womanhood." The war gave the women of the western nations their opportunity. They had "proved themselves as patriotic, as self-sacrificing, as intelligent, as alert and active, as willing to serve as men....In short, we are for Universal Suffrage."

Four letters, which helped to gain the support of conservative Haligonians, appeared in the *Chronicle* in February and March 1917, three by Judge Benjamin R. Russell, Mary Chesley's brother and a distinguished resident of the city, and one by Ada Powers of Lunenburg. In her letter to the editor on March 17, Ada Powers began by noting that until recently women who dared to speak in public on women's suffrage were considered "unwomanly and out of their sphere," which "from time immemorial was considered to be the home." But times had changed and the question of votes for women was "commanding the attention of the whole civilized world." Women already had the vote in many places, with no ill effects.

She answered at length the usual objections, that women would not use the ballot if they did get it, that women would neglect their homes, that a woman should not vote if she could not fight ("in other words if you want to vote you must go to war and kill somebody"), yet a woman risked her life for her country every time a soldier was born into the world. To the argument that bad women would vote as well as good women, she observed, revealing her middle-class perspective, that in states and countries that already had equal suffrage, the vote of "the disreputable woman" actually amounted to very little, that the slum ward of the cities invariably had the lightest woman vote whereas the "respectable residence ward" had the heaviest. Anyhow, as potential voters there were more bad men than women, only one criminal in twenty being a woman. The remainder of her letter concerned the possible improvements that could be made for women under family law if they had the vote. For instance, she noted that to have a vote even in municipal affairs, a woman must never marry or must be a widow. "Politically married women are in the same class as idiots, criminals and Indians."

The bill to amend the Nova Scotia Franchise Act unanimously passed second reading. However, on May 1, the *Bulletin* reported that Premier Murray, declaring there was "no useful purpose to pass the bill at this time," had withdrawn the bill for the time being. This became known as Murray's "three-month hoist." On April 24, throwing party allegiance to the winds, the *Chronicle* "thundered against the betrayal of liberal principles by the party which professed to sail under that name in Nova Scotia."

On September 15, the *Herald* described a meeting in Halifax of the Equal Suffrage League, which eventually became known as the Equal Franchise League. Ada Powers, who had come from Lunenburg especially for the meeting, spoke of the spread of the equal suffrage idea, particularly in the west of the country, and of the good which it had assisted in accomplishing. The league's plan was to print and distribute literature, but because of the Halifax Explosion on December 6 every able-bodied woman was required for relief work and nothing further was accomplished.

There was plenty of resistance to female suffrage at the federal level as well. George William Kyte, Liberal MP from Richmond, Nova Scotia, in the House of Commons in February 1916 worried that if the duties of men and women were "rearranged," you "would have the mother and daughters on the roof of the barn to repair the leak and the father and sons in charge of the pastry and needlework." This division of labour was "decreed by God himself and honoured and respected by man throughout all the ages....It is the sturdy trees of the forest that bear the brunt of the storms, and thus afford shelter to the tender foliage that vegetates beneath their protecting branches."[11]

Pressure on the Nova Scotia government for equal suffrage continued. The *Bulletin* noted on February 12, 1918, for example, that a petition for women's suffrage was being "signed in splendid numbers." Anyone who had not yet taken advantage of this opportunity to show "their up-to-date-ness, their loyalty, and love of freedom" could still sign at various stores in town. In answer to a man hiding under the name "Equity" in the *Progress-Enterprise* of February 13, who claimed to be opposing women's suffrage "to save the morals of the women," Ada Powers argued along with western Canadian suffragist Nellie McClung that if women were angels there was great need of more of them in public life. Her appeal to have everyone sign the petition ended by stating that anyone who opposed women's suffrage failed to read the signs of the times, which indicated more plainly than ever that women were able "to take [their] place with man in Church, Home and State." Unusually, the *Progress-Enterprise* issued a disclaimer: "This paper does not hold itself responsible for the opinions of its correspondents."

Over time, the Nova Scotia government had a change of heart. "An act to amend and consolidate the Acts in respect to the Electoral Franchise" received royal assent on April 26, 1918. That same day, a simple amendment to the statute law, deleting the word "male," conferred upon women the right to hold office and to sit in the provincial legislature. Given a general tendency among historians to consider the Maritimes conservative in such matters, Maritime historian E. R. Forbes points out in *Challenging the Regional Stereotype* that the Local Council of Women took the opportunity to declare their support, "perhaps with a note of suppressed glee," for their sisters in Ontario, who had secured the franchise but were still denied the right of election to the legislature.

In the spring of 1917, two events of great significance shifted the tenor of the war. On March 20, the *Bulletin* announced that recent developments in Russia had "fallen like a thunderclap on the world." German sympathizers there, most likely funded by Germany, had apparently been hindering the successful prosecution of the war. No doubt, the *Bulletin* surmised, the elimination of the German element would make for a constitutional government for Russia and "the dawning of a lasting freedom for the country." Russia's prosecution of the war to a victorious end was a forgone conclusion. Prime Minister Borden also thought the change might bring improvement: in his diary in March 1917 he speculated, "It should apparently strengthen the determination of Russia to win the war and render her power more effective."[12] The future would, of course, unfold differently.

Not much notice was taken of events in Russia in the Lunenburg County press. On July 30, 1918, however, the *Bulletin* reported that the ex-czar Nicholas 11 had been shot on July 16, "according to a Russian announcement by wireless," and "the former empress and Alexis Romanoff, the young heir," had "been sent to a place of security." The *Progress-Enterprise*, on September, 25, confirmed the "burning to death by the Bolshiveki [*sic*] of the Russian Empress formerly Princess Alix of Hesse and her four beautiful daughters." The whole family had in fact died in Yekaterinburg on July 17. The important point with respect to the war was that the Germans had made peace with the Bolshevik government in March 1918, thus enabling them to move many more of their troops to the Western Front.

Opinions of the events in Russia would change fairly quickly. By January 8, 1919, the Lunenburg paper was reporting on the door-to-door distribution of "seditious literature" in Toronto and the necessity of nipping Bolshevism in the bud. The sentiment was that Canada must take a warning from Russia where men of such stripe were allowed to run unchecked. There is "no room for revolutionists in Canada."

The other important happening in the spring of 1917 was America's declaration of war on Germany. The *Bulletin* of February 6, commenting on the developing situation south of the border, observed that President Woodrow Wilson had at last sent "Count Bernsdorff and his batch of intriguers" out of the country and recalled his representative in Berlin. Only an overt act would now be needed to plunge the United States into the war, "where they should have been long ago in honor to themselves....Altho the States come into the game late, they will be none the less welcome, but we, in this country, will long remember the sacrifices we have made while our neighbors of the same origin and speech were satisfied to parley and only take part in the war for the dollars that were in it for them." Then, on April 10, the *Bulletin*'s headline read: "The Stars and Stripes Better Late than Never." Congress had declared war on April 6, 1917. The *Morning Chronicle* rejoiced: "America has found her soul....[T]he United States has awakened to the immense evils which we resist, and has come to see that international righteousness requires the valiant witness of all free peoples....A free Republic has put upon a brutal autocracy the brand of scarlet shame."

Throughout most of the war, Canadians had lived beside a large and neutral neighbour. L. M. Montgomery, on a visit to Warsaw, Indiana, in September 1916, commented in her journal about how very different the two countries were. "It seems so strange to be in a country that is not at war! I did not realize until I came here how deeply Canada *is* at war—how *normal* a condition war has come to be with us." It was strange to see no khaki uniforms on the streets, no posters of appeal for recruits, no bulletin boards of war dispatches. "It all makes me feel that I ought to be back home in the thick of it."[13]

One of the concerns, particularly early in the war, was that Canada might be invaded by Germans from the United States. As Michael L. Hadley and Roger Sarty maintain in *Tin-Pots and Pirate Ships*, the danger posed by American neutrality in 1914 was virtually identical to the earlier Fenian menace; agents could foment raids or sabotage by sympathizers among the many people of German, Austrian, and Irish descent in the United States and in Canada. There were many wild rumours. One Member of Parliament was told that the Germans were mustering a force of 150,000 men to attack Canada. Prime Minister Borden knew, however, that such a group would constitute a violation of American neutrality and could not possibly escape the notice of US authorities. Another rumour was that Germans had chartered a yacht to lay mines off the Atlantic coast. Historian Martin Kitchen points out in "The German Invasion of Canada" that in fact there was considerable support among the German general staff for the idea of raids against Canada by sympathetic forces based in the United States, for Canada was an important supplier of soldiers, weapons, and raw materials. One suggestion for a large-scale invasion proposed that irregular, anti-British troops should be dressed as cowboys to avoid notice. It was thought, however, that the Canadian government might be inclined to protest the approach of 650,000 heavily armed bronco-busters with foreign accents marching toward its border.

On November 3, 1914, the *Bulletin* had appealed for the organization of a Home Guard, or Rifle Club, for "the protection of our homes against the possible ravages of an enemy." Rumours had been heard about bands of Germans forming in the United States whose object was the invasion of Canada. It was doubtful the United States would permit "any such excursions, but our duty is plain and we should not be caught napping....[T]he dread experience of poor Belgium is a fearful warning to us." There was some urgency to the notion that men eighteen to sixty should be enrolled and drilled in rifle practice and shooting. According to the *Bulletin* of December 1, the Home Guard was organized with an initiatory roll of sixty members, not only for home defence but also to train men who would eventually enlist in the regular military regiments.

The *New York Sun* on January 24, 1915, rather melodramatically declared that Canada was living in dread of a German invasion from the United States. Reportedly, the people of every city in the Dominion feared attack, but Halifax, situated on the coast, a naval station and a garrison town, was "in a turmoil of martial sentiment. War permeates the very atmosphere." Every Haligonian apparently believed there were hundreds of thousands of Germans living in the States who were "silently, longingly and eagerly awaiting their opportunity to seize the harbor, to destroy the forts and to deal mercilessly with the inhabitants." At patriotic church services, prayers were being said not only for those in the trenches and those in the North Sea but also for those along the coast of Nova Scotia who might be attacked at any moment. "To the American neutral mind all this seems rather incredible," the *Sun* continued, "but it is assuredly a big possible reality to the Canadians." The king, the mother country, and Canada form "a trinity that is the very creed of every Canadian....With courage and dauntlessness they await the dangers to come."

There were indeed rumours of imminent invasion by "German reservists now apparently slumbering in this neutral land," but the threat, though real enough, was never as severe as some imagined. Reservists, in most European armies including the British, were men who had been full-time soldiers and now could be called up anywhere in the world for duty. Despite the very few isolated cases of sabotage by German agents that occurred in later years, the prime minister had been informed that fears of an actual invasion were groundless. Perhaps the uneasiness was not entirely absurd, however. Margaret MacMillan in *The War That Ended the Peace* remarks that Helmuth von Moltke, who would have been the chief of the German general staff early in the war, on the eve of the outbreak of hostilities was convinced that the British had planned the war all along; he wondered whether Germany could persuade the United States to come into the war as Germany's ally by promising Canada to the Americans.[14] According to *The Oxford Companion to Canadian Military History*, Canada did keep fifty thousand troops at home during the war, in part for fear of invasion by German-Americans.

Americans, in their neutrality, even began to wax somewhat poetic about their northern neighbours. The *New York Times*, according to the *Bulletin* of January 11, 1916, claimed that Canadians had a right to be proud of themselves. "They show readiness to enlist, zeal in training, fine vigor and courage in fighting. Voltaire's 'few acres of snow' are a nation full of fire….A hardy, rosy, 'fit' set of fellows, these Canadian youngsters. The old breed in the new environment has improved." A writer in the *New York Herald*, quoted in the *Morning Chronicle* of March 2, 1917, exclaimed: "If the United States does not wish to ally itself with any European nation in a war against Germany, why does she not ally herself with Canada, a country as much American as she is? Here is little Canada (in population) big in country, large in manliness and courage, void of yellow streaks, who, with a population of about as much as the State of New York, at the first insult from Germany took a bulldog hold on her and has been worrying her ever since."

The *Bulletin*, on August 28, 1917, commented that "our American cousins" had been quick to grasp the significance of Canada's response to the challenge of Germany. The *Baltimore Sun*, for example, had gone overboard with praise:

Kipling called Canada "Our Lady of the Snows," but the story which the staff correspondent is telling of her war record shows that when her pride, loyalty, and her affections are enlisted she is the Vesuvius of Nations. The narrative of Canadian sacrifice and heroism is an epic which Homer might have been proud to tell. When we compare this splendid enthusiasm, this eager devotion, this unquestioned and magnificent courage and unselfishness, with certain manifestations of American indifference, half-heartedness, and calculating prudence, we feel a sense of humiliating moral inferiority. To be a Canadian must be, for the next generation at least, equivalent to being one of the elect of the earth. Some said we should annex Canada, rather better for Canada to annex us.

One irritant for Canadians was being bombarded, as usual, with information from below the border, and in the circumstances it wasn't always to their liking. In his article "Canada Invaded!" historian Paul Litt suggests that American cultural products that used American patriotic symbols could be inaccurate as well as offensive. Canadians, he continues, "found US boastfulness hard to stomach. They were disappointed by Americans staying on the sidelines during their desperate struggle to save civilization, and they gagged on smug pronouncements by American politicians that equated American neutrality with moral superiority." When the United States finally joined the war in April 1917, things changed, but not for the better. "American producers of songs, magazine pieces, movies and plays blithely exported domestic war propaganda with no adaptations to accommodate Canadian sensibilities....Canadians suddenly found themselves asked to believe that the United States was saving the world single-handedly.... [S]uch presumption and insensitivity on the part of eleventh-hour adherents to the cause bred a deep resentment in Canada." Litt concludes the war emphasized the drawbacks of Canada's dependence on popular culture that largely emanated from outside its borders.

One person who attempted to deal with misrepresentations in the news in his own zealous way was Canada's chief censor, Lieutenant Colonel Ernest J. Chambers. According to Jeffrey Keshen in *Propaganda and Censorship*, Chambers suppressed 253 publications, approximately 90 per cent of them American-based and two-thirds written in a foreign language. As for American movies, Chambers stressed that much of the US movie industry remained under the control of Germans, Poles, and Jews whose loyalties, he asserted, undoubtedly lay with the Central Powers. His decisions, Keshen maintains, were too often based on racism rather than sound evidence.

As always, there were ups and downs in Canadian-American relations, but perhaps the following verses best express the feelings of the time.

"In Flanders Fields" (ca. 1915) by John McRae

In Flanders fields the poppies blow
Between the crosses, row on row,
That mark our place; and in the sky
The larks, still bravely singing, fly
Scarce heard amid the guns below.

We are the Dead. Short days ago
We lived, felt dawn, saw sunset glow,
Loved and were loved, and now we lie
*   In Flanders fields.*

"*America's Answer*" *(1918) by R. W. Lillard* [15]

Rest ye in peace, ye Flanders dead.
The fight that ye so bravely led
We've taken up. And we will keep
True faith with you who lie asleep
With each a cross to mark his bed,
And poppies blowing overhead,
Where once his own life blood ran red.
So let your rest be sweet and deep
*   In Flanders fields*

Fear not that ye have died for naught.
The torch ye threw to us we caught.
Ten million hands will hold it high,
And Freedom's light shall never die!
We've learned the lesson that ye taught
*   In Flanders fields.*

"CATASTROPHE!" exclaimed the headline in the *Bridgewater Bulletin* on December 11, 1917, "City of Halifax Shaken to Its Foundations." A large area of the city was in ruins, and the loss of life and the list of wounded were appalling in number. The explosion was first thought to be a German raid, the paper maintained, and everybody was terrorized. Three boys from Bridgewater, named Guinan, had been killed. Some pupils from Mount Saint Vincent Academy and the Maritime

Business College had come home on Friday evening, and all had exciting experiences to relate.

The response to send aid had been quick. That same day, an item titled "Bridgewater to the Rescue" announced that a carload of building material consisting of glass, putty, tar paper, beaver-board, nails, and so on, had been dispatched to the stricken city. Railway authorities had sent a special train to Halifax of all the passenger coaches at its disposal for refuge work. Women of the town rolled bandages and collected clothing and bedding. The entire output of Telfer's woodworking factory had been purchased for use in Halifax, and Boehner Brothers of West LaHave had also received large orders for building material. Lunenburg, Mahone Bay, and Chester had "already done nobly in relief work." Like other towns in the province, Lunenburg had sent help to the stricken city and supplies, so many that the manager of the reconstruction committee wrote to Mayor Duff saying that they required only carpenters and plumbers with tools, and bricklayers, but no more common labourers or teams.

The facts of the explosion are well known. The city of Halifax was the main port on the east coast for the passage of troops and war supplies by convoy overseas. On the morning of December 6, 1917, two vessels collided in The Narrows between the harbour and Bedford Basin, causing the largest man-made explosion before Hiroshima. The Norwegian merchant ship *Imo* was on its way to New York to pick up relief supplies, and emblazoned on its side in large letters were the words BELGIAN RELIEF. The *Mont Blanc*, a French cargo ship laden with high explosives, was in the harbour to join a convoy to cross the ocean. The blast devastated much of the city's North End. Almost two thousand people were killed, nine thousand injured, and hundreds blinded by flying glass. Twenty-five thousand people with inadequate shelter faced a blizzard the following day that buried the ruined city in snow. Prime Minister Borden, who arrived in Halifax shortly after the disaster, described the devastation as "a scene of unparalleled horror."

It was indeed a catastrophe, and only a hundred kilometres or so up the coast from Lunenburg County. As able seaman Bert Griffith, who was there, wrote to his wife: "A German fleet could not have done so much damage."[16]

Rumours of sabotage abounded. Hysteria spread, especially by the *Halifax Herald*, determined to blame the Germans. Four days after the explosion, the paper gleefully announced that practically all the Germans in the city were to be arrested. Indeed, sixteen people with names like Bergmann, Calfruckhow, Meyer, Schultz, Rabnovitch, and Hornstein had already been taken into custody and locked up, though some had been released. Janet F. Kitz in *Shattered City* confirms that after the explosion anti-German feeling ran high. Windows were smashed in one or two houses whose owners had German-sounding names, but there was "really too much to be done to waste time on revenge."

On December 11 a letter from a prominent citizen in the *Herald* declared that the explosion was only a taste of what the city would experience if "the Huns" should actually arrive. "When the brutal Germans take a city they assault the women and bayonet the little children and carry off the men as prisoners." Halifax had allegedly had "its first taste of war" and although the experience did not compare with what the people of Belgium and France had suffered during the past three years, it would "nevertheless give our people a SLIGHT IDEA of what war REALLY MEANS."

The *Herald* on December 8 charged that "Behind all, as responsible for the disaster, [was] that arch criminal, the Kaiser of Germany, who forced our Empire and her allies into the fearful war." On December 12 the paper declared: "So long as there are people in Halifax who remember this past week, or whose children remember it, so long will the name German be a name for loathing and disgust." As Michael J. Bird observes in *The Town That Died*, "There was little doubt in the minds of most citizens that the real culprit was the Kaiser, for if he had not started the war the *Mont Blanc* would not have been in the harbour with such a deadly cargo." But, before long, Bird continues, "even the most gullible Haligonian began to realize the impossibility of the explosion having been the result of some deep laid German plot."

A segment from an editorial in the *Kölnische Zeitung*, quoted in the *Progress-Enterprise*, gave a rare glimpse into the thinking of the other side:

> *Not without emotion can one note the news of the devastation of the hard-hit Canadian town. And yet is it not better that these munitions should not have reached the theatre of war and the trenches, there to be used against our people in its hard struggle for freedom and independence, our people which did not seek war, and also did not produce these munitions which have now struck those who wanted to trouble us with them? From the point of view of humanity the event is regrettable but we hope the effect will be salutary, since an irrefutable object lesson will thus bring the terrors of the war home to a place where people felt themselves comfortably secure, far as they are from the guns.*
>
> *Canada is getting war experience at the front and also at Halifax. We hope that its lesson may open the eyes of the warlike section of the people to the fact that humanity has higher ideals to defend than those represented by Wilson, Lloyd George and other business politicians.*[17]

Lunenburg's John James (Jim) Kinley, in his holiday season message as lieutenant-governor of Nova Scotia, on December 17, 1997—eighty years after the tragedy—described the Halifax Explosion as "the saddest event in our province's history."

One thing is certain. History would prove that the 1880s and 1890s were not the best of decades in which to be born, for so many of the men who fought and died in the Great War came into the world in those years. What became, one wonders, of the three young Lunenburg men who so bravely volunteered to go overseas on August 14, 1914, a mere ten days after war was declared?

The young Norwegian, Emil Olsen, according to the *Progress-Enterprise* of December 1, 1915, had returned to "the town he calls his home after having faithfully done his 'bit' at the front." He was apparently the town's first returned soldier. Born in Stavanger, Norway, in 1889, Olsen had shipped to England on a steamer when not quite fifteen years old. After travelling the world for a year or so, he ended up in Lunenburg looking for work, and he sailed out of that port for the next decade. He was only twenty-four and single when he and the others went off to Valcartier, where he enlisted on September 27, 1914.

His career in the army, mainly with the 16th Canadian Scottish Battalion, was short but traumatic. At Ypres in April 1915, during the Battle of St. Julien, he suffered gas poisoning and was severely, and permanently, wounded in his right leg by a hand grenade. After stays at several hospitals in France and in England, he was returned to Canada on the *Metagama* in December, "no longer physically fit for war service." Although fined for being drunk and disorderly—likely during his time on Salisbury Plain before embarking for France—and having suffered from gonorrhoea, a common complaint among Canadian soldiers, when he returned to Lunenburg and was applying for a pension, medical records indicated that his conduct while in the army had been "manly," his habits "good," his temperance "moderate." The *Progress-Enterprise* on July 5, 1916, reported that "Bergu Emil Olson" had married Winnie Beatrice Arenburg, who was "becomingly attired in white embroiled voile and a black picture hat," in St. John's Anglican Church. As usual, the groom's attire was of no interest. Olsen lived until October 1972, age eighty-three.

Corporal Olsen, "a foreigner," pronounced the *Progress-Enterprise* on December 1, 1915, "fought for us; the conflict is still on; how many native born young men of Lunenburg will follow his example, and the example of the other gallant lads who have already enlisted?" A reception in Lunenburg to welcome him home, attended by the 75th Regiment band, Mayor Hall, and various speakers including Judge Chesley and the newly appointed recruiting officer, G. H. Love, resulted in only one new recruit, Milton Deamone.

One of the other men who left Lunenburg that August with Olsen, Edwin ("Ned") Coldwell, had a longer but equally unpleasant war experience. Almost thirty when he signed up at Valcartier, Ned Coldwell, single and a Presbyterian, was said to be an engineer on his attestation papers, but it later emerged that he was a clerk in a general store before the war. He sailed to England in October 1914 and went over to France the next April. While on active duty that August the burst of a shell led to a fall, resulting in a fracture at the base of his skull. He returned to the trenches but suffered dizziness, shortness of breath, and increasing heart trouble and weakness, reducing him to light duties for a time. Acute rheumatic fever and perforation of his right ear drum as well meant that he was in and out of hospitals in France and then England until he shipped back to Canada in November 1917, "service no longer required." Healthy before the war, he became an outpatient at Camp Hill in Halifax until it was determined that further treatment in hospital was of no material benefit. He died in December 1945.

Of the three men who left Lunenburg for the war that August day in 1914, Charles Ernst Cossmann, scion of a prominent Lunenburg family, was the one who would not return. He was killed in action on the battlefield in France on April 19, 1916.

There are several mentions of Charlie "Cossman" in letters home from Lunenburg soldiers at the front. Ned Coldwell, for instance, mentioned him in a letter that appeared in the local paper on June 23, 1915, stating that Cossmann had gone to the hospital with food poisoning from eating canned goods.

A rather incoherent letter from one C. A. Cossmann, "somewhere in France," was printed in the *Progress-Enterprise* on February 23, 1916. It was meant as a card of thanks:

Dear Everybody, That means you, if your nice. Have benefited greatly through the thoughtfulness and generosity of a number of persons and societies in the old Burg in the form of chews, smokes, eat, etc.... [C]an't thank you all but sure you will accept a joint letter through the P. E.— Am very sorry that I cannot send you all a real German for they're lots different from some I know. Oh! But they are all good fellows, when they are asleep?... [I]t is a H---! of a war, would have preferred

*a milder form for my intation [sic]. But cheer up, we'll need you all
before it's finished, if you don't believe me come and see for yourself.*

Although this letter is signed "C. A. Cossmann" (the middle initial
should be "E"), no other soldier with this name turns up in the records,
and it would seem to be our Charlie Cossmann, especially since he
mentions "the old Burg."[18]

On May 3, 1916, the *Progress-Enterprise* announced that Charles
Cossmann had been killed in action, pointing out that he was one of the
first to enlist when war was declared, and that after training in England
he had served in the trenches as a bomb thrower. He was very popular
in the community, the paper maintained, and his death had elicited
much mourning. Son of Otto A. Cossmann, he was the grandson of
Rev. Charles E. (Carl Ernst) Cossmann, DD, for many years pastor of
Zion Lutheran Church in Lunenburg. When news of the soldier's "fatal
ending" was received, every flagstaff in town, as well as the shipping in
the port, had flags at half-mast. Even though he was a Lutheran, the
chimes of St. John's Anglican Church were rung in remembrance.

The *Progress-Enterprise* on May 17 claimed that Sunday afternoon,
May 14, 1916, was a historic occasion for the congregation of Zion
Lutheran Church, for it was called upon to memorialize one of its
illustrious sons who had given his life for the Empire's cause. He had
died somewhere in France, "on the field of Honor, in the service of his
King and for his Country." A modest estimate suggested there were
1,300 in the church and Sunday school, and several hundred people
on the outside could not come within hearing distance. Among the
audience were Chaplain McKinnon of the 119th Battalion and Major
Margeson of the 219th. A detachment of the fire department, of which
Cossmann had been a member, followed in the procession behind the
ubiquitous 75th Regiment band.

The First World War personnel records in the national archives tell
us a good deal more about the war experiences of this young man. Born
in Lunenburg on June 29, 1891, Cossmann was twenty-three when he
enlisted at Valcartier in September 1914. A good-sized man, weighing

73 kg and standing 178 cm tall, the records revealed that he was single, a machinist, and he practised the Lutheran faith. Originally in the 17th Battalion, he was transferred to the 13th, the Royal Highlanders of Canada. With Ned Coldwell and Emil Olsen, he sailed on the *Ruthenia* from Quebec down the St. Lawrence River and across the Atlantic to England that October, arriving in France on April 26, 1915. Less than a month later he came down with influenza. After another bout of flu, he rejoined his unit on October 12, 1915.

His life then took a terrible turn. From December 15, 1915, he was held in confinement awaiting trial, and he was eventually convicted by a court martial at Neuve-Église in Belgium: "When on Active Service, Desertion, in that he absented himself from working party while proceeding to work in the front line." On January 1, 1916, Charlie Cossmann was "sentenced to suffer death by being shot." The sentence was confirmed by General Herbert Plumer, who commuted the sentence to ten years penal servitude. The sentence was then suspended. The above curious letter, not actually dated but published in the *Progress-Enterprise* on February 23, may have been written while he was in prison, or soon after, but it's not possible to know.

Released in February, Cossmann was granted nine days' leave in late March. On April 4 he returned to his unit, and fifteen days later, on April 19, "somewhere in France," he was killed in action. A small brown card toward the bottom of his personnel file reads: "Estates card states 'decorations not wanted by relatives'…(Half-brother) Paul Cossman, Lunenburg. N.S." A large annotation in red pencil notes: "Hold Medals."

Chapter Four

"HOW WOULD THE KAISER VOTE?"

On August 7, 1917, a public meeting was held in Bridgewater's Queen Park, with Mayor Dr. C. S. Marshall in the chair. On this third anniversary of the declaration of "a righteous war," the *Bridgewater Bulletin* reported this gathering of the town's citizens recorded its "inflexible determination to continue to a victorious end the struggle in maintenance of those ideals of liberty and justice which are the common and sacred cause of the Allies." This apparent unanimity suggested peaceful times ahead on the home front.

But a few months later, as one of the most divisive and controversial federal elections in Canadian history approached, the tone of the *Bulletin*'s reporting became increasingly strident. In a last desperate push before the voting took place on the seventeenth, the paper outdid itself on December 4 with an editorial headlined by melodramatic allegations in words large and capitalized: "Wounded Soldiers Clubbed, Stabbed, Shot and Bombed to Death—Churches Defamed and Sacred Statues Vilified—Trenches Full of Naked Murdered Women—Horrors of Hell Itself Outdone by Order of the Kaiser." The *Bulletin* proclaimed that the conduct of the German armies in the districts they occupied in Europe, constituted "the most blistering indictment of any nation recorded in history":

> *Full rein was given by the higher command to the degenerate impulses of men whom rigid discipline had long bereft of their finer feelings. Ladies of education and refinement in captured villages and towns were forced to wait upon the tables of German soldiers and officers after being stripped naked. Little children were impaled on the swords and bayonets and carried in triumph at the head of companies until the infants' hearts stopped beating, when they were pitched overhead. There was the looting of homes and destruction of property. Relics of art were seized and sent to Germany.... Young girls were buried alive with their heads above ground and left to die. Satan himself would stand aghast. British ships were sunk in the North Sea and the lifeboats shelled.... Canadian prisoners were beheaded, their comrades crucified and disembowelled. Even a Mother Superior was crucified to the door of her convent, and women within were cut to pieces and mutilated. These are not sensational soldiers' yarns but official facts.* THIS IS KULTUR. THIS IS THE THING OUR MEN ARE FIGHTING OVERSEAS. IF THEY ARE TO DEFEAT IT, WE AT HOME MUST HELP. YOUR BALLOT IS A BULLET. THE TARGET IS THE KAISER AND HIS KULTUR. TAKE GOOD AIM AND SHOOT!

Halifax Herald, *October 7, 1918.*

That same day, under the prominent headline that began, "WARN-ING!" the *Bulletin* drew closer to the point, retaining its use of upper case for emphasis:

> *German Influences are at Work in Canada Originating in Quebec. The Same Malign Influences Which Have Brought Disaster in Russia and Italy are at Work in France, Great Britain, United Sates and Canada. If Quebec Rules with Sir Wilfrid Laurier at the Head the Kaiser Will Soon Place His Bloody Foot on Our Necks. Do not fool yourselves that the Country is safe. One big German war ship could lay waste our coast cities easily....Men and Women, Vote for J. W. Margeson and for the Patriotic Union Government Composed of the Big Men in the Liberal and Conservative ranks. They will safeguard the Country.*

The leading public issue during 1917 would undoubtedly be con-scription, whether or not to force men to enlist to maintain the strength of the Canadian army overseas. The *Bulletin's* editorials above, with their heavy dose of war propaganda, reveal two of the major concerns of the time: the need to keep Sir Robert Borden's Union government in power at Ottawa, for it could be counted on to enforce conscription, and the escalation of negative feelings against the enemy.

———

Before the war, the Germans had been regarded by many as more or less ideal immigrants. They fit in well with the general population, tending to assimilate easily, and they were, to the approval of many, mainly Protestants.

At first, it seemed that all might go well. The *Bulletin*, on February 23, 1915, reported that William G. Weichel, the German-Canadian Conservative member for North Waterloo, Ontario, had proclaimed in the House of Commons that German Canadians were answering the call to duty. They were "proud of the race from which they sprung, proud of German progress in science, art, music, literature and philosophy, but, sir, not proud of the violation of the neutrality of Belgium, of the burning of Louvain, nor of the destruction of the Rheims Cathedral." So many people of German origin had left the fatherland because of Prussian militarism, Weichel maintained, left to escape military domination. German Canadians were answering a call, not of blood, but of duty and gratitude, and they would stand shoulder to shoulder with all other Canadians.

Attitudes changed rapidly, however. "From being a favoured people within the nation, overnight the Germans were vilified as the enemy," writes K. M. McLaughlin in *The Germans of Canada*. It was no longer possible to be both a German and a Canadian. The sense of pride in being German was replaced with feelings of anxiety and uneasiness. Horrible tales were told of atrocities committed by the barbarous "Hun." The conflict had become not just a war against Germany but a war against the very idea of "Germanness."

There was increasing hostility toward all things German. The *Halifax Herald*, always the most hysterically xenophobic, led a backlash against German names. Its headline on September 15, 1915, proclaimed that "German Street Names Are Offensive": "What inspiration can the present generation draw from names like Brunswick, Dresden, Gottingen, Hanover, Coburg, Jacob, Rottenburg. Streets should be named after the Duke of Kent, the Duke of Argyle, King George and other royals, Cornwallis, the founder of Halifax, and we should be honouring the 'Noblest Soldier of them All,' the King of the plucky Belgians....We are sending our young men across the water to fight the German barbarians. It's not too much to ask that these obnoxious German names be removed."

Some names were indeed changed. On May 15, 1917, the *Bulletin* informed its readers that the Nova Scotia legislature had passed a bill permitting Alfred George Kaiser and his family, owners of a long-standing fur business on Granville Street in Halifax, to change their name from Kaiser to Kingdom. The *Herald* wrote approvingly, on June 12, 1918, that Berlin, Iowa, had done the "proper thing" by altering its name to "Lincoln." Of course, the British royals did their bit during the war by changing—for patriotic reasons—the family name from the House of Saxe-Coburg-Gotha to the House of Windsor.

Some proposed name changes did not take place in the end. Not surprisingly, New Germany's name was controversial. As the *Bulletin* put it on April 29, 1919, "The name, Germany, stinks in the nostrils of the great bulk of our people," and it was no wonder many of the good people in the village wanted a change. On the other hand, "the word 'New' purifies the word 'Germany' to some extent and perhaps enough to let the name stand."

The people of Lunenburg County were aware of the unpleasant incidents that occurred in the city of Berlin in Ontario, with its proud German heritage. A crowd of unruly soldiers in the 118th Battalion, before going overseas, had removed a statue of Kaiser Wilhelm from its pedestal in the local park and threw it in the lake; once the statue had been retrieved and located in a German club, they proceeded to trash that building. On another occasion, an alderman of German background was escorted from his office to the city hall and made to kiss the Union Jack, amid cheers from the assembled crowd. On September 1, 1916, the name Berlin was officially changed to Kitchener.

One of the more bizarre naming affairs occurred closer to home. A correspondent in the *Progress-Enterprise* on October 2, 1918, claimed that a child in a section of Lunenburg County had recently been christened with the name "Berlin William." It is "almost impossible to believe that there would be parents insane enough to hang a name like that on a poor innocent baby." The *Bulletin* commented sarcastically on October 8, "It has been said there are no pro-Germans in Lunenburg County!"

Even animals, it seems, were not immune to the anti-German feeling across the country. Dachshunds, it was said, were attacked in the street unless wearing patriotic colours, and German shepherds quietly became Alsatians. There was only one lonely dachshund at the Canadian National Exhibition show in Toronto in September 1917. "This long elongated native of sausage-land was discovered in a pitiful state of depression and low morale. While all the other fellows were being patted and petted, this forlorn alien enemy looked around it with a woebegone expression and actually whined and shed tears when a charitable onlooker stroked it. If it had been a real Hun it would have bit the hand that fondled it, but the dogs of Hunland are more humane than some of their masters."[1]

Several major incidents heightened the animosity toward the Germans. Although it quickly became apparent that Germans had nothing to do with either event, German saboteurs were blamed initially for both the burning of the Parliament buildings in Ottawa on February 3, 1916, and for the Halifax Explosion in December 1917. These hasty reactions were understandable, if misguided, but on May 7, 1915, a German U-boat did in fact torpedo and sink the RMS *Lusitania*, a British ocean liner en route from New York to Liverpool. More than 1,100 people perished, including many Canadians and more than 120 neutral Americans. Halifax's *Morning Chronicle* called this act the "blackest crime in the long list of outrages, on land and sea, which have made the name of German vile." Later that year, British nurse Edith Cavell was arrested for helping Allied soldiers escape from occupied Belgium. Accused of treason by the Germans, she was shot by firing squad in Brussels on October 12, 1915. Both of these incidents increased hatred of Germans among the Allies and helped turn American public opinion against Germany, thus eventually precipitating the United States' entry into the war.

During the war, more than 8,500 "enemy aliens" were incarcerated in camps across Canada, including a couple thousand Germans, mainly army reservists, as well as nationals of the Austro-Hungarian and Turkish empires. Many of these men were permitted to leave the camps when labour shortages arose in 1916. According to Desmond Morton and J. L. Granatstein in *Marching to Armageddon*, German-born officials and civil servants were fired and university professors and teachers were driven from their jobs, orchestras stopped playing the works of Wagner and Beethoven, and in 1918 the government banned all publishing in "enemy" languages, later relenting provided English translations were run alongside the foreign text. "On the scale set by

European horrors," the authors note, "such persecution was minor but it left ugly memories and uglier precedents." Facing such widespread hostility, Germans in Canada were uneasy throughout the war.

The German people of Lunenburg County were not "immigrants," at least not recent immigrants. Having been in Nova Scotia for several generations, most of them undoubtedly saw themselves as Canadian, and few Canadians would have regarded them as "alien." They had left their homeland in Europe before Germany became a unified nation, and though proud of their German heritage, few connections to or feelings for Germany remained. Still, with their German names and German past, they were sometimes, albeit usually fairly gently, tarred with the same brush.

Faced with mounting casualties at the front and a decline in the number of volunteers stepping forward at home in Canada, the likelihood of enactment of conscription was increasing. Both Britain and New Zealand had brought in compulsory military service early in 1916, though Australians in a second referendum in December 1917 had once again said no. The Selective Service Act in the United States authorized the government to raise a national army through compulsory enlistment on May 18, 1917, shortly after the country declared war on Germany.

For the first couple years of the war, conscription in Canada had seemed unlikely. Prime Minister Robert Borden himself had famously told the Halifax Canadian Club on December 18, 1914, that "under the laws of Canada, our citizens may be called out to defend our own territory, but cannot be required to go beyond the seas except for the defence of Canada itself. There has not been, there will not be, compulsion or conscription." He went on to say that "Freely and voluntarily, the manhood of Canada stands ready to fight beyond the seas."[2]

It was expected, then, that Canada would fight the war by voluntary recruiting. The editor of the *Bulletin* on October 3, 1916, wondered if conscription should even be talked about, for there were "phases of the question affecting Canada which cannot be fully or wisely discussed." He agreed that there was a strong feeling in favour of conscription, but, with considerable foresight, he went on to say, "if we were resisting actual invasion we would probably establish conscription even in this country, but surely, when we consider the various elements which constitute our population, the problems which will face us when peace comes, and the long international boundary, conscription for a war in Europe is difficult."

However, it was a fact that as time passed fewer volunteers were coming forward. As Jonathan Vance notes in *Maple Leaf Empire*, "the public recruiting meeting, long a staple of the voluntary system, was now widely regarded as useless, for the able-bodied male rarely turned up to be publicly harangued." Desmond Morton remarks in *A Military History of Canada* that by the summer of 1915 two of the "sharpest goads for enlistment" had disappeared: few people now believed the war would be short and exciting, and no one needed work. It seemed that men who lived on farms, were married, had jobs, or men who had deep ancestral roots in the country, were least likely to enlist. Morton further observes that these characteristics applied to the eastern provinces as much as to Quebec, where recruiting was low, and it was "no coincidence the Maritimes ranked only a little ahead of Quebec in recruiting rates."

An important, and ominous, development took place in the first week of 1917—a national registration of manpower. National service cards were delivered by post office authorities to all men residing in the country between the ages of sixteen and sixty-five years. Filling in the cards and returning them, with information on one's age, parentage, nationality, physical condition, profession, marital status, dependants, and willingness to change place of work at the same pay during the war, was compulsory under the War Measures Act.

The *Bulletin* on January 9 explained that the object was to gather information and eventually organize the manpower of the Dominion. It did not mean compulsory military service. Quite the opposite, in fact, "for we believe that we have still in Canada enough willing young and virile men who are ready and anxious to join their fellows in the field of battle as soon as they can be relieved of their present duties." Men were needed to run the farms and the fisheries. If a man was successful as a fisherman on the banks and was needed there, then care would be taken that he would not be asked to enlist in the army. Likewise, farms, railways, mines, and coal and steel industries must be operated. If men were chafing to go, then someone must be found to replace them. "All this can be done by the systematic organization and direction of the muscle and the brains of the country. We are all patriots."

The *Progress-Enterprise* on January 10 also approved of the registration, saying that the man who filled in the card "had done something at least to vindicate his good name in days when Canadian soldiers cheerfully forsake everything for the battle-scarred road of duty." If unfit for the battlefront himself, a man could work in some position and relieve some younger or more robust man who could then take a place in the firing line. The *Canadian Fisherman*, the trade journal of the fishing industry, in its January 1917 issue, strongly urged every fisherman, fishhouse worker, canner, and those actively engaged in the production and distribution of fish foods to fill out their national service cards. The fisheries were necessary to the life of the country. The fishing industry might be asked to speed up production to supply food at home and overseas, and it was necessary to have a list of the men engaged in the industry. "Fill out your card and send it in!" This national registration scheme, alas, did little to increase voluntary enlistment.

Contrary to his earlier assurances, in the late spring of 1917 Prime Minister Borden returned from Europe convinced that, despite serious opposition from Quebec, compulsory military service was necessary to maintain the strength of the Canadian army in the field. At the Imperial War Conference in London he had been given access for the first time to secret information about the war, and he had also visited the front in France. In the House of Commons on May 18, 1917, announcing conscription, he "spoke movingly of the 'call from the wounded, the men in the trenches, and those who have fallen.' He was answering their call." His visits to wounded soldiers in hospitals had affected him deeply; he had promised the soldiers that the CEF would be kept at strength, and it would not lose its effectiveness or be broken up for want of reinforcements. "I should feel myself unworthy if I did not fulfill that pledge."[3]

Like most of the press in Canada, the Lunenburg County newspapers ultimately supported conscription. The *Bulletin* on May 22 assumed that recruiting by the voluntary system was practically at an end. Canada had done wonders and had "electrified the world," but the time had come to gather in the slackers, "a good bunch of them in Quebec." Right in Lunenburg County, however, there were "a number of sturdy young men hanging around home in safety"; they had better get into the game before they were forced, for it was much more honourable to be a volunteer than a conscript. The *Progress-Enterprise* on June 13 remarked that all the conscription talk at Ottawa could not help but convince everyone the situation was serious. If there was such absolute need to force men to join, then "the dream of the beauty of the voluntary system melts into empty air." Slackers and shirkers existed in every locality. "Take Lunenburg, for instance, many have gone; many have not, who could and should."

"What Else But Conscription?" asked the *Bulletin* on June 19. Germans were committing rape, burglary, assault, arson, and murder on French towns. Senseless atrocities and vandalism were being committed by the kaiser's troops. According to a German commanding officer, they were making war not just against the French army and territory but "against everything that belongs to the French blood and race." In one instance, alleged the *Bulletin*, little André Labot had been beaten with a cane for failing to salute an officer, then forced to salute a dummy draped with a German uniform until he fell exhausted; finally he was bayoneted and killed. "What other method can be proposed than the selective draft?"

The churches, too, were on side. The Anglican archbishop of Nova Scotia, Clarendon Lamb Worrell, summed up the common argument of those crying out for conscription: "Why men of infinite value to the community should be called upon to sacrifice themselves in order that a number of worthless and non-producing creatures may go on in their animal enjoyment is beyond comprehension." The *Bulletin* on July 3 reported that members of the Nova Scotia Methodist conference in session at Springhill had stood plainly in favour of conscription, even declaring that ministers should take their places in the firing line with other men (clergymen and divinity students were exempt from the draft).

Reasonably, but radically for the times in Canada, the Methodists also favoured the conscription of money and labour and the nationalization of all national resources and public utilities. Historian Michael Bliss, in his article on the denomination in *Conscription 1917*, maintains that the war became a "divine cause" for Canadian Methodists. "By the end of the first year of the war the church had 'transfigured' the war into a crusade for Christianity rather than a simple defence of liberty." The church would play an active role in recruiting. In the journal the *Christian Guardian* children were taught to badger men on the street in the hope of shaming them into enlisting.[4]

The Military Service Act (MSA) passed in the House of Commons in July 1917, by 102 votes to 44, and would go into effect early in 1918. The *Bulletin*, needless to say, expressed satisfaction with the vote but was upset at Nova Scotia's poor showing. Outside Quebec "and the few petty partisans from Nova Scotia," the paper pointed out on July 31, opposition was negligible. "It must be said, to Nova Scotia's disgrace, that her sons in parliament, lacking in patriotism and loyalty, had voted in greater numbers than those of any other province, with the exception of Quebec, to paralyze Canada's effort in the war." Ontario, where only two out of eighty-five MPs voted against conscription, stood as the "banner province."

Conscription was highly controversial in Nova Scotia, according to Brian Douglas Tennyson in *Nova Scotia at War*. All eight Conservative MPs, one of them Dr. Dugald Stewart from Lunenburg County, supported the conscription bill, but only two of the eight Liberals; the six men opposed remained loyal to Sir Wilfrid Laurier, declaring that they supported the war but not conscription, and they wanted no coalition with the Conservative party. Farmers were generally opposed because their sons were essential labour, especially when the government wanted them to produce more food. There was some evidence, Tennyson writes, to suggest that fishermen felt the same way, "although historians interested in the conscription issue ignore them."

The *Bulletin* argued on October 23 that the MSA had been framed not only with the object of securing the necessary support for the men who had gone voluntarily, but it was also so designed that it protected all productive industry. The bona fide farmer, fisherman, shipbuilder, and all other necessary producers, would be given fair consideration and fair play in their applications for exemption. "We must keep the soldier fed, we must keep everybody fed and we must also keep the soldier supported with proper assistance." But the matter would not rest there.

Conscription became law in Canada on August 29, 1917. To give legitimacy to such a potentially divisive law—ardently supported by patriots and fiercely resisted by most French-speaking Quebeckers— the Borden administration decided it needed to form a coalition government. The Union government was proclaimed in October 1917, Borden's governing Conservatives combining with a substantial rump of Liberals who supported conscription. Sir Wilfrid Laurier, the aging Liberal leader, had declined to join the coalition, and was supported in opposition mainly by an alienated Quebec and some long-standing and loyal Liberal supporters in the Maritimes. An election had been called for December 17, and the major campaign issue would be conscription.

In Lunenburg County the candidates for Member of Parliament were, for the Unionists, Joseph Willis Margeson, paymaster for the 25th Battalion and Conservative member in the local legislature, and William Duff, merchant, shipowner, and mayor of Lunenburg, running for the Liberals. Duff announced in the *Progress-Enterprise* on

November 5 that he would contest the county as a "straight Liberal," intending to go to Ottawa "free and untrammelled, making no pledges and giving no guarantees." He was the only candidate in the field so far, and the only one with practical knowledge of two of the county's greatest industries, fishing and shipping. If his Conservative friends were sincere in their desire for Union, he respectfully submitted that they would prove to the country their sincerity by allowing him to be elected by acclamation. That was not to be.

The *Bulletin* on November 20, the day of the nomination proceedings, described Major Margeson as "a returned soldier, an active young man with rare parliamentary ability." Duff's address that day, the paper claimed, was mainly notable for its avoidance of the war and excuses for not allowing the chief recruiting officer to speak at the fishermen's picnic that year. Duff had explained, to the *Bulletin*'s disgust, that he thought the picnickers should not be bothered with recruiting speeches. Against charges that he did not support the war, Duff responded that he had never said anything against the MSA and his well-known attitude toward recruiting was that as long as he did not go to the front himself, he would not urge anyone else to go.

The election was, quite frankly, rigged. In September Borden had written in his diary: "Our first duty is to win at any cost the coming elections in order that we may continue to do our part in winning this war and that Canada be not disgraced." Solicitor General Arthur Meighen had suggested to Borden in the fall of 1916 that the lifting of the vote from the disloyal and its award to the patriotic would be a "splendid stroke." And that's more or less what happened. Based on this thinking, two pieces of legislation were passed by the government in the fall of 1917, thus paving the way to victory.

The Military Voters Act gave the vote to all military personnel and nurses, no matter how long they had lived in Canada, and the act also allowed the government to allocate the votes of those soldiers overseas who said they did not know their home constituency to ridings where the government needed a few more votes to win. The second bill, the Wartime Elections Act, gave the vote to the female relatives of soldiers, the first women allowed to vote in Canadian federal elections. At the same time, the vote was taken away from immigrants who had come to Canada since 1902 from enemy nations—mainly Germany and the Austrian Empire—and from anyone exempted from the draft such as conscientious objectors. The election was clearly stacked in the government's favour. Borden's biographer, Robert Craig Brown, describes the measures taken to win as "a bald, reprehensible gerrymander." "Against the unscrupulous tactics of the government," write J. L. Granatstein and J. M. Hitsman in *Broken Promises* (their history of conscription in Canada), "Laurier and his party were helpless."

On September 11 the *Bulletin* complained that once again the *Morning Chronicle* had risen "to the pinnacle of tommyrot, finding fault with the government for disfranchising a lot of Germans, Austrians, Bulgarians, and Turks, wolves in sheep's clothing who were understandably deprived of their votes in a war election." Such people, "newly naturalized Huns," insisted the paper's editor on September 18,

Canadians Voting up the Line. The soldiers overseas voted overwhelmingly for the Union government.

would cast their vote against "Borden's Win-the-War government." The "average alien enemy is usually a miscreant with no sense of honor or decency when there is a question at issue between his native country and that of his adoption."

A notable incident took place in Ontario in November. At a public meeting on the twenty-fourth, in Kitchener, Prime Minister Borden had been prevented from speaking. "As everyone knows," the *Bulletin* expounded on the twenty-seventh, "that city is largely German and it was natural to expect that Sir Robert would not be well received, but Canadians are scarcely prepared to find, right here in Canada, a hotbed of German sympathizers who openly give expression to their feelings....[E]very loyal Canadian should resent with his vote the devilishness of the Kitchener Germans." The *Halifax Herald*, excessively excited as usual, wondered if it might have been another deliberate plot to murder Borden, who had been "insulted, howled down, and prevented from speaking."

Attacking "the Quebec French-Canadians, the Germans, Austrians, Bulgarians, Doukhobors, Mennonites, Galicians, and other Foreigners...more than ONE-HALF of our population," the *Herald* warned, "the loyal people of Nova Scotia do not yet realize the FACT that the British population of Canada is only 55 per cent, of whom over 400,000 of the Flower of the Race are in khaki, or overseas fighting to the death the enemy of mankind." Borden could ask for no better recommendation for himself and his war policy than "this behaviour by the pro-German section of Kitchener (ex-Berlin)," the *Bulletin* concluded on December 4, then asked, "How Would the Kaiser Vote?"

On November 27, the *Bulletin* had argued that "a vote for Duff means desertion of our soldier boys in France." Duff, the paper allowed, would follow a policy which if persisted in would "send all our Canadian army to sure slaughter....Save your boys by supporting Union Government," and by voting for Margeson.

Given that women were voting for the first time—albeit only selected women—special efforts were made to encourage them to vote, and of course to vote for the right party. The *Bulletin* on December

4 maintained that "as their sons, brothers, and husbands at the front bear the burden of proving the valor and steadfastness of Canadian men, so the women must bear the burden of proving the capacity and intelligent patriotism of Canadian women." If they voted for the Union government, then the general belief would be that women as a whole could be safely trusted with the ballot. But if these pioneers should fail, if they should "be deluded by some weird wizardry into deserting their men in the trenches, then the cause of women suffrage would be put back a black half-century." The paper claimed, probably correctly, that the soldiers looked to their women-folk to vote solidly for the steady stream of reinforcements.

That same day, the *Bulletin* succumbed once again to intolerance. "Are we going to change the name of Canada for 'Quebec'?" The thinking was that if Laurier won, Quebec rule would supersede Canadian rule. "On December 17th the people must declare for Canada and Canadian soldiers or Quebec and Quebec's slackers. They must choose between patriotism and pea soup." By contrast, the Bridgewater paper urged, Canadians must think of "the future of our Country, its destiny and the character of its people"; at stake are "their most cherished possessions, British institutions, British traditions, and British ideals of liberty and civilization."

The *Morning Chronicle*, too, on December 15, gave a last-minute "Dire Warning": "We already have a government made up of the best and most trustworthy statesmen of both political parties, with but one purpose, apart from honest and fair administration in view—service in the war.... Should our first and only practical line of defence in Europe give way, and the Germans descend on our shores, surely every rational and true Canadian will say no to partisanism."

Just days before the election, Major General Sydney C. Mewburn, the minister of militia and defence, announced that farmers' sons who were honestly engaged in the production of food would be exempt from military service. Farmers were fearful that the MSA would take their sons from the fields just when they were needed to respond to the government's demands for greater food production. On November 27, in a last-minute, rather dishonest, attempt to sway voters in Lunenburg County, the *Bulletin* assured its readers that Sir Robert Borden had stated that all men engaged in fishing would be exempt from military service. Fishermen should not listen to anything in the contrary.

In the battle for votes, Duff wrote to the "Fishermen and Ship Owners of Lunenburg County," appealing to them on the grounds that he was particularly well qualified to protect their business interests. Of course, the *Bulletin* on December 4 took exception, declaring that the people in the fishery were as patriotic as everyone else and not only concerned with their financial interests. That same day, a letter to the editor appeared from W. C. Smith & Company of Lunenburg, titled "A Deliberate Lie Nailed," denying a statement that the firm was not in favour of Union government. "We were and are now prepared to support the Union Candidate irrespective of what might have been his former politics."

The turbulent campaign came to an end on December 17, 1917. It rapidly became clear that the aftermath was going to be as nasty as the campaign itself. The day after the election, the *Progress-Enterprise* referred to "Unionist Gutter Snipe Journalism," which sought to portray Sir Wilfrid Laurier as disloyal because he had once said the Germans were a noble people. New Brunswick, the paper pointed out, still kept the name of a German state, and yet the province was loyal. As well, the British people retained on the throne a family of German descent on both sides, the king himself of German descent, though he had changed the family's name to a distinctly English one. Laurier was "ungrudgingly devoted to the service of the King, the empire, and his beloved Canada"; yet, "the miserable scribblers in the Tory press, slackers and skulkers," who were too cowardly to volunteer for service abroad, although of military age, "wrote the foulest calumnies upon him, merely because he was Roman Catholic and a French Canadian."

By contrast, the Lunenburg paper's rival in Bridgwater the same day expressed rage against William Duff, who had won the election for the Liberals. "A new partnership—Lunenburg County and Berlin," the paper's headline read, for though the country, apart from Quebec, had voted overwhelmingly for the Union government, Lunenburg had not. Duff could now take his seat with the Quebec "insulters of soldiers." The elected Laurier supporters mainly represented "purely French and pro-German constituencies." Though the votes had been fairly evenly split in the larger towns in the county, many small communities had voted Liberal: the village of Blue Rocks 113 to 14 for Duff over Margeson; Italy Cross 110 to 47; and Midville Branch 97 to 30. The reasons for this unfortunate voting behaviour, sniffed the editor of the *Bulletin*, were obvious to anyone who knew "Lunenburg County's peculiarities and prejudices, coupled with an unstinted and barefaced use of rum and money." The county's very name, the paper implied, would forecast the result, plus "the treasonable and shocking canvass of the Laurierites against conscription." The

only object of these "misguided and misdirected people" was to "punish the government for its humane and patriotic endeavour to win the war and save our soldiers not already killed from annihilation....How small those constituencies must feel that have thrown away their golden opportunity to help defeat the dirty Hun and to cement the great British Empire the world over."

There had been a big turnover in Lunenburg, according to the *Morning Chronicle* of December 19. Duff had carried the county against Margeson by a majority of 1,216 votes—the largest

William Duff.

majority that any candidate had ever received in the constituency. Many of the old formerly Conservative districts had given Duff handsome majorities. His personal popularity and the intense opposition of the masses to Borden's government had made the difference. Province-wide, the Liberal opposition had won four seats: Lunenburg, Antigonish-Guysborough, and two Cape Breton ridings. The Union government won twelve seats in Nova Scotia, but the popular vote was much more even, 48 per cent for the Unionists compared to 45 per cent for the Liberals. Political scientist J. M. Beck claims that several ridings, five in Nova Scotia, had been won only with the questionable use of the military vote under the Military Voters Act. As David Mackenzie observes in *Canada and the First World War*, support for the Union government and conscription was "hardly overwhelming in Atlantic Canada."[5]

The supporters of the Union government were of course convinced that the people of Lunenburg County had made a terrible, and foolish, mistake. But why had they got things so wrong? The *Halifax Herald* was first off the mark, on December 19. There were "special reasons why Duff secured the majority of the Stay-at-Home vote in Lunenburg"; though not stated outright, the implication, once again, was that Lunenburg's German background had mattered. More than any other part of the country, Nova Scotia and the other Maritime provinces should have voted for the "Union-Victory government." Forsaking screaming capitals for once, the paper resorted to bold type instead: "These provinces next door to the Mother Land, these provinces that have so splendidly responded to every call in this Crisis, these provinces...would be the **first to be attacked and to suffer defeat**." "New Scotland" aligning itself with Quebec was "deplorable" and "humiliating."

The *Bulletin* on December 25 expressed similar disgust. Surely the vote "places this good old county in a deplorable and disgraceful position of which many of its citizens are heartily ashamed....[A]ll the howling and rioting of the Laurierites of Blue Rocks, Midville, New Cornwall and some other sections will not detract the attention of the public from the fact that they encouraged the Kaiser and his murderous

Huns." *La Presse* had written that outside Quebec women had voted en masse for Borden. Not so in Lunenburg County, where many women seemed to have betrayed their boys in the trenches and helped to keep them there. "They will yet weep bitter tears over their foolishness." In spite of its chagrin at Lunenburg County lining up with Quebec, in its joy over the great victory nationally for Union government the paper wished its readers "a very peaceful and happy Christmas."

Naturally, the unfortunate loss in Lunenburg County had to be explained. Regrettably, some ugliness had taken place during the election campaign, and on voting day there was "organized rowdyism, threats and intimidation," according to one irate correspondent in the *Herald* on February 19, 1918. A gang of ruffians had bombarded the Drill Hall in Bridgewater, shouting insulting epithets at the speakers, smashing windows, and battering with rocks the sides of the building, which was crowded with people, including a large proportion of women. The policemen had gone home to bed "sick." At Rose Bay, too, a building had been stoned, and Major Margeson had only been able to speak between interruptions. Speakers in favour of the Union government had also been denied a hearing at New Canada, a small community well inland from Bridgewater. On the day of the election, "unseemly disturbances" had taken place at Blue Rocks, where "some hoodlums broke in the polling booth, upset the stove and did other disgraceful acts." "Talk about Quebec!" scolded the *Bulletin*'s editorial on December 25.

On May 28, 1918, the *Bulletin* still apparently smarting from the loss, complained that "the political air" at the time had been "fetid with Duff rum....It came, not by flasks, but by the barrel and puncheon." The men at Blue Rocks who assaulted the presiding officer, and threatened to throw him and the polling clerks off the high cliffs into the sea, were "a gang of rum-crazed Duff supporters." Had it not been for Duff's "stubbornness and narrow conceited pride," Lunenburg would now be represented in the House of Commons by a cabinet minister instead of someone who spouted "cheap claptrap, tenth-rate-ward-heeler stuff." On the same day, the Bridgewater paper printed a letter

on "Hooliganism" from New Ross: there were "disgraceful acts of hoodlums and boodlers in this community during the election campaign…
daring acts of boodling and seditious vapourings." The very name of
the county indicates German sympathies, charged the correspondent,
for once calling a spade a spade, labelling himself a "Loyal Subject of
Our King." But New Ross, "founded by loyal soldiers of King George
the 3rd, that she should fall away from her long cherished traditions
is beyond comprehension after the large contribution she has made to
King and Country in this great struggle for liberty."

"Lunenburg occupies pre-eminently a rather unenviable position
compared with the rest of English speaking Canada," lamented the
editor of the *Bulletin* on January 2. In any case, as the paper had warned
on the day of the election, "the slackers that were so prominent at the
polls had better get themselves measured for uniforms."

For some, there was a serious flaw in the Military Service Act, and that
flaw was the possibility of exemption. Under the act, men were divided
into six classes, based on their age, their marital status, and whether
or not they had dependants. In the important class one, the first men
to be called up were twenty to thirty-four years of age, unmarried or
widowers, with no children as of July 6, 1917. Local civil tribunals
would consider applications for exemption. In April 1918, in response
to the mounting casualties caused by the German spring offensive
on the Western Front, by Order in Council the government lowered
the age of the men in class one to nineteen, and abolished all exemptions for men under age twenty-three. As Patrick M. Dennis puts it
in *Reluctant Warriors*, "In a single stroke Borden had overcome two
great obstacles to harnessing Canada's untapped supply of draft-age
men…the extremely troublesome issue of exemptions and the need to
establish a continuous and reliable flow of reinforcements to the front."

The *Bridgewater Bulletin* on December 4 reassured its readers that
under the selective draft, the first category of class one would supply

all the men required to reinforce the Canadian army. Other categories would not be called up, and no man whose work was vital to the production of food or other wartime necessities would be taken from their present employment. Schoolteachers, the paper advocated, should be exempted, because teachers were scarce and "the children of our land have to be taught whether the war continues or not." Farmers, on the other hand, were apparently more expendable, for on May 14, 1918, the *Bulletin* maintained that it was more important to send men to reinforce the front than for them to stay on the farms: "Let us hear no further word of exemptions—let the demand rather be for the privilege of serving."

Farmers across the country were, in fact, outraged. Once the election was over, the government disavowed General Mewburn's statement that farmers' sons would be exempt, claiming that it was not within the minister's authority to grant a blanket exemption.[6] The *Progress-Enterprise* on April 24 observed that there was "an entirely erroneous… prevailing impression" in some parts of Nova Scotia that the employment of a class one man in industries such as lumbering, fishing, or farming would give him an exemption. A farmer, for instance, must demonstrate that he was as valuable, if not more so, to the state as a farmer than as a soldier; he must produce sufficient food to supply his household but also contribute to the general food supply of the country. Fishermen were in the same position. The *Canadian Fisherman*, in its November 1917 issue, made the case for fishermen of military age, saying they should be exempted on

"*Miss Canada: Just change implements for a little while, my boy. I will look after your pitchfork while you are tossing Huns instead of hay.*" Halifax Herald, *May 24, 1918.*

condition they remained at their occupation for the duration of the war. They were highly skilled food producers that could not be replaced: "For winter fishing, especially, it takes young men able to stand the hardship of seafaring and fishing in rough, cold weather."

One of the nastier sides of the issue was that the public was invited to snitch, to provide information that would lead to cancellation of exemptions obtained by false or misleading statements. Certainly potential conscripts did attempt to use devious means to escape the draft. Ian McKay quotes a historian of Pictou Couty who observed that "youths who had never pulled a cow's teat had themselves classified as farmers by ingenious means—growing potatoes at summer cottages, feeding pigs in the back yards of town houses." Some fishermen in Lunenburg attempted to defy the law by refusing to take their registration notices from the post office before returning to the fishing banks.[7] William Duff stated in the House of Commons in May 1918 that a number of young men, "sons of good Tory fathers," not wanting to join the army, had got jobs aboard the *Niobe* "as oilers and wipers and so forth." He thought the ship should be "renamed the HMCS City of Refuge."

The response to the MSA among men of military age was overwhelmingly negative, not surprising perhaps, for if they had wanted to go to war they likely would have enlisted already. In fact, though, some of these men had attempted to join up earlier but had been turned down as unfit; now, desperate for troops, even men with hernias were moved up into higher classes under the act. According to *The Oxford Companion to Canadian Military History*, of those eligible for call-up well over 90 per cent sought exemption; by the end of the war 124,588 men had been taken on strength with the CEF, with only 24,132 conscripts arriving in France by armistice on November 11. It "was evident that popular enthusiasm for military service had been bled dry, and not just in Quebec," note Robert Craig Brown and Donald Loveridge in "Unrequited Faith." Farmers, they claim, saw the exemption promise as "a cheap political trick," and 97.4 per cent of the farmers who were in class one applied for exemptions. In practice, farmers were aided by the granting of harvest leaves, and registrars were ordered to call up men from urban addresses first.[8]

By the spring of 1918, the net was tightening. Every person residing in Canada at this time—male or female, British or alien, of sixteen years and over—was required to fill in a card on Registration
Day, June 22, 1918. The registrar for Lunenburg County would be D.
Frank Matheson, with deputies for the districts being D. J. Rudolf, J.
H. Creighton, and L. H. Smith. Registration was the law, announced
the *Progress-Enterprise* on June 19, and failure to register would result
in a maximum fine of $100 and one month's imprisonment, also an
added penalty of $10 for each day the person remained unregistered
after June 22. Everyone must contribute to the war effort, but it would
be the men tracked down to join the army who would be most affected.

As Patrick Dennis remarks in *Reluctant Warriors*, the conscripts, by
not voluntarily enlisting earlier, had "lawfully exercised their rights as
citizens in the face of exhortations by the press, the churches, and a
good part of the enraged Canadian citizenry (most of them beyond the
age eligible for military service)"; they faced "an unprecedented and
Hobson-like choice—join the CEF and serve one's country honourably
or invite dishonour and a level of public opprobrium that can only be
imagined today." Now, for many, there would be no choice.

Meanwhile, overseas, the soldiers were wearying of the war and
increasingly desperate to be relieved by new troops from home. An
unusually graphic letter from Steve Conrad, 25th Battalion, "somewhere in France," was printed in the *Bulletin* on November 27, 1917.

*Now I know the boys around home are saying, "They can win the
war without me," but if a few men in each town thruout the Empire
stays back, they are putting the lives of other men in danger. We, that
have come over here, are still carrying on even though in every battle
we see men die; scorched like moths in a furnace, blown to atoms,
gassed, tortured. We are ready to step forward and take their place,*

*not knowing what will be our fate. Bodies may die but the spirit
grows greater as each soul speeds on its way, and the courage and
determination never dies.*

Private Conrad, from Bridgewater, a boilermaker before the war,
was finally demobilized as a sergeant in April 1919, having embarked
for the battlefields of Europe in July 1916, in what must have seemed
another lifetime.

Private Raymond Whynacht, of Voglers Cove, also in France, made
his forceful plea for others to join the fight in a poem, "To Our Boys":

A certain kind of vermin,
  Has come out since war began,
And I cannot quite determine,
  Why it should be called a man...

I guess you're having darn good fun,
  With rushing round the girls,
But wait until our job is done,
  Then see who wears the curls...

You read the papers every day,
  And would curse if we should lose,
But who are they who have to pay,
  So you should get good news...

Now one last word I want with you,
  Before I drop my pen,
You're the smallest thing that ever grew,
  And tried to live like men.

A letter from Sergeant Elden Schwartz, 26th Battalion, dated May
18, 1917, began, "Well, I suppose you people over there know that

the war is still going on." The letter went on to express the soldier's homesickness.

Well, father, how is old Lunenburg?...Sometimes I sit and wonder if I shall ever get the chance of getting down again to old Lunenburg. If all goes well, and I don't fall in this struggle, probably I shall be married to a very nice English girl—if some other better looking fellow don't come along while I'm at the front. I suppose the fishermen are into it with their sleeves up. Good luck to them all, and hope they will beat each other on the trips....Remember me to all, especially the old maids and widows, and let us hope, if God spares me, we shall meet this year. I will close by signing—"Fight the Good Fight."

Schwartz, a seaman, had joined up in April 1915 at Woodstock, New Brunswick. He died of serious wounds to his abdomen and knee on August 16, 1917, and is buried in Noeux-les-Mines Communal Cemetery in France.

Guy Tanner of Blue Rocks told his father, in a letter printed in the *Progress-Enterprise* on May 16, 1917, that he was lonesome in the Port Pitt Hospital in Chatham, England. "I now take the pleasure of dropping you a few lines, but I cannot say that I am smart, for I am not. I am in the hospital wounded." He had had a narrow escape, a serious wound behind his ear, a short distance from his temple. "But thank the Lord I have pulled through all right. I have no cigarettes or no tobacco and no pipe, for I lost it all the night I got wounded.... [T]he war is still going on as strong as ever, it may end this year, but I am doubtful of it."

Millions of letters crossed the Atlantic during the four years of war. Regrettably, most of the letters sent to the men from the home front have been lost, because battlefield conditions made it difficult for the soldiers to preserve them. But, as Modris Eksteins remarks in *Rites of Spring*, "Reading matter from home was essential to sanity in the front line." The soldiers needed to know they were remembered.

And of course those at home wanted desperately to hear from their men at the front. As Jeffrey Keshen observes in *Propaganda and*

Censorship, most troops in letters home reinforced rather than undermined the idealistic notions of war that many people held. This was partly due to censorship, but soldiers also wanted "to project those manly attributes that had prompted them to take up arms." To whine would make the soldier look weak and unmanly, and it would also depress and worry those at home. The soldier's burden was to bear the brunt stoically.

Letters home, Keshen maintains, were also shaped by the fact that most of the troops were not well educated, most not having gone beyond grade six. Field Service Cards with "I am quite well" checked were sent home by the millions. Citizens at home were "never enlightened as to the indiscriminate slaughter often accompanying advances nor the gruesomeness so often associated with death." Thus arose the notion of "a *field of honour* from which heroes emerged, and where death was clean, quick, painless and saintly—the small bullet hole in the left breast, while the victim, with arms outstretched, urged his comrade on to victory." Tim Cook in *Vimy* claims that letters home from survivors of a battle to the families of friends who had died were "almost always couched in the language of cheerful sacrifice and a clean death in battle."

Most letters home tried to reassure relatives that all was well, and really, it was all a wonderful, even ennobling, experience. An unnamed soldier in the field, whose letter was printed in the *Progress-Enterprise* on June 28, 1916, assured his mother that he was not alone. "Every man who wears the King's uniform and stands shoulder to shoulder with you in the battle is a brother to you." The feeling of brotherhood and "the confidence you put in the man on your right and left...makes us laugh in the face of danger and death....I have seen death hundreds of times over here but I never saw a soldier die but he passed the Great Divide with a smile on his lips." It's questionable as to whether such sentiments would reassure a mother.

The *Bridgewater Bulletin* observed on August 28, 1917, that the town of Lunenburg and the county generally had been hard hit by the recent heavy fighting in the war. One loss the paper mentioned particularly was that of Captain Owen Gates Dauphinee, who had left his farm in Pine Grove when the call came for volunteers: "an exemplary young man, a good soldier, and an excellent citizen...a bright young man in the prime of life."

Born in Bridgewater in April 1881, Dauphinee was thirty-five when he enlisted, a member of the Church of England, according to his officer's declaration paper. He had spent eighteen years in the 75th Regiment and also served in the King Edward Coronation Contingent, a guard of honour assembled for participation in the coronation ceremonies of the monarch in London. He thus joined the 112th Battalion with the rank of captain. He crossed the ocean on the *Olympic* in July 1916. Restive in England, he reverted to the rank of lieutenant "in order to get quickly to the firing line" and went to France with the 25th Battalion in June 1917. Less than two months later, on August 20, he was killed in action at the battle for Hill 70, on the outskirts of Lens. His "giving up his life for King and Country at once stamps him as a hero," but it was a sad blow for his wife and three children.

Also killed in France about the same time was Robert Hunter Duff of Bridgewater. A civil engineer, he had enlisted in December 1915, almost twenty-eight years old, sailing to England on the *Olympic* the following July. In England he reverted to the rank of private at his own request in order to proceed to the front. By June 1917 he was in the 2nd Canadian Pioneer Battalion, a unit whose purpose was to consolidate positions captured by the infantry by doing tunnelling, mining, wiring, railway work, and trench repair.

The unsigned item about Robert Duff's death in the *Progress-Enterprise* of September 5, 1917, is extraordinary for its passion and eloquence.

In the order of nature and progress of the spirit, all true life is an example of sacrifice. Yet there is unutterable sadness in the seeming defeat of the purpose of individual life when the young spirit of health and promise is killed in the rage of war. And the sadness would be overwhelming and unbearable to the thoughtful heart, if life were summed up only in years. But "we live in deeds, not years," and in this time of vastest and most frightful battle and murder and sudden death, there is the consoling, strengthening, and abiding faith that our dead heroes have achieved the noblest life of manhood in their supreme sacrifice of self for the world's salvation.

The writer tells us that Duff was likely killed on the battlefield of Lens, that before the war he was an engineer with the Canadian Northern Railway in Ontario and later the Canadian Pacific, that two of his brothers were also serving overseas, and that his wife Sheila, from Toronto, had been left behind with a small son.

The war's impact was felt throughout the county. On September 4, 1917, the *Bulletin* reported on the centennial celebrations of the founding of New Ross. It was said that the "gallant boys" of the village had "heard the call from the Motherland across the sea, and no fewer than eighty of our noblest have answered the call and thirteen of them have already paid the supreme sacrifice." A few days later, on September 11, the *Bulletin* reported that Chester was probably the first Canadian town to erect a "War Shrine" to her overseas soldiers. A shrine with a roll of honour had been placed in the post office through the efforts of the women of the Red Cross. With a population of seven hundred, this little town had sent forty-two men to the front, and seven had died on the "Field of Honor." It was proposed that after the war a suitable monument would be erected on the parade as a lasting memorial to Chester's heroes.

The name of one soldier on the Lunenburg war memorial appears as well on the Ypres (Menin Gate) Memorial in Belgium. The personnel records reveal that Ellsworth Edward Smith of the 85th Battalion had been reported wounded and missing after action and "now for official purposes presumed to have DIED on or since 30 October 1917." His body was apparently never found, for no further information is given. Tim Cook in

Ellsworth Smith.

Vimy describes "bodies so badly mangled in battle that in death they could not be identified. To have lost one's life is to have given everything one can give. But to lose one's name and to be lost forever to one's family is something unimaginably terrible." This, it seems, was Ellsworth Smith's fate.

The bodies of the soldiers who died overseas were not brought home. As the *Progress-Enterprise* remarked on October 16, 1918, "they sleep in the shade of a little white cross on a foreign but friendly soil."

It was also time to welcome home the wounded. A reception was held at the LaHave Islands on April 24, 1918, in honour of Private John Publicover, who had been a sniper in the 85th Battalion and had just returned from overseas. A fisherman before the war, Publicover enlisted in Bridgewater in March 1916 at the age of twenty-six and served in both England and France. Wounded in the back and chest at Passchendaele in October 1917, he had also developed a tumour on his left mammary gland. He was discharged on June 26, 1918, medically unfit to continue as a soldier. At the reception he modestly responded to an address, was loudly cheered as a hero, and presented with a gold watch and chain and an Oddfellows' ring. The *Progress-Enterprise* of May 8 noted that he was one of fifteen men who had nobly volunteered from the islands in September 1915, eleven of whom had already laid down their lives. Having been in and out of hospitals in Europe, Publicover now faced further treatment in Halifax.

On June 25, 1918, the *Progress-Enterprise* reported that a "goodly crowd" had assembled at Western Shore, with flags flying on all sides, to greet "our first returned hero." Private William Sawler of the Royal Canadian Regiment was coming home from the front, the first man from the parish of St. Martin to go across. Born in Gold River in 1896, Sawler had enlisted at Halifax in August 1915, at age nineteen and a mere 51 kg. He had "done his duty nobly and sacrifice made complete" at Passchendaele. At the South Gold River schoolhouse, Rev. C. H. Talmay voiced the feelings of the people in a few words, "partly of sympathy but chiefly of gratitude."

Sawler was a hero, but he was also a severely damaged man. Because of injuries sustained in the battle on October 29, 1917, both of his legs had been amputated. After stays at numerous hospitals in France and England, he spent time at Camp Hill in Halifax, and then went to Toronto for artificial limbs. He would go to Toronto again for further hospital treatment and "some educational course that he may begin a new and more peaceful sphere in life." In one way only it is possible to think of Private Sawler as a lucky man. He returned home from Liverpool in June 1918 on the Canadian hospital ship *Llandovery Castle*. On her next voyage from Halifax back to England the *Llandovery Castle* would be torpedoed by a German submarine and sunk off the southern coast of Ireland.

Chapter Five

A "NEAR RIOT," SUBMARINES, AND SPIES

How many young Nova Scotians "are going to deliberately incur the ODIUM and penalties of DESERTERS from Our Citizen Army?" asked the *Halifax Herald* on November 6, 1917. The paper warned that every man who had not registered under the Military Service Act would be considered a deserter from the Canadian army, liable to imprisonment and "all the odium that attaches to a deserter at this period of the world's history, when desertion and cowardice is doubly odious." If not on the registration list, a man would lose his right to claim for exemption.

The *Bridgewater Bulletin* on January 1, 1918, was equally concerned that potential conscripts comply with the law. The first draft was about to be called, and Ottawa had made it clear that strong measures would be taken against defaulters. Rewards were offered to any civil service police or peace officer who apprehended and delivered a deserter into military custody. Class one men who failed to comply would be liable for any term of imprisonment not exceeding five years, with hard labour.

The *Progress-Enterprise* customarily took a softer approach. On January 16, the Lunenburg paper reported that several men from the nearby village of Blue Rocks who had failed to register had voluntarily surrendered themselves and had gone to Halifax to report to the authorities. The men, all fishermen, had just arrived in from the sea; they were not wilful violators of the act. The men of Blue Rocks were reportedly as willing as any to do their share, but had no definite knowledge of the new laws and ordinances. The public should remember that if these men were taken, this section would have supplied more fishermen that any other district in the county. The *Bulletin* on January 22 agreed with this assessment, but claimed that it was well known the men had been wilfully misled to understand that they had no need to register. They were allegedly told to defy the authorities and ignore the calls for registration. The men were not so much to blame as those who knowingly led them astray. And thus began a bit of a spat.

On February 11, the *Herald* immediately got on its high horse, claiming that William Duff, mayor and MP, was responsible, that he had some kind of special "pull," and that he should be punished for inciting men to defy the MSA. There seemed to be some underground "influence" working against registration for the act, and no other county had shown up so badly. Men had been told that registration was a "bluff," that they were foolish to register unless they wanted to be killed, and so on. So they became defaulters, and the "influence" was William Duff. A sergeant and two men had gone down from Halifax, boldly invaded the little community of Blue Rocks, and twenty-six men had surrendered. They were taken to Lunenburg and put on parole to report at the railway station in time for the Halifax train next morning. At the time for departure, only two showed up. The police returned to the village and gathered up fourteen men. "One or two of the Blue Rocks young bloods had 'taken to the woods.'" Lunenburg County had been placed in a most unenviable light, not only in Nova Scotia but all over the Dominion.

In the *Morning Chronicle*, William Duff, not surprisingly, denied the charges, saying that "the story had emanated from an individual who was actuated by malicious motives against him." The *Herald* on February 19 contrasted Duff's "injured innocence" with what "the Blue Rocks fellows" who had been arrested and taken to Halifax were saying about how they had been "tricked and duped and finally Left-in-the-Lurch by their 'friend.'" In a statement published in the *Herald*, James Tanner protested that Duff had told his father, Enos Tanner of Black Rocks, that "we were not to attend the exemption board and that 'He would get us clear.'" Ruggles Knickle claimed, "Duff told me not to sign and he would look out for me." Stafford Romkey said Captain Allen had told him that Duff was going "to 'arrange matters' so that we would be exempted." Similar statements came from several others. The *Herald*'s editor exclaimed, "If the Military Service Act is to be enforced and respected and made a thing of vitality, it must be enforced against men of the type of Duff and Allen of Lunenburg town, as well as against the Tanners, the Romkeys, the Knickles, the Greeks, the Walters, the McDonalds, and the Frittenburgs of Blue Rocks. OTHER-WISE the Selective Draft law will be brought into contempt."

The *Bulletin* on February 19 claimed that William Duff's "connection with the Blue Rocks military scandal," and his "alleged interference with conscription," had become "common talk all over the county." Keeping up the attack, the paper maintained on May 14 that Duff's antagonism toward the MSA had made it lonely for him in Ottawa, and "as he is not a fluent French scholar his conversation with his seatmates is far from animated.... [H]e has made several foolish attempts to listen to his melodious voice in parliament, but each time he put his foot in his mouth but failed to keep it there."

The *Progress-Enterprise* expressed a slightly different, and more compassionate, view of events. "Some of our boys have been summoned to Halifax for 'mobilization,'" the paper observed on February 6. Although they were "conscripts," many of them had volunteered earlier and had been turned down as physically unfit, "but now in the great anxiety to raise the promised 500,000 they are taken." Others had had good reason for not volunteering; perhaps some had been slackers, but it was hard for anyone to judge. They were going now at "a very trying time and under trying circumstances and deserved the full sympathy and consideration of all the citizens, perhaps even more than those who went earlier." On April 17 the paper published Duff's "absolute and unqualified denial," in which he stated "I am as loyal as any man in Canada." As for the war, he believed "the cause is a noble one, and is in the interests of democracy, liberty, truth and righteousness." He vowed he would do everything in his power, whether as a private citizen or as a member of the House of Commons, "to bring this war to a successful conclusion."

On May 15 the *Progress-Enterprise* printed Duff's speech on the budget in the House of Commons, in which he pointed out the investment in gear the fishermen had already made, and declared that fishing and shipbuilding could not be done by old men and boys.[1] A paper in Halifax, "one of the Government organs," had "flung in our teeth that the fishermen and sailors of Lunenburg county were slackers and cowards." According to Duff, nothing of the kind.

I think the members of this House will agree with me that men who leave their homes on the 15th of March, when the ice is on the coast,

Lunenburg harbour and railway wharf in winter, March 1916.

and the March winds and gales are blowing, and go out and anchor one hundred and fifty miles from land, and every morning at daylight start off in the dories and haul their trawls, and continue that occupation for perhaps a month before they see land again—men who pursue that occupation all through the summer fogs and during the August and September gales, before returning home, cannot be called slackers or cowards.

The men on the schooners were discovering, perhaps to their surprise and no doubt chagrin, that they were considered less valuable as fisherman, contributing to the food supply, and more useful as soldiers at the front. At the same time, their vessels were being threatened offshore by German submarines.

The tension in Lunenburg continued. On June 18, 1918, the *Halifax Herald* reported that a "near riot" had occurred on the waterfront, "on the part of an excited crowd." The military police, two men named Cameron and Heron, had been in Lunenburg for several days endeavouring to apprehend those who had come in on the fishing fleet. Since many of the men did not have the proper documents, exemption papers or marriage certificates, there was much trouble. The fleet was about to sail again and the fishing captains complained bitterly. Perhaps more concerned about their profits than their crews, suggested the *Herald*, they were charging that the police should have done their work before the vessels were ready to sail, in time for them to get new men.

The *Progress-Enterprise* on the nineteenth insisted that the police had "acted in a particularly obnoxious manner not using any judgment or discretion," and had caused considerable inconvenience; there were particular accounts to substantiate the claim. Austin Knickle, the father of twelve children, had been arrested and put in jail. Allen Weaver, who had been married for eleven years, was taken off his vessel and ordered to walk the six kilometres to Blue Rocks to bring in his marriage certificate.

Greville Knickle, who was also married, was ordered at the point of a revolver to produce his papers. A crowd had gathered on Smith's Wharf, among them a forty-year-old man of feeble mind and certain innocence, only just out of the Nova Scotia Hospital a few years. Even he was arrested in the sweep but later freed. Finally, a young man, inopportunely named Kaizer, was about to board his vessel when accosted by the police. He explained his papers were on-board but one of the policemen drew his revolver and forced him into the county jail. After a great deal of trouble, the captain had him liberated.

The Lunenburg chief of police was informed by one of the military police that "they were running the town." "Are these police men to be allowed to terrorize peaceable citizens and threaten to shoot, or can civil law protect its law abiding citizens?" asked the *Progress-Enterprise*. Considering the lighter side of things the next day, the paper remarked on the randomness of the approach to men in the town: "It is lovely to think that the residents of Lunenburg preserve such a look of pristine innocence and delightful freshness, that men who have been married for years and are the fathers of a dozen children are accosted as youth of 20 or 22."

The *Bulletin*, naturally, did not let things lie: "It is an ugly fact, but we are obliged to admit that there is room for some reincarnation of the spirit of loyalty in some parts of Lunenburg County." Ever since the first mention of the MSA, there had been a growing sentiment in the county antagonistic to its provisions. "How often did one's ears become tired with the thread-bare remarks 'Canada has done enough,' 'wait till the Germans come over,' 'Vote against Borden and keep the boys home.'" This sentiment had been "fanned and nursed and fostered and cultivated" until in the election last December the county had given William Duff a majority of some 1,300 votes. Picking up on the *Herald*'s language, the *Bulletin* claimed on August 13 that the sentiment showed further evidence of being alive "when a near riot occurred in the Town of Lunenburg in opposition to some Dominion policemen who were attempting to carry out the law."[2]

"Like Saul," exclaimed the *Progress-Enterprise* on August 21, "the Editor of the *Bulletin* is breathing out threatenings and slaughter, against the fair name of many of our best citizens, and our good old County, and the shire town in particular." The *Bulletin* had stated that the only aim of a certain class of Lunenburg's citizens was "the price of fish and the money making prospects of vessel property....[O]ur people are certainly alive to the value of the almighty dollar and to the means of making money, but we can't see why their loyalty should be impugned or their lack of military enthusiasm questioned." Before conscription, "the percentage of our people who enlisted voluntarily compares favourably with any other portion of the Dominion."

It would be hard also to surpass Lunenburg's record of giving to all the various patriotic causes. Evidently the majority for Duff was what "stuck in the editor's crop" and caused him "to cry out disloyal" and "attempt to brand the fair name of the County with a Hun brush." Why was Lunenburg considered more disloyal than the other counties that had given large majorities antagonistic to the government? The "Scotch people of the east," in Cape Breton, were "on the same par as the population of this noble County." And Australians, too, had voted against conscription. As for the "near riot," the *Bulletin* "should confess" that at least one of "the so called Dominion Police" had been intoxicated, that he had flourished a revolver under the noses of peaceable and inoffensive citizens, threatening to shoot them for no cause whatever. The *Bulletin* had maintained that "the Hun is here," inferring that there were "spies and disloyal people in our midst." If they were not interned, asserted the *Progress-Enterprise*, then the government was not doing its duty. "Cease besmirching as honest and loyal a population as can be found in any British Colony."

Of course, there had been disturbances in other parts of the country, and some were very serious. At Quebec City on March 28, a riot had occurred when the federal police tried to arrest defaulters. A mob burned the military service registry office, including its records, and pillaged English-Canadian businesses. Rather foolishly, soldiers had been brought in from Toronto and, trapped by an angry crowd, they opened fire, killing four civilians. Quebec and Ontario farmers also demonstrated in Ottawa because exemptions were being denied their sons.[3] At

Niagara Camp in Ontario, according to the *Bulletin* on August 20, ten conscientious objectors had been tried by court martial and sentenced to penal servitude for life. This had been commuted by the government to ten years' imprisonment, to be served in the Kingston Penitentiary.

Overseas the war was taking a turn for the worse. In March 1918, German commander-in-chief General Erich Ludendorff launched the last great German offensive of the war, code-named Operation Michael. The French and the British, reinforced by the Canadians, were able to hold the Germans back, up and down the line. In August the Canadian Corps participated in the Allied counteroffensive at Amiens, the battle that some said turned the tide on the Western Front. This significant defeat caused Ludendorff to call August 8 "the black day of the German army." The battle at Amiens was the beginning of what became known as "Canada's Hundred Days," which historian Wade Davis describes as "a nonstop engagement as the Allied forces, with the Canadian Corps in the vanguard, pushed the Germans east until their final surrender."[4] The end of this push, for the Canadians, came at Mons in Belgium on November 11, the location where the British had first met the Germans in conflict in 1914.

Military historian J. L. Granatstein calls the hundred days in 1918 Canada's "greatest victory," and it was during this period that the Canadian Corps became known as "the shock troops of the British Empire." It was also the time when the corps suffered its heaviest casualties of the war.[5] According to Patrick Dennis in *Reluctant Warriors*, approximately 45,000 Canadian troops were killed, wounded, or taken prisoner in the period from Amiens to the armistice. He contends that the more than 24,000 conscripts—contrary to the commonly held belief that they were too few and had arrived at the front too late to make a difference—had in fact provided the crucial manpower to reinforce the corps, and allow General Arthur Currie "to execute an aggressive and continuous series of offensives which led to successive

triumphs in the Hundred Days." As well, Dennis maintains the conscripts on their way across the ocean would have enabled the army to
be kept up to strength if the war had carried on into 1919.

It was in 1918, too, that the war at sea had reached its peak, and
Nova Scotia, with its long coastline exposed to the Atlantic, would
be more affected than the rest of the country. As David Mackenzie
comments in "Eastern Approaches," Atlantic Canada was the part of
the country closest to the war in Europe and the one part directly
touched by enemy activity. Halifax, the main point of departure on the
east coast for supplies, munitions, and troops crossing the Atlantic, had
been a key player in the war from the start. Further down the shore, the
principal industry of Lunenburg was fishing, and access to the sea for
the schooners was essential.

In the early years of the war, the people of Lunenburg County, as
well as the rest of Nova Scotia, had felt secure because the vast expanse
of the Atlantic Ocean separated them from the strife in Europe, and
they knew as well that they were protected by the Royal Navy. As the
Progress-Enterprise remarked on August 26, 1914, every official source
had explained that the Atlantic was free from German cruisers and
that it was being patrolled by British men of war. "The ocean highway
is clear, the Grand Banks is safer than Cross Island." The *Canadian
Fisherman* asserted in August 1914, "The cruisers of the mother country have kept the Atlantic shores of Canada clear of German war vessels and there is absolutely nothing to prevent Canadian fishermen
from prosecuting their business as usual. Even if there were a number
of German warships prowling around the fishing banks it is safe to say
that they would never bother fishing vessels....[M]odern nations do
not war on fishermen."

The situation would change dramatically, however, when German
raiders, and especially submarines, began to appear in the western
Atlantic. No longer a barrier, the ocean had become a pathway to
deliver the terrors of the European war to North America's shores.
Early in the war, it had generally been thought that submarines could
not make it all the way across the ocean. In *U-Boats against Canada*,

Michael L. Hadley explains that German submersibles of the First World War could only stay under water for an extremely limited time, and thus they operated as surface raiders. They would go to their operational zone on the surface, then submerge on sighting a distant target, and surface suddenly at close quarters to attack.

The *Bridgewater Bulletin* on February 22, 1916, revealing surprising compassion, gave some insight into the anguish of the men fighting on the other side in the U-boats (*Unterseeboote*). In order to avoid the horror of a lingering death by suffocation, crews of German submarines caught in nets laid for them by the British hastened their end by committing suicide, according to a Canadian army surgeon who had witnessed the aftermath of a captain lining his men up and shooting each one in the head in turn. It "almost baffles the imagination to conceive of a discipline so marvellous," said the *Bulletin*, contemplating the "mental torture of waiting to be put to death in this way instead of yielding to the natural instinct of struggling to reach some exit from their imprisonment at the bottom of the sea."

Compassion aside, it was now known that the U-boats, as well as creating havoc with ships in the waters off Europe, could indeed cross the ocean, for by mid-1916 they were showing up on the coast of North America. And on January 31, 1917, Germany declared unrestricted submarine warfare, abandoning all international restrictions on the use of submarines in its campaign against Allied merchant shipping. The Germans realized this act would bring the United States into the war, but if enough shipping could be destroyed before America's weight could be felt, then Britain might be defeated. Merchant ships crossing the Atlantic on their own were suffering enormous losses. There seemed to be no solution to "the deadly depredations of the U-boats," remarks Milner in *Canada's Navy*. But the solution came in July 1917, when convoys were introduced to escort merchant ships safely to Britain. Troops, food, and supplies thus continued to cross the Atlantic to help win the war.

Although the Royal Canadian Navy played a useful role helping to defend the convoys, it was more difficult to protect the vessels fishing on the banks, for they were dispersed, and with no radios the fishermen could only notify naval authorities of attacks after they had rowed ashore. The navy did patrol the coast in a fleet made up of "armed yachts, submarine chasers, trawlers, and drifters," according to Richard H. Gimblett in *The Naval Service of Canada*. Instead of building up the navy, however, the Canadian government provided Britain with Canadian seamen. In 1914 Ottawa had established the Royal Naval Canadian Volunteer Reserve composed of qualified mariners and a volunteer reserve of amateurs. By 1916 so many men had come forward that the minister of naval service created the Overseas Division of the RNCVR to recruit Canadians for the Royal Navy. The *Bulletin* on January 9, 1917, reported that Lieutenant Chorley of the Royal Navy had met a few citizens in the council chamber in Bridgewater to raise men for the British navy. Only men from ages eighteen to thirty were wanted, and they had to be English or native-born. They must "have no German odor about them," which seemed an odd way to appeal for recruits in Lunenburg County.

The British government and the Admiralty consistently advised the Canadians against expanding their navy, and with Canada's "industrial resources and manpower so heavily committed to the overseas army," as Milner explains, the "motley flotilla" of patrol vessels had nothing with which to fight the submarines. And because the convoy system worked so well, the U-boat captains were forced to look for easier prey. They mainly settled on the unarmed and unprotected schooners of the fishing fleets. As Michael Hadley and Roger Sarty put it in *Tin-Pots and Pirate Ships*, "the merchant ship convoys ultimately defeated the U-boats," but the little schooners that the submarines went on to attack were "small fry that scarcely repaid the enormous effort involved in transatlantic voyages."

German raiders were already active on the east coast of South America by 1915. In February that year the auxiliary cruiser *Kronprinz Wilhelm* sank four British steamers as well as the three-masted Lunenburg schooner *Wilfrid M.*, sailing from St. John's to Pernambuco, Brazil, with a valuable cargo of codfish—the first Canadian vessel to fall victim to German commerce raiders according to the *Bridgewater Bulletin* of February 23. Owned by William Duff, J. J. Kinley, and others, the captain of the vessel was Cyrus Parks of Parks Creek, and one of the crew members was the son of the manager of Robin, Jones, & Whitman of Lunenburg. The *Bulletin* reported that the mate was Sedley Young of Lunenburg, who had had "a varied career of shipwreck, travel, and romance on the high seas, and this appears to be the culminating event in his exciting experiences."

A shock came when the *Deutschland*, the first submarine to cross the Atlantic Ocean, arrived in Baltimore on July 10, 1916, and was greeted warmly in the neutral United States. The first U-boat to carry cargo, the submarine had dived under the British blockade, and it would return to Europe loaded with important industrial materials, bulk crude rubber, nickel, and tin, much needed by the military forces in Germany, at the same time proving that submarines could cross the Atlantic without support.[6] (The *Deutschland* was eventually converted for war and patrolled as U-155, laying mines, virtually unopposed, off Halifax and the Nova Scotia coast in the early fall of 1918.)

In October 1916, U-53 arrived in Newport, Rhode Island, and after a short stay departed and promptly sank several Allied steamers. The *Progress-Enterprise* reported on the eleventh that the "submarine arm of the German navy" had ravaged shipping off the eastern coast of the United States, sinking four British, one Dutch, and one Norwegian steamer off the Nantucket shoals. "Under the light of the hunter's moon" the US Atlantic fleet picked up passengers and crews and brought them into Newport. The war at sea was inching closer. As Milner declares in *Canada's Navy*, "The U-boat war had come to North America."

One of the first Lunenburg vessels to be lost was the *Harry W. Adams*, captained by Fred Acker of Mahone Bay, on its way from Newfoundland with a cargo of dried fish for La Coruna on the northern coast of Spain. On Christmas Eve, 1916, not far from its destination, the schooner was approached by a German submarine. Forced to disembark into the dangerous waters of the Bay of Biscay, the crew was put aboard a captured Norwegian steamer, and eventually landed at Ferrol. The *Harry W. Adams* was torpedoed and sank in less than half an hour. Another schooner, also owned by Adams & Knickle, the *Mayola*, was torpedoed near Gibraltar in February 1917.

A similar fate overtook the tern schooner *Perce* in the South Atlantic that spring. Headed for Santos near São Paulo, with a cargo of lumber and fish, Captain Carl J. R. Kohler of Lunenburg had taken his new bride along for the trip. Captured by the German sea raider *Seeadler*, the crew was transferred to a French steamer and eventually landed at Rio de Janeiro. Having bombed and sunk the *Perce*, the raider departed in a southerly direction while its band played "Deutschland über alles." Some "malicious persons" circulated damaging reports about the loyalty of Captain Kohler, a naturalized Canadian born in Germany, but, because of favourable statements by captains of British vessels also captured, he was exonerated. The *Progress-Enterprise* commented on May 2 that the submarine menace was serious and could be an important factor in deciding the outcome of the war.

On June 13, 1917, the Lunenburg paper observed that the local fishermen had practically all returned from the banks. The fleet had been remarkably clear of casualties that year, and the catches had also been good. "What a contrast to the unfortunate fishermen of Europe. By virtue of the might of Britain our fishermen have not as yet been molested by any raider or submarine. The battleships of the Allies have kept these murderers away. Our Lunenburg fishermen are grateful and they realize their protection lies with the fighting forces of the Empire." Later that year, on September 25, the *Bulletin* claimed there were rumours of an enemy submarine in American waters, in the vicinity of the Nantucket lightship, but these should be taken with a grain of salt. The *Halifax Herald*, however, was taking it all more seriously. A special cable from London on October 19 had contained a warning from a naval expert that a change was taking place in German u-boat policy. Thus, reports of "North America as a war zone must NOT be dismissed as bluff."

Then, on October 30, 1917, the *Herald* announced that the commander of the military district had ordered all lights in private houses, shops, warehouses, and other buildings must be obscured by the use of blinds, and lights from public buildings, such as places of amusement, clubs, churches, and hotels, must be obscured so as not to throw a glare into the sky or seawards. The area affected included Halifax, Dartmouth, and vicinity, and penalties for contravening the order could be as high as $5,000 or imprisonment for up to five years. The upper half of lights on motor cars was also to be darkened. On November 26 the *Herald* complained that not everyone was complying, and thereafter no leniency would be shown. Street lights facing seaward were to be darkened on the seaward side and the remaining portion of the lamp frosted. John Griffith Armstrong in *The Halifax Explosion and the Royal Canadian Navy* maintains that the "virtual blackout made Halifax unique among Canadian cities and served as a constant reminder of the growing danger off the coast."

During the late spring of 1918, the German submarines were increasingly active along the American east coast, and many vessels had been sunk. The *Bulletin* noted on June 11 that New York City, on orders from Washington, had "joined the grim company of the cities of darkness," with blackouts like London and Paris. Submarines had also been sighted near Bermuda. The *Herald* on June 4 declared that submarine warfare on this side of the Atlantic was now an accomplished fact. Halifax presented a most desirable goal for submarine commanders' ambitions, for everybody knew it was the chief port for the embarkation of troops on this side of the water. "We cannot expect to be left in blissful immunity." The city may be bombed, but even so, "we must carry on in the British way. There must be no evidence of panic, wild excitement or unreasoning alarm." Citizens were assured by military and naval officials on June 15 that an airplane raid or bombardment by submarine were remote contingencies. Contrary to such assurances, the sinking of a schooner off Portland, Maine, prompted the *Herald* to proclaim in a headline on July 25, "The War Is At Our Doors."

And then there was the little matter of spies. The *Herald* warned on July 25 that German spies had done "dirty work hereabouts," and nothing had been done to "round up these gentry." Earlier, on July 10, the *Progress-Enterprise* had cautioned that Nova Scotia "now wants to get her eyes open." There were "mysterious fires in mills and ship yards, tractors with mangled machinery, forest fires without end and many other promiscuous happenings that seem to dictate the fine hand of the brutal pacifist…and last and worst there is the crowning horror of the sinking of the Canadian hospital ship *Llandovery Castle* which has some very sinister signs about it. Signs that point clearly to the enemy within our gates who is too peaceful to fight." "Is there a Hidden Hand in Halifax?" queried the *Herald*. "Who is the spy, or is there a small coterie of spies, operating in this city?"

The *Llandovery Castle* was returning to Liverpool from Canada, having delivered convalescing soldiers to Halifax. Approaching the coast of Ireland on June 27, 1918, about 160 kilometres southwest of Fastnet Rock, the ship was torpedoed by U-86. A hospital ship, unarmed and running with full lights, it was clearly identified by a brightly illuminated red

Halifax Herald, *July 11, 1918.*

cross. The Germans apparently thought the ship was carrying American flight officers and other military personnel as well as ammunition. The ship sank in ten minutes. In what the *Morning Chronicle* described as the "culminating act of cynical brutality," the submarine then machine-gunned the survivors in the lifeboats, in an attempt, it seems, to kill the witnesses to what the *Herald* called "this infamous Teuton act." Only one lifeboat survived, saving only 24 of the 258 people on-board, many of whom were men of the Canadian Army Medical Corps.

The few survivors were picked up after thirty-six hours by the British destroyer HMS *Lysander*. Fourteen Canadian nursing sisters, including the matron Margaret Fraser, daughter of a former lieutenant-governor of Nova Scotia, perished when their lifeboat was capsized in the whirlpool caused by the sinking ship. A distinctly Canadian, solemn requiem mass for these victims was chanted in early August in St. Etheldreda's chapel in London; the catafalque was draped with British and Canadian flags and covered with the words CAMC, CEF, and the Nursing Sisters' insignia.[7] It was widely believed that the U-boat commander, Helmut Brümmer-Patzig, had been fed information about the voyage from German spies in Halifax. The sinking of the *Llandovery Castle* was the deadliest Canadian naval disaster of the war, and, not surprisingly, the incident outraged public opinion.

The *Bridgewater Bulletin* on August 13, 1918, observed that Lunenburg was getting anxious. The sinking of several fishing schooners "by Hun subs at our very doors has caused great excitement and consternation," not only in Lunenburg town but also throughout the whole county, for the fishing fleet was now on the banks and liable at any moment to be attacked and sent to the bottom "by the ruthless Hun, who spares neither friend nor foe when he has his own ends to serve." It might be truly said that the people of Lunenburg had never before realized what this war meant to them. It could also be said that "Lunenburg now fully and very painfully realizes that the advent of the Hun sub may mean destruction to its splendid fleet of vessels and probably the death of many of the members of the crews." Every part of the county was represented on the schooners, about three thousand men, the "bone and sinew" of the county. A woman from Blue Rocks remarked that she was sorry her son was not over in France instead of at sea at the mercy of the submarines.

The same edition of the *Bulletin* acknowledged that the people of Lunenburg County had just reason to feel grievously alarmed. "The submarine crew have given it out that they have orders to destroy the fishing fleet and that they will do their very best to carry out their diabolical orders there can be no doubt.... [T]he success they have already achieved shows that the Hun ship will spare none, neither American or Canadian, Gloucester or Lunenburg, and that Lunenburg's turn may come at any moment." People anxiously awaited the arrival of the *Herald* with the daily news, phones were busy between the outlying districts and the town, and one met so many worried faces. "For war has at last come home to us in reality."

Three American schooners from Gloucester and Boston had been sunk in early August by u-boats operating off Seal Island in Yarmouth County, within sixty kilometres of the Nova Scotia coast. The crew of one of these vessels, the *Muriel*, was mainly Nova Scotian, including Captain Eldridge Nickerson of Shag Harbour. A Yarmouth schooner, the *Nelson A.*, homeward bound from a fishing trip, had been sunk by a bomb off Shelburne—the first schooner sunk on Nova Scotia's Atlantic coast—after the vessel had been ransacked for provisions. The crew had landed safely in Lockeport.

On August 3, u-156 had attacked and set fire to the recently launched four-masted schooner *Dornfontein*, on her way from Saint John to South Africa with a load of lumber. The crew, having spent five hours in the bowels of the submarine, had been released and came ashore on Gannet Rock off Grand Manan at the entrance to the Bay of Fundy. The submarine then proceeded up the south coast of the mainland, finally on August 5 attacking an oil tanker bound for Mexico, the *Luz Blanca*, off Halifax, about twenty-seven kilometres southwest of the Sambro lightship. Although struck by a torpedo, the ship had not sunk, and when the submarine resurfaced to finish the job with her deck gun, a three-hour battle ensued. The merchant vessel's inferior twelve-pounder gun was no match and she eventually sank. Two of the seamen were killed by shellfire.[8]

The *Herald* was certain that now that "the Hun Sea Wolf" was actually at the mouth of the harbour, the people of Halifax would "awaken to the reality of WAR!" The paper quoted a naval man as saying, "Vividly and poignantly they now realise that the Hun is unmistakeably and actively AT OUR VERY GATE. Today our merchant seamen were murdered on the waters of the Atlantic." The *Herald* offered a $5,000 reward to anyone who discovered the submarine base that must surely exist somewhere along the Atlantic coast or in the Bay of Fundy, and a $500 reward for the conviction of an enemy spy. On August 7 the paper pointed out that Halifax was fortified, and therefore a German commander was more likely to "take a crack at" some of the unfortified towns along the shore. Hubbards and Chester were likely safe, being at the end of deep bays, but Lunenburg, Yarmouth, Sydney, and many other coastal towns "might look like easy prey." The *Herald* further observed, "No country derives greater wealth from the ocean in proportion to its population than Nova Scotia, and likewise, no country of its size and population has so many of its citizens engaged in seafaring life."

The *Bulletin*, too, was convinced that there must be a submarine base somewhere, and certainly there were spies. The conviction that the Lunenburg fleet was in great danger was enhanced on August 5 with the sinking by U-156 of a Newfoundland vessel, the tern schooner *Gladys M. Hollett*, and a cargo of herring bound for New York, about twenty-four kilometres off West Ironbound Island. Captain Cluett reported that the Germans spoke good English and were experts at handling a dory, which led him to believe they had formerly been fishermen. The bomb placed on-board did not do as

> **Who gave the Huns information about our Fishing Fleet?**
>
> **Where is the Hun Submarine Base on our coast?**
>
> **Where are our Secret Service men?**
>
> **Get busy, the Hun is in our midst.**

Bridgewater Bulletin, *August 13, 1918.*

much damage as intended, and the schooner was eventually towed to Dartmouth partly submerged, was successfully raised, and lived to sail again. Most disturbing, however, was the news from Captain Cluett that the "pirate captain" had taken the Newfoundland sailors into his confidence, evidently thinking he was on a Lunenburg vessel. He told them that he had "full and complete knowledge of all the Lunenburg fleet," a record of all vessels, names of skippers, number of men in the crews, tonnage, destinations, and so on. He said he was out to destroy the whole fleet, but had no intention of hurting or molesting the sailors. The *Bulletin* on August 13 speculated that this information must have been communicated to the Germans by "someone cognizant of the facts, someone in close touch with Lunenburg and its shipping." The public must be warned.

———

Speculation in the local media about spies only increased with time. A claim was made in the *Herald* of August 7 that there were five hundred Austrians, Bulgarians, and Germans in Halifax, "unskilled laborers and navvies," every one of whom might "naturally and properly be regarded as a spy!" and they were "running loose in the imperial city of Halifax TODAY!" There were "HORDES of alien enemies" throughout the province, and the *Herald* maintained that they should be interned. To aid in the possible round-up, the names of those in Halifax were published in the paper. The next day's *Herald* queried with emphasis, "Can You Imagine the Great Hun Naval Port of Kiel Being 'Wide Open' With 500 Nova Scotians and Newfoundlanders Running at Large There?" It was not surprising that people were increasingly anxious. Lieutenant Colonel E. C. Phinney, formerly second-in-command of the 85th Battalion, and now a returned soldier alarmed by the number of "alien enemies" wandering freely about the city, had stated categorically in the *Herald* of August 10 that he was convinced that "before this war ends Halifax and our coast towns, not possibly, but with the highest probability, virtually a certainty, will be shelled either by U-boats or by fast Hun raiders." The columnist warned of "the Hun octopus almost within a stone's throw of the houses."

Alarmingly, that same month, the *Herald*, having attempted to remove the "Hun peril" from Halifax, claimed to have uncovered a nest of spies in Chester. Beginning on August 1, 1918, the *Herald* became increasingly obsessed with the idea that there was a German spy operating in Lunenburg County on a lonely island off Chester Basin. According to the paper, the latest mystery in Chester was not Captain Kidd and fabulous buried treasure on Oak Island, but the "Swiss" gentleman who curiously had been German when he first arrived, among the many American summer people, a couple of years before the war began. Supposedly he had come back now to buy a bungalow, but instead he had gone off to that "lonely and almost God-forsaken rock for three long months PAINTING PICTURES." There was no scenery there "save the ever-swelling and storm-tossed ocean." The editor of the *Herald* was suspicious. With his speedy motor boat it would be easy to intercept a ship along the coast, and the island was a great place to signal a hostile craft or an enemy submarine, which the *Herald* had called "the sea's hidden and undiscoverable grim reaper." Or he could run into Halifax and contact the many spies that were surely there. After all, "how many artists are there on our coast? And has the war created a demand for Nova Scotia coast scenery?"

On August 20, the *Bulletin* ran the headline, "Who Is Signalling?" The "reputed landscape painters" spending the summer on the islands off Chester? There had been lights at night, signals flashed from Chester to a point on or near Tancook Island, and reflashed to a motor boat out to sea. The Intelligence Department in Halifax had been informed of the activity of "mysterious men in Chester," but the complainants had been told that there was nothing in their suspicions. However, there had been signals at Chester on the nights before the sinking of the oil tanker, claimed the paper. There are "too many suspicious neutrals 'summering' along the coast of Nova Scotia." A correspondent in the *Herald* from Mahone Bay observed that there were "points on our coast never visited by our people, coves and capes and bays and islands." Why was there no patrol of all this coastline?

One rather distinguished supposed spy was living in plain sight at Lunenburg. James Liechti had been a professor of modern languages at Dalhousie University, and had retired and returned to live in Lunenburg in 1906. He had married Minna Cossmann, daughter of Rev. Charles Cossmann, in 1866. Regrettably, in the midst of the wartime hysteria, Professor Liechti had been accused of signalling Germans from his home on the Cossmann farm at the edge of town. This was a great wrong, declared the *Bulletin* on September 3, and it had caused Liechti and his daughter much annoyance and grief. Those

Professor James Liechti and his family. An unlikely spy.

who knew him were "very loth to believe that he would be a party to anything detrimental to the well-being and best interests of the British Empire and the Allies in general....[H]e is an old man, a gentleman, a scholar, and, we believe, true to the country of his adoption."

The accused man published a lengthy denial: "I have enjoyed the protection of British Laws in this province of Nova Scotia for many years and I will prosecute to the extreme penalty of those laws, under which I live, all or any persons who seek to impugn my loyalty in this present crisis to the British Empire or any of its Allies or to question the same, or to attribute to me sentiments or sympathies antagonistic to the Allied Cause." The whole story had come about because a hired man with a lantern had been attending to necessary farm duties late at night. The facts were substantiated by official investigation. The irony, perhaps, was that Professor Liechti was not even German; he had been born in Winterthur, Switzerland, in 1835.

The early days of August had been bad enough, but worse was to come. The submarines were not just lurking along the coast; now they were attacking the fishing vessels on the banks. The *Progress-Enterprise* on August 21 printed a telegram from William Duff, MP, to A. K. Maclean, acting minister of marine and fisheries in Ottawa, notifying him that there were about 125 fishing vessels on Quero, St. Pierre, and Grand Bank containing cargoes of fish for food estimated at $2.5 million. Owing to the submarine menace he suggested, unsuccessfully, that the government arrange for convoys of naval vessels to bring the schooners home from the fishing grounds.

In late August, U-156, commanded by Kapitänleutnant Richard Feldt, began to create havoc off Canso, having captured the steam trawler *Triumph*, operated by the National Fish Company of Halifax, and converted it into a "Hun raider...an engine of Devastation, Deviltry and Destruction," as the editor of the *Herald* aptly described it on August 22. Captain Gjert Myhre and the crew had been taken aboard the submarine and were offered refreshment and cigarettes. Put in a dory, they had to row the ninety-five or so kilometres to shore. Before they left, the Germans had already put two light guns on the trawler, fore and aft, and fitted up a small wireless apparatus. Manned by sixteen sailors off the enemy submarine, the *Triumph*, well known to the other crafts in the area, was able to approach and sink unsuspecting fishing vessels. Captain Myhre, of Norwegian origin, was a very experienced seaman, and had once opined, "If most of the people who eat fish, especially in winter time, had to catch them, the word would soon disappear from menu cards."

With a steady procession of men rowing and sailing in from the open sea at Canso, the extent of the devastation soon became apparent. The *Canadian Fisherman* in its September 1918 issue commented approvingly on the practice of fishing in dories—light, easily stowed, and seaworthy—because these boats gave the fishermen better chances to make land in rough water than the small yawls and lifeboats used by British fishermen, many of whom were lost through being swamped in over-crowded boats.

One of the crews among the eighty-odd survivors at Canso came from the *Lucille M. Schnare*, a vessel belonging to W. C. Smith & Company of Lunenburg, overtaken on the Middle Ground overflowing with fish. Captain Artemas Schnare and his men had been treated with "exceeding courtesy," according to the *Morning Chronicle* of August 22. Crew members of the *Schnare*, on arriving home in Lunenburg, described the end of their vessel in the *Progress-Enterprise* of August 28: "About three-quarters of an hour later, while in full view in the moonlight, the light and riding sail which could be plainly discerned, slipped into the deep to join the ghosts of others sacrificed to the rage of the German Mad Dog."

Two American schooners, the *Francis J. O'Hara* from Boston and the *A. Platt Andrew* from Gloucester, were sunk by the *Triumph* at the same time, as were two other Lunenburg County vessels. Many of the men of the *Uda A. Saunders* of the LaHave Outfitting Company, Captain Enos Publicover, were out in their dories taking care of their nets when the trawler appeared flying British flags; the German colours were hoisted after the schooner had been boarded.

The Mahone Bay vessel *Pasadena*, captained by Enos Wentzell, had been fishing on the Middle Ground banks. Through the haze, the small steam craft that had approached looked very much like the familiar *Triumph*. On August 26, the *Bulletin* printed an account: "Lying motionless on the banks on a calm night, a voice called out of the darkness: 'We are a German submarine. Send your captain on board at once.'" The captain told his men to take to the dories immediately because the "Germans did not seem at all good natured." Owned by J. Ernst & Sons, the vessel's crew was from Martins Point, Western Shore, Indian Point, and Middle River.

There were so many survivors in Canso that while some of them put up at the Seaman's Institute, many had to spend the night upon benches in the police station. One old salt advised that instead of sending the fishermen to France they should be given armed schooners, and they would finish up the submarines in no time. Captain Myhre, after arriving in Canso, described "the seventy to eighty crewmen" on the submarine as "all very young and emphatically Teutonic in the cast of their features."

The *Triumph* completed its day's work by sinking two other vessels, the surviving crews landing in Cape Breton: the crew of the American schooner *Sylvana*, sunk while fishing on the Quero Bank, had landed at Arichat on Isle Madame, while part of the crew of the French topsail schooner *Notre Dame de la Garde* out of St. Malo, sunk off Banquereau Bank, had landed at Gabarus. One nearby schooner, the *Silver Thread* from LaHave, Captain James Getson, narrowly escaped, with a cargo of fish valued at not less than $10,000, because of darkness and a warning from another vessel. Captain Getson believed the Germans must have a supply base on the coast, according to the *Herald* on August 26: "The submarines are NOT running off to Germany or to Mexico every time they want petrol or provisions, but any seafaring man knows that they could not be operated for any length of time without assistance from near the scene of their operations."

The Germans were not the only ones to resort to trickery using decoys. Three Lunenburg schooners, the *A. H. Whitman*, *Amy B. Silver*, and the *Helen M. Coolen*—two from Digby, and one from St. John's— were fitted out as Canadian fishing craft but with false nested dories concealing guns to confront German submarines. Frederick William Wallace served as master of the *Albert J. Lutz* out of Digby, and he discussed this "so-called 'mystery fleet'" in his autobiography *Roving Fisherman*. These "special service vessels" were under the direct authority of the commander-in-chief, North American and West Indian Squadron of the Royal Navy, and they were manned by naval ratings as crew. By late 1917 the decoy boats had become so well known to the enemy that most of them were taken out of commission.

The *Triumph*, which had been followed closely by U-156, ran out of coal in a few days' time, and was scuttled. The U-156, however, was not finished. On August 25, working eastward, the submarine sank four fishing schooners, plus the wooden sealing steamer *Erik* out of St.

John's, off Pointe Plate on the French islands of St. Pierre and Miquelon. One of the schooners lost was the *J. J. Flaherty*, owned by Gorton-Pew Fisheries, the largest vessel in the Gloucester fleet. Three Lunenburg vessels suffered the same fate: the handlining schooners *E. B. Walters* and the *C. M. Walters* of Zwicker & Company, commanded by two Walters brothers, Cyrus and Stannage, and the *Verna D. Adams*, of the Lunenburg Outfitting Company, Captain Roger Mosher, launched at Chester Basin only about six weeks before sinking. The next day, in heavy fog, the LaHave Outfitting Company schooner *Gloaming*, Captain Fred Richard, was added to the tally. The *Gloaming*'s crew rowed to Langley Island near St. Pierre. An old man saw them climbing up the bank and thought the Germans had invaded; he sounded the alarm so when the men reached the houses there was no one there. Eventually, they were taken in and fed, and spent four nights in a hayloft.

From St. Pierre, the crews made it to North Sydney, then home. Captain Cyrus Walters of the *E. B Walters*, in the *Progress-Enterprise* of September 11, related that the German officer told him he was "no stranger in Atlantic coast waters," and even claimed to have a brother sailing out of Lunenburg, apparently a man named Emiel (Paddy) Mack.[9] "The hardest blow I ever experienced in my life," said Captain Walters, "was when the cold blooded assassins, just previous to sinking my vessel, walked over and looked down into the hold which contained the results of our summer's work, and unable to suppress their fiendish glee at the thoughts of sending to the sea's bottom many thousands of dollars worth of food, gave vent to their gratification by loud hurrahs." An unidentified fisherman in Peter Barss's *A Portrait of Lunenburg County* expressed similar feelings: "But it wasn't so nice. You know, to lose all your clothes an' all that fish an' everythin' gone to the bottom. Nothin' to live on. Nothin'. An' that's how

Sketch by F.W. Wallace. Halifax Herald, *November 4, 1918.*

it went…fishin' durin' the war." Noting that Lunenburg County "continues to be in a high state of excitement and anxiety" regarding the fate of the fleet, the *Herald*'s editor commented on August 27: "the war is NOT confined to England, France, Belgium, Mesopotamia, Palestine, Siberia, and other Eastern and Mid-Europe places, but is NOW being waged along the coasts of Nova Scotia and the United States."

Some citizens in Lunenburg County became so distraught by the sinking of their vessels by U-156 and the possibility of spies in the area that they "undertook witch-hunts of their own," according to Hadley and Sarty in *Tin-Pots and Pirate Ships*, and watched for suspicious lights and movement during the night. One woman wrote to the Department of Militia and Defence in Ottawa, outraged by the government's apparent inaction, pointing out that the men of Lunenburg were "in Khaki" so it was up to the women and children to be on the lookout for spies. "For Heaven's sake can nothing be done; are these devils to be allowed to carry on this work in aid of Germany and enjoy some protection and liberty as loyal British subjects? I tell you, men, if you don't take notice, we sisters, mothers, etc., who have given all will do something to those traitors.…[I]n that case I suppose the 'Law' would protect the Hun and traitor, and hang its own countrymen."

The colonel commanding in Halifax was besieged by similar letters and by clues about "the unsolvable 'Lunenburg mysteries.'" The "Lunenburg district is a heart-break," he sighed. "Our small intelligence branch can do nothing to catch anyone in the act." Exasperated, he wrote to militia headquarters claiming that apart from sending in a few secret service officers, the "only other possible way of doing it is to send half a company of infantry there and place the region under martial law, but I presume the politicians would not allow this." In the end, investigations convinced him that "the solution lay in bridling the tongues of gossip-mongers."

Shortly after sinking the four schooners off St. Pierre, U-156 was spotted by HMCS *Hochelaga*. Instead of attacking the submarine, the Canadian patrol vessel, with its apparently inferior weapons, turned away and called for reinforcements, which only arrived after the U-boat had disappeared. Eventually, the captain of the *Hochelaga*, Robert D. Legate, was dismissed from service for failure to carry out his duty to engage the enemy.[10] In the meantime, U-156 continued on its way home but did not make it, striking a mine in the North Sea as it attempted to pass through the British blockade. Captain Feldt, who perished in the submarine along with his men, had been ordered to cause as much fearfulness (*schrecklichkeit*) as possible, and that he had done.

Meanwhile, U-156's companion submarine U-117, under Kapitän-leutnant Otto Dröscher, had also been busy. Nine fishing schooners, all American, had fallen victim to U-117 on Georges Bank off the coast of Maine on August 10. Then, on August 24, U-117 attacked the three-masted schooner *Bianca*, from Newfoundland, southwest of Sable Island on her way from Brazil to Halifax with a load of tobacco. Scuttling charges were set off, but the tobacco cargo swelled with seawater and sealed the holes in the hull. Abandoned by the crew on order of the U-boat commander, the *Bianca* was picked up adrift by the Boston schooner *Commonwealth* three days later and towed into port.[11] A couple days later, the Boston fishing schooner *Rush* was torpedoed and sank about 175 kilometres off the Nova Scotia coast. The captain, Alvaro Quadros, survived, like almost all the fishermen on the sunken schooners, but he would be tossed overboard the *Mayflower* to his death in a storm on the Western Bank in the August gale of 1927.

On August 27, continuing its homeward voyage, the U-117 sank a large Norwegian merchant ship 175 kilometres southwest of Cape Race. Then, on the thirtieth, the U-boat sank two Lunenburg County schooners on the Grand Bank off Newfoundland: the LaHave schooner *Elsie Porter*, Captain Irvin (Dickie) Eisenhauer,[12] owned by Reinhardt Brothers, and the *Potentate*, Captain Frederick Gerhardt, belonging to the LaHave Outfitting Company. Captain Eisenhauer had been taken on-board the submarine for what the *Morning Chronicle* of September 4 called a four-hour "Joy Ride." The German war records, according to Hadley and Sarty, claimed that the crew members "were without exception German-speaking German-Americans." The crews eventually ended up in St. John's. Indeed, the *Evening Telegram* estimated that upwards of seventy Bank fishermen whose vessel had been sunk by the German raider within the past few days were making for land in their dories. Captain Gerhardt asked, "'Why are you sinking defence-less fishing vessels?'" and was told, "'You are helping to feed America.'"

As the submarine menace increased, there were more calls for black-outs. The *Herald* on September 4 quoted an experienced master mar-iner who argued that buoys should be taken in and lights extinguished all along the coastline from Brier Island to Cape North. The *Bulletin* on September 10 reported that Lunenburg was in darkness, orders having been issued by the general officer commanding Military District No. 6 that all town lights must be dimmed nightly until further notice. This order included stores and residences, which, when illuminated, must have their blinds or curtains drawn so that all rays would be thrown to the ground. The orders also covered headlights on autos, the lenses either painted or shaded from the top to across the centre at least.

On the twenty-fourth, the *Bulletin* pointed out that the regulations now applied to all inhabitants in communities along the coastline of Nova Scotia, and to every light of every description, fixed or moveable, inside or outside, except single coloured lights, illuminated route signs, and certain lights on vehicles. Lights should be obscured in such manner as to render them invisible from the harbour, the sea, or any other body of water. Lights outside buildings were to be extinguished by 11 PM unless permission was granted otherwise. Failure to comply could mean a large fine or prison. In Ontario, Toronto, too, was "going dark." Street lighting was prohibited between five and eight in the evening, and every second street light was turned off, but this was because of hydro shortages,[13] not because of the danger of attack as on the east coast.

Although U-156 and U-117 had left Canadian waters, U-155, formerly the *Deutschland*, arrived in mid-September and laid mines ten to fifteen kilometres southwest of Chebucto Head and Sambro Island, at the entrance to Halifax Harbour.[14] On September 12, south of Newfoundland, U-155 torpedoed and sank the Portuguese steamer *Leixoes*, then tried, unsuccessfully, to cut the transatlantic telegraph cable near Sable Island. The *Leixoes* sank in fifteen minutes, and there was no time to get adequate provisions or water. Some of the men were six days at sea in an open boat in rough water before landing. When the captain of the U-155 learned through a megaphone that the ship was not British or American, according to the *Morning Chronicle* of September 18, he cried, "Ach du lieber Gott, I have wasted a torpedo."

As late as October 15 the German U-boats were still active, for on that day the new LaHave tern schooner *Industrial* was torpedoed on the northern edge of the Gulf Stream, only a short run from her home port to which she was bound with a cargo of salt from Turks Island. On November 27, the editor of the *Progress-Enterprise* expressed anxiety for the safety of the Lunenburg fishing schooner *Vera M. Lohnes*, missing since September 6. It was thought that the schooner had foundered or was torpedoed by a submarine, for the German boats were active off the coast about that time.

On October 9, 1918, the *Progress-Enterprise* reported on the third annual Lunenburg Fishermen's Picnic and Reunion. Despite the country being engaged in "the most gigantic war of history," it was felt that the day should be observed, to give the toilers of the deep a welcome as well as a genuine day of sport. A handsome arch erected at Nash's Corner, at the entrance to the town, decorated with evergreens and the flags of the Allies, greeted the visitors. "This year is not so much a day of rejoicing as a sort of celebration of the safe return of the major portion of our hardy toilers who during the summer faced the gravest danger in the prosecution of the County's greatest industry. No avocation was pursued in the Dominion, under conditions of greater peril than that which threatened the men of our fleet and though seven or eight of the vessels and cargoes were sacrificed on the altar of the Hun's vengeance, there can only be a feeling of thankfulness that the men were spared." The editor of the newspaper wondered if the crews were spared because the men on-board the U-boats were formerly American fishermen, or because they were so far away from Germany that they did not fear punishment on return for not being brutal enough. No one could know, but as long as the fishermen were safe there was little need of argument. "Our fishermen are worthy of the highest tributes of respect, as they endure bitter cold and blizzards of which landsmen have no conception, together with the every day dangers which beset them at all times, all without complaint."

The men in the merchant marine were not so fortunate. How many scores of times, exclaimed the *Bulletin* on December 10, since "the Hun began his dastardly campaign of terror on the high seas," had these words, "Some of the Crew Were Lost," been heard in curt Admiralty announcements. "To anyone who KNOWS the tradition of the sea, who knows the splendid heroism that men of the mercantile marine displayed in the face of certain death, little imagination is needed to read a glorious romance between the lines of these official bulletins." Unarmed and often unprotected, the "peaceful mariner… carried troops, munitions, and more important than all, food, across mine and U-boat infested waters with utter disregard for personal safety." Of the 300,000 men of the merchant marine, about 15,000 perished, leaving women and children behind with no government pensions, no separation allowances or patriotic fund to care for them.

A branch of the Navy League of Canada was organized in Lunenburg in October 1918. The main speaker at the meeting in the Oddfellows' Hall, with Mayor Duff presiding, dwelled on "the duty all owed to the sailors of the Mercantile marine." The *Progress-Enterprise* had commented earlier, on July 3, "If there is one county in Nova Scotia that should have a virile, active organization of this kind it is Lunenburg." The aim of the league was to better conditions for sailors of every class, whether of the navy or the merchant marine.[15] December 9–14, 1918, was to be Sailor's Week, when the Navy League would hold a drive to raise $100,000, the objective for Nova Scotia, $10,000 of it from Lunenburg County. This would be the first and only direct campaign for funds for "the men in blue" since the war began, according to the *Herald* on November 19. "Let us make this last drive a great, big, glorious success—a triumphant windup to our patriotic givings."

Chapter Six

"WITH VICTORY SO NEAR"

"This Is the Limit," proclaimed a headline in the *Progress-Enterprise* of Lunenburg on September 4, 1918, in response to a letter printed in the *Halifax Herald* on August 30. Written by one J. W. Daly, PhD, there was a sentence, "beautifully wrapped up and padded in patriotic effusions," that was bound to raise the ire of Lunenburgers. Entitled "There is No 'Profiteering' among Fishermen," Daly's letter was mainly a defence of "the fishers of Canso," who far from being profiteers were paid miserably for their long hours of hard labour. In some of them, Daly professed, there was "the fervor of mighty spirited France; the veins of others tingle with the rich red blood of Scotland." But "in none is there a trace of the cursed foe of God and man, that dread despoiler of mankind, the slayer of innocents—the devilish Hun. The men of Lunenburg are all strong German, yet they reap the harvest of British waters."

"What is the meaning of such an assertion?" asked the editor of the *Progress-Enterprise.* "What sense or reason is there in it?" Many of the men of Lunenburg were indeed of German origin, but "their forebears left Germany to get out from under the reign of terror; the Prussian Militarism, tyranny of the Hun, which, even as early as 1753, the time the first settlers landed here, was making the fair country of Germany unbearable, and which later turned it into an inferno which let loose a brand of demons that have outdone the mildest and most vivid conception of Satan himself." Had the forefathers of "our brave toilers of the deep" been so "strong German," they would have stayed in the country with which they sympathized. "The fishermen of Lunenburg are a mighty long way from Germany and they are carrying on their share in the war by procuring food to release bacon and beef for our troops." Fish was now an accepted ration for "our brave lads overseas." The editor concluded on a strong note, "Let us see no more such infernal drivel in the press."

A few days later, on the eighteenth, the *Progress-Enterprise* published a letter from William Duff, MP and mayor of Lunenburg, entitled "Lunenburg Fishermen Not More German Than Our Gracious King," which condemned Daly's letter and addressed his "ignorant and impertinent" remarks. Duff's response, in which he refuted the charges in the offending sentence, was intended for the *Halifax Herald*, but that paper refused to publish it. While eulogizing the fishermen of Nova Scotia, Daly had included a sentence that appeared to Duff to be "very objectionable": "British waters?" The waters outside the three-mile limit were international, Duff maintained, and citizens of every nation could fish them. As for the men of Lunenburg being "all strong German," Daly was clearly not well versed in historical facts. Lunenburg County was divided into three townships: Chester, New Dublin, and Lunenburg. The first two had no "signs of German in them." The people in Chester, New Ross, New Dublin, Petite Riviere, Voglers Cove, the town of Bridgewater, and so on, had come from the British Isles or from New England.

Lunenburg Township was more complicated. Duff repeated the myth that the first emigrants had come from "Lunenburg in Hanover, Germany"; others from Switzerland, Montbéliard, and Holland. Rev.

Jean-Baptiste Moreau, prior of the Abbey of St. Matthew at Brest, who had been appointed missionary to the settlers, came under the protection of the British government; Moreau spoke three languages, not just German. One of the original settlers in Mahone Bay, Alexander Kedy, had come from London; the first settlers at Northfield were Scottish. The people in New Germany had moved over from the county of Annapolis and one man had come from Cornwall. In short, Duff insisted, the present generation had descended from various races and consequently there was no good reason why the people of Lunenburg County should be styled Germans. They had nothing in common with the land of their forefathers and were as good British and Canadian subjects as were to be found in any part of Canada.

And, to the main point, Duff continued, even if it were a fact that about one-third of the present generation were of German origin, they were in good company. If Daly would "delve into history," he would discover that "in 1714 George Louis, elector of Lunenburg, Hanover, Germany, ascended the throne of Britain as George 1st"; and if he followed "the genealogical tree," he would find that "the late lamented Queen Victoria, grandmother of His Gracious Majesty, King George 5th, King of Great Britain and Ireland and the Dominions overseas, and Emperor of India, was a direct descendant of this same King George 1st of Lunenburg, Germany." Victoria's husband, Prince Albert "of Saxe-Coburg, Gotha," was "a grandfather of His Gracious Majesty on the paternal side." Any person should be very careful at this time in referring to the people of Lunenburg as Germans, Duff warned, "as they consider it not only an insult to themselves but as an insult to our Gracious Sovereign."

Drawing to a close, Duff's words rose to a crescendo, with a peroration glorifying the Lunenburg County fisherman:

A race of men who go down to the sea in ships and do business on the great waters, in spite of the submarine menace; a breed of manly men, who left the ports of Lunenburg and LaHave, during the past 60 days, when they were warned against submarines, to carry the merchandise of this country to foreign lands; hearts of oak, some 3000 of them, who left this county in March last, in their 100 ton boats to pursue their avocation, amidst the storms, fogs and perils of the Atlantic; vikings, who departed from their homes to do their bit by producing food, knowing full well the submarine might show her nose across their bow at any time during the trip and send them to a watery grave. And yet brave and fearless heroes of this stamp are dubbed the hated name "German," by J. W. Daly, Ph.D., and persons of his ilk.

The *Progress-Enterprise* affirmed that Duff's letter was a fair presentation of the facts. Given the important part the Lunenburg fishermen were playing in winning the war, "men in many cases who are almost 60 years of age and have gallant sons overseas fighting for a clean world," it was hardly to be expected that such insult would be lightly borne. In the 165 years since the settlers had come from Europe, the different races had become so blended that about all that remained were the names brought across the ocean by the forefathers of the present generation.

Duff's history may not have been entirely accurate (the settlers did not come from Hanover or Lüneburg but from southwestern Germany), and the people were likely prouder of their German heritage than he and the *Progress-Enterprise* assumed, but Dr. Daly had surely been put properly in his place.

———

Despite the submarines, and in spite of unwarranted allegations of disloyalty, the fishermen of Lunenburg County prospered during the war. The *Canadian Fisherman*, the journal of the fishing industry, claimed that the 1917 trips to the banks had resulted in "the largest catch in the history of the fleet." Ninety-five vessels had gone to the banks, with 1,884 men. "Every year the resume of the banner industry of Lunenburg spells prosperity; this year, however, it is synonymous with affluence." The *Bridgewater Bulletin* on November 6 reported a banking catch of 256,215 quintals worth $2,562,150; some of the crews had shared over $1,000 per man. The catch might have been even larger, but a salt famine that had been prophesized for months had become a distressing reality in August; the usual supply of salt, an indispensable commodity for curing fish, from Trapani in Sicily, had dried up because of the war.

The next year had been even more profitable, as the *Progress-Enterprise* on January 8, 1919 attested: "When it comes to big values, 1918 fairly 'rings the bell,' as fish prices went up and up, until the phenomenal figure of $15.50 was reached for several cargoes at Halifax, with from $14.50 to $14.75 a ruling price." In 1917, $10 had been considered a good figure for Lunenburg bank cod. It was the "biggest year in the history of Lunenburg's greatest industry…the most profitable since the inception of the Lunenburg fishing fleet." And shipbuilding also progressed apace: a large number of vessels, ranging from small coasters and shore-fishing craft to big three-masted schooners like the *William Duff* had been built. The fishing vessels sunk by the German submarines were being rapidly replaced, according to the *Bulletin* of January 5.

The overall catch was down slightly compared to 1917 because of the presence of the submarines, but the unprecedented high prices meant that the profits were greater. Only lobster fishing did not flourish. The *Morning Chronicle* reported that the total catch for 1918 was 247,395 quintals, valued at $3,461,476.60; some crews had shared over $1,400 per man. The torpedoed vessels and cargoes were insured, though not to their full value; however, the men who lost their summer's work were at least in part reimbursed. The *Chronicle* concluded that the fisherman's occupation was a remunerative one.

Because of the war there had been less competition from European fishermen, but, as well, more fish were being sold because a campaign had been launched in 1915 to get Canadian fish onto the menus of soldiers in training at camps and barracks throughout the country. The *Canadian Fisherman* noted in April 1915 that a large number of Canada's soldiers had been born in Britain, and they knew what it was to eat fish regularly. The Canadian Fisheries Association, founded in

March 1916, also lobbied Ottawa to make fish part of the soldiers' rations. With Sam Hughes's support, the militia department passed an order whereby a soldier in Canada could ask to have half a pound of fish daily or half a pound of meat.

Sam Hughes also supported the idea of sending fresh frozen and smoked fish to the men overseas in France and England, and later these fish, along with cured and canned fish, were shipped over to help supply the imperial army. "The fishing interests of Canada owe a great deal to the Minister of Militia and we have no hesitation in saying that his action has been the best means of advertising the value of Canadian fish and bringing prominence to the industry than ever before attempted." That December, after Hughes's dismissal, the *Canadian Fisherman* regretted the loss and declared Sir Sam "Canada's greatest advertiser....Canada's Army and Canada's Fish are the two big things he has brought into startling prominence. We thank him for both."

A persistent problem that faced the fishery, despite its profits, was the shortage of workers, caused by fishermen enlisting for overseas service in the army. The *Canadian Fisherman* in April 1916, in a special issue on the Smiths of Lunenburg, noted that five members of W. C. Smith & Company had given a son to the service of the Empire: the only son of the president, W. C. Smith, was a lieutenant with the 112th Battalion; the only son of G. A. Smith was in the postal service at the front; other sons of company members were serving at Halifax or in France.

In its next issue, the journal commended this patriotic spirit but remarked that a serious situation would arise if fishermen continued to enlist. Boat owners were signing up and hauling up their crafts, and vessel owners were becoming hard-pressed for crews to man the off-shore schooners. "The man who stays at home and does his work as a producer and developer of natural resources is doing his duty to the Empire just as much as the man in the trenches." Agnes McGuire, in the February 1917 issue of the *Canadian Fisherman*, cautioned, "Men and men of good physique and courage are alone able to engage in this calling. It is no work for weaklings nor can women carry it on. And fish is today so important a food in the army and navy that men must be left to carry on this industry."

Increasingly, as the war went on, there were calls for greater production of fish. The *Canadian Fisherman* in May 1917 observed that meat was becoming dear and scarce, potatoes were not plentiful—"both with bread are the staple foods of the Anglo-Saxon races." The journal maintained, "There is one great food resource which we have that requires no tilling, seeding or preliminary investment to harvest. That is our fisheries. God put the fish into the seas, rivers and lakes. They are there yet and can be easily harvested for the use of mankind. Fish is the only substitute for meat....It is up to the fisherman and fish producers of Canada to 'do their bit' now." The acting minister of marine and fisheries in Ottawa contended that fishermen had an opportunity but also "a clear cut patriotic duty"; the "ranks were seriously reduced by enlistments but those who remain have to more than make up for the deficiency by persistent increased effort."

On March 27, 1918, the *Progress-Enterprise* asserted that "Fish as food, conserves meat for our troops, without meat they cannot fight, for it is a proven fact that an army fights on its stomach....Persons whose patriotism leads their judgment astray, who sneer at slackers, and insist that 'fishermen should enlist,' should realize what it would mean to the troops if all or a major part of the fishermen were taken from this calling. It would mean disaster for those for whom it would be intended to help." Given the conscription of fishermen that took place that spring, apparently this line of thinking did not altogether resonate with the powers that be.

The Canadian Fisheries Association's "banquet" in February 1917, according to the *Canadian Fisherman*, had become instead an "annual dinner," a

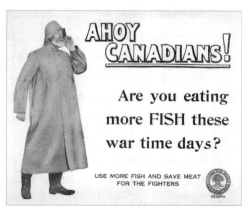

Canada Food Board advertisement.

purely informal affair, for it was thought to be "bad form" in a war year to be ostentatious. Nonetheless, the plain meal was "designated with more aristocratic nomenclature," with items such as "Shemogne Oyster Cocktail, Vol au Vint Paulhusiane, Flageolets Beans, and Ice Cream Spoonerian." The only non-fish principal dish was "Gosling Stuffed Avec Sauce Hagerine." The menu was bracketed top and bottom with the surprisingly insensitive sayings: "Thank God we don't have to eat war rations here!" and, "Just think how they'd appreciate this dinner in Berlin now!" The menu card was "elaborated with some doubtful poetry," supposedly written by Alfred Noyes:

Not only the men at the Front
With bayonet, bomb and gun—
Not only the men of the Fleets,
Are engaged in strafing the Hun.
Remember the ones at home—
The toilers at net and trawl
Who're fighting the waters in storm and shine
Providing food for us all.

Food security was as almost as much a real concern on the home front during wartime as it was on the front lines. The farmers of Lunenburg County, like the fishermen, were urged to produce more and more food, even as their sons enlisted or were conscripted into the army. The labour shortage left farmers struggling to plant their crops and harvest them, just when, for once, their produce could command good prices. They were helped somewhat by farm workers being granted leave from the army at crucial seasons. Nonetheless, city dwellers blamed the farmers for the high prices and also, unfairly, for their supposed failure to enlist.

There had been concerns about possible food shortages from the beginning of the war. As early as September 30, 1914, Premier G. H. Murray had made a plea to the farmers of Nova Scotia, in the province's newspapers, to plough as much acreage as possible for next year's crops. All the able-bodied men in Europe were engaged in the fighting, he pointed out:

> *Farmers of Nova Scotia, this is your hour of opportunity. Remember it is the products you can produce which will be in greatest demand—grains, roots, bacon, pork and beans and apples....[A] solemn duty has been laid on your shoulders as farmers....I cannot emphasize too strongly the facts that this work is just as truly practical patriotism as is the work of the soldier in the trenches. Our kinsmen in the Motherland have to be fed....You in peaceful Nova Scotia are now in a position to do much for the cause of humanity and for the enduring benefit of our Empire.*

On May 18, 1917, the Lunenburg columnist of the *Halifax Herald* complained that there were thousands of small plots and fields lying idle, cultivated neither by men nor women, and it was time for Lunenburg County to wake up. The brave "boys" at the front must be fed. Should

For All We Have and Are---

Saving food and sending it to the men in the trenches. Canadian Fisherman, *September 1917.*

they suffer a setback through lack of nourishing food, "that would be a nation's shame, which would sear each one of us." Lunenburg had given its sons, its money, and the work of its women freely, providing hospital and Red Cross needs; "let us also join the national service for greater production and do our bit with the hearty good will with which we have participated in all the patriotic work that has fallen to our hands." One Lunenburg citizen who did his part to increase food production was R. C. S. Kaulbach. He offered free lots ranging from one-eighth to two acres on his "magnificent property, Kaulbach Park," to those who wished to plant beans and potatoes.

As a means to increase food production, a massive registration of man- and woman-power took place on June 22, 1918. The information gathered, the *Bulletin* assured its readers on May 28, would be used "to proceed intelligently with the mobilization of the entire resources of the nation, towards the successful prosecution of the war." There would be data of military value, but the main purpose was the better distribution of agricultural labour, given the imminence of a food shortage. The conflicting social pressure to enlist did not let up, however. Men who looked like they belonged in class one under the Military Service Act, and therefore should have been conscripted, would be required to carry documents proving their age, nationality, marriage status, whether or not they were clergymen, or proof that they had been legitimately exempted from service. The editor of the *Progress-Enterprise* wryly commented on July 10: "A humorous friend suggests that before long the men will have to carry knitting bags to hold their birth certificates, passports, medical examination sheets, registration cards, etc."

Women, of course, helped out on the farms, as they always had. To secure extra help, boys from fifteen to nineteen were recruited as "Soldiers of the Soil" to work on the land; many were no doubt helpful, though farmers complained, according to Desmond Morton in *Fight or Pay*, that "amateur labour damaged crops and reduced harvest yields." Children, too, could help to produce more food. At a meeting of the Women's Institute, reported in the *Progress-Enterprise* of June 12, it was agreed that an effort should be made to encourage boys and girls of school age to do more than ever toward food production. To this end, the institute offered three prizes to girls and three to boys for the best collection of at least three kinds of vegetables.

By the spring of 1918, it was looking like the food shortage would become critical. The food controller in Ottawa, William J. Hanna, resigned in February due to ill health, and his duties, to "ascertain the food requirements of Canada and to facilitate the export of the surplus," were assumed by the new Canada Food Board, run by the Department of Agriculture. Isabel M. Ross, of the educational division of the board, rather unkindly listed in the *Herald* on April 26 over thirty occupations that she saw as expendable, if not essentially useless. Among the favoured she named were shoe shiners, soda fountain dispensers, insurance agents, all store clerks or salesmen, lunch counter waiters, bell boys, bookkeepers, typists, theatre ushers, shipping clerks, chauffeurs, streetcar conductors, elevator operators (not lawyers, one notices!). Her intention was to get men out on the farms and to rid the cities of their "hundreds of young 'idlers' and men doing women's work." An "anti-loafing law" had also been enacted by Order in Council on April 4, threatening punishment for any man or boy between sixteen and sixty who could not prove that he was gainfully employed.

Mrs. Obed S. Veinot of Upper Northfield, in her letter to the editor of the *Herald* on April 24, 1918, described herself as "a farmer's wife...writing to the gentlemen of the militia." Just as William Duff had defended the fishermen who did not enlist, she spoke with feeling about the plight of the farmers, declaring that they should be allowed to have their sons, on whom they depended. The "poor farmer boy knows what it is to work from sunrise to sunset under the boiling sun." The old folks had done their good share and they needed the help of young hands. "I do all that my strength will allow but cannot fill a man's place....How can food be produced alone?" The farmers were "doing their bit as soldiers of the soil and while there are plenty to fill up the space in the pool rooms and gamblers den, they are the ones who are no good to their country....If the farmer should fail for want of help our little town will soon see the wolf prowling around the door before long, so look well before you make any desperate leaps. Give the farmer all the help you can and you will surely win a glorious victory."

The *Progress-Enterprise* on June 29, 1918, pronounced, "Let us not forget, that the war is fought in our kitchens as well as on the battlefields of France. Every pound of food saved is a contribution towards victory."

Increasingly strict regulations and guidelines were issued by the Canada Food Board to recommend and enforce the voluntary rationing of items such as sugar, butter, wheat, and meat. The *Bulletin* on April 19 explained some of the new food regulations. Beef and veal could be served at evening meals only, and not served at all on Wednesdays and Fridays. No wheat or wheat products should be served at the midday meal. Sandwiches made from wheat bread and pork, beef, or veal could be served only at railway lunch counters and only to bona fide travellers. Bread should not be placed on tables in public eating houses until the first course was served.

Bridgewater Bulletin, *August 6, 1918.*

Wheat flour dumplings in hot pies, meat stews, or soups were pro-hibited. Not more than 10 per cent of fats were to be used in ice cream. The regulations became stricter as time passed.

The *Progress-Enterprise* on July 10 reminded churches that regu-lations applicable to public eating places also applied to public enter-tainments, lawn socials, bazaars, tea meetings, dinners, picnics, fairs, exhibitions, meetings of lodges, clubs, fraternal societies, and so on. The paper found it "passing strange" that some people wanted to evade the orders, because the reason for them was to save so the troops would have no shortage of food: "Extravagance at all times is vulgar, now it is sinful." One saw accounts of weddings in which occurred the expression, "The guests sat down to a sumptuous repast," or, "Today 'sumptuous repasts' should be regarded in the light of stealing. Stealing from those who need it most, the boys overseas."

Henry B. Thompson, the new chairman of the food board, had said on June 19 that enactment of regulations had been prompted by the need to save wheat, meat, fats, and sugar. "The little discomfort to which the picnicker, or other person patronizing a function of this kind, may be put, is negligible in the face of the stern necessity of war conditions." People were also asked by the fuel controller to save gas-oline to help "the boys over there." None should be wasted on Sunday motoring for pleasure.

The Women's Institute in the county was endeavouring to promote the conservation of food by home canning surplus vegetables, accord-ing to the *Progress-Enterprise* of July 10. Recipes for efficient can-ning appeared in the "women's pages" of the paper, as did a recipe for "Economy Cup Cakes." The *Herald* on October 10 advised that carrots boiled until tender and nearly ready to fall apart, drained, mashed, and pressed through a coarse cloth or strainer, formed an excellent substi-tute for eggs in puddings.

The *Progress-Enterprise* complained on October 9 that the food con-troller had "a job" in Lunenburg. Although "Land sharks and confidence men and evil doers" were to be expected in the big cities, "when it comes to our own God-fearing, Church going, law-abiding, HONEST citizens this is positively incredible....Did you ever notice how many persons there are in Lunenburg who think some particular food restriction 'crazy' as soon as it touches him or her individually? Wars may wage, men may be slain, women and children may starve, but the minute these people are asked to stop icing cakes the restrictions are 'crazy.'"

An item in the *Bulletin* of December 10 about the relaxation of food board rules following the armistice on November 11 gives some idea of the pleasures that had been curtailed during the last year of the war. Restrictions on the amount of bread served at public eating places were removed. Manufacturers could now make and sell doughnuts, Scotch shortbread or cake, and French pastry, provided they used vegetable fats only, and manufacturers—provided they did not exceed forty pounds of sugar to every hundred pounds of flour—could make and sell iced cakes and biscuits filled with icing. Conservation regulations of beef were still in force, however, and the regulation of the consumption of sugar was necessary until the end of the year, after which it was hoped the new crop, mainly from the West Indies, would be available.

—⋅—

The campaigns for funds to support an assortment of worthy causes continued throughout the war. Only five days before the armistice, the *Progress-Enterprise* reported that the Boscawen Chapter of the IODE was preparing Christmas boxes for the men overseas: "gay little tartan bags" to hold loaf sugar, candy, raisins, and cake, "a good thick pair of warm socks, then a trench candle, wax candle, milk chocolate, chewing gum, letter pad and envelopes, lead pencil, shoe laces, soap, can of coffee, cigarettes, tobacco and lastly a card with a special message to each boy." Each box contained articles valued at three dollars.

Especially appreciated by the troops were the Young Men's Christian Association huts, located near the front. Money was raised at home for the YMCA's efforts through their Red Triangle Fund. In a letter to his mother printed in the *Bulletin* on May 14, 1918, written after twenty-one days in the trenches, Private Loring Mackenzie described the "hardest march yet": "Talk about slipping, why we were falling, sliding into shell-holes and doing all kinds of fancy steps, and it was so dark our hands were not visible (it might have been because they were so dirty)." Finally he arrived at a YMCA stall, and "felt 500 per cent better after three big mugs of cocoa." According to Desmond Morton in *When Your Number's Up* the YMCA ran canteens, cinemas, and coffee bars with writing paper and reading rooms, and used the profits to buy sports equipment for the baseball leagues and sports tournaments they organized. The YMCA, he asserts, was more important than any chaplain in most soldiers' lives.

From August 19 to 24, 1918, the Knights of Columbus War Fund campaign was launched to raise $100,000 in Nova Scotia to erect army huts "for the good of our boys...to build and maintain recreation centres in all the camps, to provide chaplains here and abroad and furnish home atmosphere and comforts to the men who have gone to fight for us." H. L. Bentley of the Royal Bank in Bridgewater acted as treasurer, according to the *Bulletin* of August 20. The huts were intended to be a home where soldiers could "spend social hours, listen to music, play games, write to the folks back home." Right on the edge of the trenches, behind the lines, coffee, cigarettes, and so on would be given to the men "to strengthen them as they pass by to the firing line," and presumably to offer some sort of relief if they managed to come back. The huts would be "open to all classes, all colours, all creeds." The Salvation Army also had huts to care for the men's health and spiritual well-being.

One way to encourage people to donate more to the various causes was to publish the list of donors in the newspapers. A Red Cross collection in Blue Rocks and Black Rocks was printed for all to see in the *Progress-Enterprise* of November 13, 1918: Mrs. Arthur Hynick and Mrs. Jacob Hynick had each given one dollar, while Mrs. Theop Knickle and Rodger Knickle gave fifty cents each. Perhaps next time the Frittenburgs, Tanners, Greeks, and Morashes would dig deeper into their pockets.

Sometimes it all seemed too much. The *Bulletin* on April 3, 1917, had claimed that there was widespread opinion that there should be a period of rest, a breathing spell, between the operations for funds. There was "such a thing as overdoing patriotic endeavour and if the liberality of our people is to be depended upon in exigencies it must be fostered and encouraged rather than be crowded to the wall....[W]e are but the mouthpiece of public sentiment and trust these remarks will be so judged."

———•———

"The Soldier's Family—Is It Overpaid?" read the headline. The *Bulletin* of February 13, 1917, answered its own question: "No, A thousand times, no!" The paper noted that some people were complaining that a woman who received money from the Canadian Patriotic Fund was better off than when her husband was at home. But the complaints were far from warranted, for that woman had given her husband to the country. "Is our paltry silver and his precious life to be placed in the scales over against each other? The man—God save him!—is standing between us and German bullets, facing toils, wounds, death. The woman—God bless her!—is bearing loneliness and anxiety, the pangs of fear that convert every door-knock into a death-knell. Shall we stay-at-homes, some of us slackers, few of us doing our whole duty, all of us beneficiaries of the sacrifices of this man and woman—shall we add Grim Want to the spectres that accost them?"

The campaign to support the Canadian Patriotic Fund was one of the most important of the charitable causes during the war. The original CPF, dating from the War of 1812, had funded pensions, some medical care, and even campaign medals, but the CPF re-established by the government in August 1914 limited itself to providing financial support to soldiers' families. The money contributed to the fund was to come from voluntary subscription, and was intended to supplement a soldier's pay, not replace it. Since the soldier received only $1.10 a day and the separation allowance paid to the wives of married men was $20.00 a month, it was obvious that many families would need further assistance. The Canadian state and the soldiers themselves were larger sources of financial support for most military families, claims historian Desmond Morton; however, the need to support the families of married soldiers did inspire "the largest single charity Canadians had yet created." The chief architect of "the Patriotic" was Sir Herbert Ames, a Montreal MP and businessman, who stated in the House of Commons on February 29, 1916: "Our slogan has always been 'Fight or Pay.'...If you cannot put the 'I' into fight, put the 'pay' into patriotism." Although Sir Herbert had insisted that the CPF was not a charity, Morton concludes that it "surprisingly resembled one in its submissiveness to powerful donors and its manipulative approach to its beneficiaries."[1]

Like the rest of the country, Lunenburg County played its part in supporting the CPF. Writing about the fund on January 5, 1915, the *Bulletin's* editorial had insisted: "Those of us who cannot go to war MUST help those who do. Shirking service or aid is equally cowardly. No man with rich, red British blood in his veins wants to be in the coward list." The towns of Lunenburg and Bridgewater had responded nobly to the call for funds, the *Bulletin* observed on May 25, but the county's municipal council had "funked, or wilfully neglected to do its duty by our brave soldiers."

Campaigning for "the Patriotic."

The *Progress-Enterprise* on October 6 reported that money in varying amounts had come from private subscriptions, from Halifax & Southwestern Railway employees, from the LaHave Lodge of the Independent Order of Odd Fellows, a town grant from Lunenburg, and from Lunenburg Academy teachers. But "Lunenburg, above every other county, cannot afford to stand aloof and not assist in supporting the families of the men who are risking their lives at the front in defence of our country." There are "slackers among the wealthy who are over age and unfit for service as well as among the young shirkers," the *Progress-Enterprise* alleged on June 13, 1917. "In these times of stress and trouble every one has a duty to perform. Conscription of wealth would be much more popular in Canada to-day than conscription of men."

The Patriotic Fund had two responsibilities, to raise funds and to spend them on soldiers' families on the basis of need. But there was also what Sir Herbert called the "Third Responsibility," to act "as counsellor and business agent to families who, deprived temporarily of their managers, found themselves faced with difficulties that singlehandedly they could not overcome." In theory, according to Morton, the purpose was "to supply the wisdom, frugality, and moral rectitude that the absent male might ideally have provided." Historian Alan Bowker describes the third responsibility as "guardianship, which often meant in practice that middle-class volunteers monitored the welfare of wives and widows, checked up on their behaviour, and provided advice and instruction on how to manage their households, spend their income, and raise their children."[2] Morton and Granatstein in *Marching to Armageddon* remark, "Organizers congratulated themselves on teaching thrift to soldiers' wives, discouraging foolish purchases, and depriving immoral mothers of their children." As Morton puts it in *When Your Number's Up*, the women had to deal with both paternalism and authoritarian meddling.

The Lunenburg County municipal council continued to be a reluctant contributor. Though "heartily in accord" with the idea of the fund, the council was convinced that collection and administration were "rapidly getting beyond reasonable bounds." Provisions for the families should be taken out of the hands of a charitable organization, the council argued in the *Progress-Enterprise* of March 13, 1918, and "placed where it belongs rightfully," either in the hands of the Department of Militia and Defence or a federal government committee specially appointed for such a purpose. Sir Herbert Ames rose in Parliament on April 30, 1918, to report that the CPF was paying out about $1 million a month to support more than fifty thousand families. Over its history, the fund had received upwards of $50 million in patriotic giving, but the government's efforts to raise revenue through taxes and war savings bonds were now encroaching on CPF income.[3] On July 10, the Lunenburg paper notified its readers that legislation empowering the federal government to take over the CPF and to furnish the necessary funds from the general revenues of the country would be introduced at the next session of Parliament.

———

In November 1918, the people of Lunenburg, Chester, Bridgewater, and all the villages en route had a treat in the shape of a visit by two hydroplanes from the United States Naval Air Station at Eastern Passage, near Dartmouth. In Bridgewater, the *Bulletin* reported on the fifth, hundreds lined the riverbanks "gazing at a spectacle few expected in their life time and brought about by the war." As the machines glided up over the river, the droning of their engines could be heard. They "circled over the town as smoothly as eagles in their flight" and alighted near the Acadia Gas Engines factory. Ensign Hinton delivered a message to Mayor Marshall from Premier Murray, sending personal greetings and "congratulations upon the vigorous way in which your town has entered upon the Victory Loan campaign." No appeal, said the premier, was worthier. "It is to me a matter of profound pride that I am privileged to entrust this message to the gallant and intrepid aviators of our great Ally and neighbor, who, in assisting in this unique way to stimulate our Victory Loan campaign, is giving a striking demonstration of the bond of union which unites us in a common cause."

In Lunenburg, Mayor Duff also received a message from the premier, while J. J. Kinley, MPP, got one from G. D. Campbell, provincial chairman of the Victory Loan campaign. Here the wharves were packed with crowds eager to witness the manoeuvres of the aircraft. The *Progress-Enterprise* on November 6 marvelled that it was a unique way of stimulating the Victory Loan campaign, adding, "The South Shore has always responded splendidly to every patriotic call." The planes flew on to Liverpool, Shelburne, and Yarmouth.

The Canadian government had begun to appeal to the public for money to help finance the war effort in 1915. The fourth such effort, in November 1917, was called the Victory Loan campaign; further appeals were made in 1918 and in 1919, since spending continued after the war ended. As an advertisement explained in the *Bulletin* of October 22, 1918, "money must be borrowed from the people of Canada" because "a nation at war must make tremendous expenditures in cash to keep up her armies and supply them with munitions, food and clothing," and "Canada must finance many millions of dollars of export trade in food, munitions and supplies which Britain and our allies must have on credit." The high-interest, tax-exempt Victory Bonds were popular and the campaigns a great success. Unlike other wartime causes, people were able to make an investment, not simply donate.

The *Progress-Enterprise* announced on September 25, 1918, that work for the organization of a new Victory Loan campaign had begun. J. J. Kinley would be the county chairman, D. W. Smith of Lunenburg the secretary, and committees were appointed in Mahone Bay, Chester, Riverport, and Rose Bay. The *Bulletin* on November 19 reported that subscriptions were "away over the top and still pouring in"; Kinley had telephoned to say that the results of the campaign were "most gratifying and puts the great county in the front rank." According to the *Morning Chronicle* of November 25, final returns showed that Nova Scotia had contributed over $33 million, more than $8 million in excess of the unofficial objective set for the province. Though the largest amounts had come from Halifax and Cape Breton, Lunenburg had collected almost $1.5 million. The *Bulletin* on November 5 announced that

Conquerall Bank had won a Governor General's honour flag for raising its Victory Loan objective in the first day's canvass—one of many
such flags that were coveted and won throughout the county.

A letter in the *Progress-Enterprise* of November 6, 1918, signed
by Scott Corkum, Artemas Schnare, Benjamin C. Smith, and Henry
Winters, declared that Lunenburg's fishing captains supported the
Victory Loan. "For the fishermen of Nova Scotia, as for all classes of our
people, the Victory Loan offers an investment that is safe as a church
and sound as a bell. Behind the loan is the credit of the Dominion, the
whole wealth of our country." As well, the investor rendered patriotic
service by maintaining the Canadian army in France and providing the
capital for carrying on industries and business at home. "And so the buy-
ers of Victory Bonds will be keeping faith with the boys who are holding
the line for freedom, and will be doing their country a good turn."

The clergy also enthusiastically supported the drive for funds.
Rev. A. D. MacKinnon, pastor of St. Andrew's Presbyterian Church,
according to the *Progress-Enterprise* of November 6, urged buying
Victory Bonds to the point of personal sacrifice. And Methodist pastor
Rev. A. R. Reynolds went much farther, proclaiming that the Canadian
government was offering citizens the privilege of helping to win "the
greatest and most significant war in all history" with their savings, in
the form of a safe and profitable investment. "It is the struggle not
between Germany, Austria, and Turkey on the one side and almost the
whole civilized world on the other; it is the struggle between the false
ideal and the true, between autocracy and democracy—indeed we may
well say between the Kingdom of Darkness and the Kingdom of Light.
Out of the struggle will ultimately emerge a new civilization, vastly
better than any the world has ever yet known; a civilization in which
the principles of the Great Prince of Peace, and the righteousness of
God shall have the pre-eminence."

Much of the success of the campaign was due to unequalled publi-
city in the press. A typical advertisement appeared in the *Progress-
Enterprise* on November 6, 1918: "Be a Soldier at Home, Buy Victory
Bonds." The security was the finest in the world, the paper contended,

and 5½ per cent would be paid on your money. Such ads were often followed, after John McCrae's death in January 1918, by references to the poem "In Flanders Fields," with poppy fields and torches and such poignant lines as, "Be yours to hold it high!" and, "If ye break faith... we shall not sleep."[4] Local businesses donated space in the newspapers for ads promoting Victory Bonds with titles like "Put Your Dollars in Khaki," by Frank Powers and the Lunenburg Foundry; "A Business

Lunenburg's Answer to the U-boats. Halifax Herald, *November 4, 1918.*

Proposition," by Kinley's Drug Store; and "Come Men—'Over the Top,'" by "The Hubley Co. Ltd., The Store of Quality." The *Progress-Enterprise* itself donated space on October 30 for, "'Hun Hellishness Halts Here,' say our boys at the front. Do you say 'Amen' to this? Then buy one or more Victory Bonds."

But the pièce de résistance was the full-page advertisement in the *Halifax Herald* of November 4, with the headline "Lunenburg's Answer to the U-Boats." It was contributed by a group of patriotic and prominent Lunenburg businessmen: Kinley's Drug Store, Lunenburg Outfitting Company, Smith & Rhuland, W. C. Smith & Company, John B. Young, Adams & Knickle, Lunenburg Foundry Company, Frank Powers, Zwicker & Company, and Robin, Jones & Whitman. Almost the entire ad consisted of a sketch depicting a schooner being destroyed by a U-boat, with members of the crew of the doomed vessel adrift in lifeboats about to make for shore; a submarine lurked in the background. Alongside the sketch are the words:

Only a few weeks ago the Hun U-boats were carrying out their foul work off our shores.

Our Lunenburg vessels with their crews of dauntless fishermen fell victims to the treacherous Hun. These underwater pirates true to the barbaric spirit first manifested in the criminal sinking of the Lusitania *sent the men of our schooners adrift in open boats without food or water utterly regardless of weather conditions and totally devoid of any feelings of humanity.*

Now these murderers, these slayers of peace, the authors of countless vile and unspeakable atrocities are whipped and defeated—beaten to their knees.

We hear from them the squeal of the thrashed cur—they plead, these criminals, for Mercy!

This is Lunenburg's answer, proud of her crews who refused to be affrighted and who carried on in spite of Hunnish hate. No Mercy for you Huns until you first surrender!

This Victory must be final and complete. Our Lunenburg soldier

*heroes must be backed to the limit. Buy Victory Bonds! Put the finish-
ing touch to the gigantic conflict—*
    Now then—all together over the top with the Victory Loan.
    *Buy in the same way as our Nova Scotia soldiers fight—without
stint right up to the limit.*

The *Herald* declared that the appeal was "both striking and original
in design....Depredations of the Hun U-boats off the Nova Scotia
coast had come very close home to Lunenburg,...and many of that
county's fishermen had endured much hardship." These comments
appeared on a separate page in the same issue of the paper, below the
sketch with similar subject matter by Frederick William Wallace (see
page 147). The next day, the *Herald* maintained that the "appealing full-
page Victory Loan advertisement by the Lunenburg merchants was an
inspiration, and gave an impetus to everybody to buy bonds."

The *Bulletin* on November 19 congratulated the Lunenburg County
Victory Loan workers on the magnificent result of their canvass, and
it also congratulated the purchasers of bonds on their ready and willing response to the call. Bridgewater had been allotted a much larger
sum than it was thought it would or could raise, but "the local workers
went at it with a vim." The allotment of $220,000 had been passed by a
comfortable sum, despite the fact that in the first two days of the previous week nothing had been done on account of the peace celebrations.
Influenza had also interfered with the canvass.

"When Will Lunenburg Clean Up," protested the *Progress-Enterprise*
on May 15, 1918. There were hideous dumps near the railway station
and on the approach to town along the Mahone Bay road, which comprised "articles dating from the time of Adam to the latest German
offensive....Nature has done so much for our beautiful town that the
citizens...should be ashamed to have its appearance marred by rubbish
heaps and gutters littered with torn paper, banana skins and the tide of

living during the long winter." A clean-up week was necessary from an aesthetic but also a sanitary point of view. Refuse in cellars harboured every germ in the catalogue: "Scarlet Fever, Diphtheria, Sore Throat, Tetanus, these are a few who just love a nice pile of cellar refuse in which to grow fat and deadly." There was, however, much worse to come.

In Canada, nearly fifty thousand people died during the global pandemic known as Spanish influenza. At least fifty million perished worldwide, more deaths than in the war. Despite its name, the disease did not originate in the Iberian Peninsula, but its presence was first broadcast in neutral Spain. The sickness came in three waves, according to Mark Osborne Humphries in *The Last Plague*: the first, in the spring of 1918, causing comparatively few deaths. But the second wave, in the fall, was extremely deadly. Compared to earlier epidemics, this virulent strain struck hardest at otherwise healthy young adults, who developed the more severe symptoms and ultimately died from complications like bronchopneumonia. As Eileen Pettigrew maintains in *The Silent Enemy*, this was particularly devastating because the war had also taken so many young people of the same age group. The disease struck again in the winter of 1918–1919, but not as severely.

Some historians believe that the influenza arrived in Canada with soldiers returning from the war. According to *The Oxford Companion to Canadian Military History*, there were cases among the CEF troops as early as June 1918, and 776 would die of the disease by 1919. But Humphries points out that most soldiers had not returned from Europe before the epidemic had peaked in North America. Rather, he argues convincingly, the flu had been brought to Canada by American soldiers on their way overseas to join the fighting.

In what appears to be the first mention of the Spanish influenza in the *Halifax Herald*, on September 23, 1918, the paper reported that about five hundred American soldiers had arrived at "An Atlantic Port" suffering with the flu. The worst cases were taken to military hospitals, but many were put up in curling rinks and two church halls commandeered by the military authorities. Because of wartime secrecy, we cannot be sure of the boat they arrived on or the port. However,

Humphries notes that the ss *Nestor* had sailed from Hoboken, New Jersey, on September 17 filled with apparently healthy American soldiers destined for Europe. Three days after sailing, because of sickness the ship was forced to put in to Sydney, Cape Breton. With the hospital there overwhelmed, supplies and personnel were sent up from Halifax, and when the ships returned to the capital they carried the disease to the mainland. About the same time, a huge congress of Catholics, mainly from the United States, was held in Victoriaville, Quebec, which led to the earliest account of deaths from the flu within Canada's civilian population.

Humphries maintains that the fatal second wave did spread outwards from Western Europe, likely from Great Britain, but it arrived in Canada by a circuitous route: "it was American soldiers and civilians who were travelling *to* Europe *via* Canada that spread the disease to the Dominion." Humphries also claims that the influenza was spread across the country by newly mobilized soldiers travelling by train to the west coast to join the expeditionary force on its way to cross the Pacific to fight the communists in Siberia.

By late September 1918, alarming news was coming north to Nova Scotia about the spread of influenza and the number of deaths in New England. The situation was so desperate in Boston that an urgent appeal had been made for nurses. Haligonians, remembering the help that had come from Massachusetts at the time of the explosion, sent nurses, according to Pettigrew, but before long they were needed at home. On October 2, the *Herald* announced the deaths of two Gloucester sailors in Yarmouth. That same day, the *Progress-Enterprise*, mentioning the disease for the first time, reported that the Gloucester schooner *Rhodora*, bound for the banks—having put in down the shore at Liverpool with five of her crew ill with Spanish influenza—had been quarantined in nearby Brooklyn.

"Heartily believing in the old adage that 'an ounce of prevention is worth a pound of cure,'" the Lunenburg board of health closed until further notice all institutions and public meeting places, such as schools, churches, and theatres. The editor of the *Progress-Enterprise*

on October 9 commented that "without doubt the wise precaution-
ary measure will be heartily endorsed." There were no cases in the
town, but several houses in Riverport had already been quarantined.
Drastic measures would be taken if any resident concealed illness
in the home. That same day the *Morning Chronicle* predicted that
the influenza in Halifax was not likely to be as bad as in Boston.
Province-wide, the paper said, apparently Lunenburg was the worst,
with seventy cases reporting in the last twenty-four hours. R. C. S.
Kaulbach, in the Lunenburg paper on October 23, noticed that these
cases had occurred a few days after the fishermen's picnic, which had
brought people into the town from all over the province and should
have been cancelled.

On October 10, Leslie Tanner, the promising sixteen-year-old son
of William and Sevilla Tanner, became the first fatality in Lunenburg,
dying from bronchial pneumonia following an attack of Spanish influenza. A few days later, at the Ovens, Ivan Winters, son of Gabriel
Winters, succumbed after only two days' illness. The *Herald* reported
on October 16 that there were four thousand cases in Nova Scotia,
with sixty deaths. The situation in Lunenburg County was indeed bad,
especially along the LaHave River. There was "not so much talk now
of 'Common Colds,'" scolded the editor of the *Progress-Enterprise* on
October 23. "All around the continent people were dying faster than
they could be buried, but in Lunenburg there were only 'Common
Colds.'" The alarming number of funerals had changed that tune, and
"sadly and slowly the fact has sunk in, that Lunenburg 'Has the Flu.'"

The provincial health officer, Dr. W. H. Hattie, called for any young
woman to volunteer for nursing, even if she had no training. The *Bulletin*
on October 22 claimed that there were about ninety cases in Bridgewater,
thirty-five houses under quarantine. The local board of health notified
the postmaster to close the public waiting room in the post office on
the arrival of all mails and to keep the doors locked until the mail had
been sorted; all persons "loafing" in the post office would be penalized
with a fine up to fifty dollars. Barbers were told to keep their shops in a
sanitary condition and to prohibit unnecessary loafing; failure to do so

would result in closing. With churches closed in Halifax, Archdeacon Armitage of St. Paul's held an open-air service on the Parade, thus preserving the continuity of service not broken in a hundred years.

Of the numerous deaths thereafter, only a few can be mentioned. J. Wilfred Mossman of Rose Bay, aged thirty-five, "an active, industrious Christian gentleman...passed into eternal rest" on October 16, leaving to mourn his widow Lavinia, two small children, aged parents, and eight brothers. Robert Burnley Hume Robertson, barrister and stipendiary magistrate of Bridgewater, "passed to the Great Beyond" on October 21, also age thirty-five, "in the prime and strength of his manhood." Because of the infectious nature of the disease, his burial took place outside in the rain, in front of his residence; floral offerings, it was said, were magnificent and filled an automobile and a wagon. Mrs. Frank Garber left behind a husband and two children. The *Bulletin* declared on October 29 that she was "a woman of sterling character and worth," and the community would not soon forget "her radiant optimism and cheery manner and loving disposition.... [T]he sadness of her departure is tempered by the knowledge that she died faithful to her Lord." Crewman Lorraine Burgoyne of the schooner *Charles A. Ritcey* took sick after the vessel left Lunenburg on October 15. Arriving in Halifax, he was refused entry to the Victoria General Hospital. After several days, according to the *Herald* of October 23, Captain C. D. Ritcey finally got him admitted to the Morris Street hospital, but his fate was already sealed. On November 20 the *Progress-Enterprise* reported that widow Jane Jefferson had died in New Germany, leaving behind seven children, including her son Howard, "now serving his King and country." The *Bulletin* on November 5, in a tiny item compared to accounts for "grander" folk, simply noted that Elva, wife of John Labrador of Bridgewater, a soldier serving overseas, had died a few days ago, leaving three children behind.

The Women's Institute in Bridgewater supplied soup, gruel, and other food to persons afflicted with influenza and unable to cook for themselves, as well as solid food for those nursing. Some days there were up to forty cases to look after. Obviously, concluded the *Bulletin*'s editor, the need for a hospital was now alarmingly apparent. In the meantime, the board of health proposed using the assembly room of the school building as an emergency hospital.

Many cures were proposed, most of them useless. One typical supposed cure was published in the *Progress-Enterprise* on November 6: "1 oz. gum camphor, 1 oz. turpentine, 1 oz. ammonia, 1 lb. lard. Melt the lard and camphor together and let cool, then add the turpentine and ammonia. Spread on a linen cloth and place flannel over the top and apply to the chest. The above is said to give instant relief in the worst cases of influenza." The *Bulletin* the day before had quoted the *Boston Globe*: "Carrying around mothballs in your pocket and using chopped onions and garlic for a poultice may not make you immune to the Spanish influenza…but it may tend to get you more room in a crowd."

On November 12, the *Bulletin* announced that "the 'flu' is flying away." Workers were returning to the factories. More important, it seemed, the paper hoped that the embargo would be lifted by the twentieth so the Empire Theatre could reopen in time to show the new serial *The Brass Bullet*, which was apparently "a wonder." On the nineteenth, the paper thought the "influenza scourge" was now at a low ebb, and there was no valid reason for keeping public places closed any longer. Christmas was rapidly approaching and "this 'closing' menace to business without adequate cause is all wrong."

On November 27, the province's Department of Public Health felt confident enough to declare that the epidemic stage of the influenza had passed. Nova Scotia had been fortunate on the whole since the number of deaths was "less proportionately than in many other places." On December 10, the embargo was lifted from churches. The *Bulletin* observed that they had been closed for eight Sundays, "so now that the pastors have had plenty of time for reflection and preparation we may expect a great flow of oratory." To the paper's delight, the Empire Theatre also reopened, the main attractions being "the feature picture *The Devil's Assistant* in five startling acts" and P. C. Shortis, the great manipulator of the banjo and violin who had played before crowned heads. However, after a "sharp recrudescence" of influenza in a number of communities, the department again closed the churches, schools, and theatres on December 11. The crisis was not quite over.

In Lunenburg County, 104 people died in 1918 from Spanish influenza. There had been 18 deaths in Bridgewater and 12 in Lunenburg town.⁵ The officially recorded number of deaths in Nova Scotia was 1,769; however, Dr. Allan Marble of Dalhousie University estimates a figure closer to 2,000, the overall death rate being 3.4 per cent, substantially lower than in other parts of the country. He noted that the pandemic had resulted in one important change: Canada finally got a federal Department of Health in 1919.⁶

They say it's not *that* you die that matters, for all of us must, but rather *how* you die. J. Howard Smith of Lunenburg, like so many others at the time, did not have a good death. Born in Lunenburg on November 3, 1888, Smith, a carpenter in his father's shop, enlisted at Sussex, New Brunswick, on August 25, 1915, at almost twenty-seven years of age. He arrived in England in October 1915 and served in France with the 5th Canadian Mounted Rifles from April to October 1916. He was in and out of hospitals in France and England, suffering from shrapnel in his neck and a bayonet wound to his right thigh that he received at Sanctuary Wood. He was also treated for both gonorrhoea and syphilis, and pediculosis, infestation with lice. In February 1918, he apparently received bad news from home and became depressed, ending up eventually in the Lord Derby War Hospital, Warrington, Cheshire, where severe cases of shell shock were treated.

He had not been ill before he enlisted, although both his grandfather and his father were said to have been insane and had committed suicide, according to his records. Smith himself tried to cut his throat with a razor. Disinterested in his surroundings, he had bad dreams, severe headaches, and nosebleeds, he heard shells bursting, and imagined people talking to him, sometimes in a voice sounding like his father's. Diagnosed with "melancholia," he was invalided home to Canada on October 14, 1918, for further treatment. He was admitted to Camp Hill Hospital in Halifax on November 3 and died there on January 11, 1919, from "influenza complicated by pneumonia." He left behind his wife, Annie, and a small boy. His funeral was at his home at Masons Beach.

"Melancholia," similar to what we now call post-traumatic stress disorder, was not particularly well understood in the First World War. As Morton and Granatstein remark in *Marching to Armageddon*, shell shock in returned men was seen as "a manifestation of childishness and femininity." Amputees, they contend, may be the popular image of war-wounded, but fewer than three thousand of Canada's eighty thousand war pensioners had lost limbs. Most were victims of illness, not wounds. And, in the words of Wade Davis in *Into the Silence*, it took the "unprecedented scale and horror" of the battles of France to make medical and military professions understand the truth about shell shock. "Strong men, young and old, reduced to hysteria, twisted and contorted, mute with fear, shak-ing with tremors, eyeballs pro-truding with the brightness of madness. These were the refu-gees from a place that Siegfried Sassoon described as 'the loom-ing twilight of hell.'"

Nurse Addie Tupper, who had died in December 1916, cer-tainly knew about shell shock. In her last letter home to her mother, she had written about the necessity of welcoming sol-diers home from the war: "Any man, woman or child whose health permitted should wel-come these boys home. If not, I fear the home people have little realization of what these boys go

Donald Roy Purcell.

through. Day after day in trenches of mud and water, cold and weary, seeing their companions, often their friends, killed, blown in pieces beside them, expecting the next shell will be their death, perhaps seeing comrades buried by shell bursts or being buried themselves. Or, worse yet, seeing such shell-shock that makes the boys blind, deaf, speechless or, often, insane."[7]

Just a few hours before the tidings of Germany's eventual surrender reached Lunenburg, a cable was received announcing the death of yet another soldier. Donald Roy Purcell of the 85th Nova Scotia Highlanders, only twenty, had been mortally wounded and died shortly after in No. 1 Clearing Hospital in France on October 29, 1918. A waiter before the war, Purcell, like so many others, had sailed to England on the *Olympic* in October 1916. One time in France, in July 1917, he forfeited five days' pay for being improperly dressed, wearing shorts on parade. His cousin, Private Norman Tanner, had also fallen fighting. Both boys had been brought up by their grandmother, Mrs. John Conrad, who, not surprisingly, was inconsolable. It seems doubly hard, lamented the *Progress-Enterprise* on November 20, that Private Purcell should fall "with Victory so near."

Chapter Seven

"THE DAWN OF PEACE"

n the fall of 1918, Canadian troops were moving eastward, helping to liberate the French countryside from German occupation. In a letter home, Roy Martin Whynacht told his mother in Lunenburg that his unit was "following Fritze up now," and it was "great fun going up through French villages." The civilians who lined the streets had miraculously unearthed many French flags. The battalion went through in a body and the band played "La Marseillaise," the first time the people had heard it in four years. A couple of young women plastered the bandmaster with flowers and kisses, and "the crowd was dancing, laughing, crying and just about beyond themselves." Whynacht, a bookkeeper and stenographer in Digby before the war, had enlisted in the 219th Battalion in February 1916, sailed from Halifax on the *Olympic* in October that year, and served in France with the 85th Battalion. He returned to Canada as a lance corporal on the *Adriatic* in June 1919. In his letter, which was printed in the *Progress-Enterprise* on November 27, Whynacht remarked, "You people in Canada cannot begin to form the most remote idea of what these poor souls have suffered during the past four dark years of their existence. I didn't realize it myself until I lived with them a few days. I can't realize how Hell could be worse."

The war was coming to an end. Like most of the Allied press, the newspapers of Lunenburg County were merciless and unforgiving, and had no doubt who was to blame for the carnage. "Kick the Kaiser!" the *Bridgewater Bulletin* headline virtually roared on August 6. "The Hun Is in Retreat." The Allied forces were close on the heels of "the flying Germans," capturing prisoners and guns.

"Peace but peace through victory is the only thing to consider," concurred the editor of the *Progress-Enterprise*—presumably Agnes McGuire—on September 18. The Germans were laying mines in villages in their bid for peace. "They can kill whole villages of women and babies; they can crucify our soldiers; they can outrage every tenet of decency and civilization, yet when the Allies after suffering years of unprovoked bloody murder give them a taste of it…Kaiser Bill and his horde of hell hounds [now think themselves] the most ill used and abused people on earth."

The *Bulletin* printed a letter on December 24 from Steve Conrad to his brother, saying that he was in Mons, where the British had made their retreat in 1914. Canadian forces had captured the Belgian city on the last day of the war. Hundreds of people in the streets went "wild with happiness" when they saw the troops marching in. They "thought the world of the Canadians." Private Conrad was happy that the enemy had been beaten, and announced that he would be starting the next day for Germany. The infantry battalions of the Canadian first and second divisions would march east into Germany, crossing the bridge over the Rhine at Bonn on December 13, a momentous occasion for sure, but given the steady downpour of cold rain that day, most of the men, one assumes, would likely rather have been on their way back to Canada.

———

"The Dawn of Peace," declared the headline in the *Progress-Enterprise* on November 13, 1918. "The longed for time is here, the most glorious news in the history of the civilized world has been received....God grant that never again will there be anything but 'Peace on earth, good will to man.'"

"GOD SAVE THE KING. THANK GOD! THE STRUGGLE IS OVER," read the main headline that day. The citizens of Lunenburg had been awakened on the eleventh with the glad pealing of the peace bells, which immediately followed the flashes of the electric lights that announced the "joy-tidings" of the ending of the war. News of the kaiser's abdication had already been received with jubilation. Flags were strung up and work at once suspended. Automobiles were "gaily decorated with bunting and all sorts of patriotic devices." That afternoon, a huge crowd assembled in the post office square, and stood at attention at the bandstand "while the King was played after which all sang 'Praise God from Whom All Blessings Flow.'" Hymns of praise were fervently sung at a thanksgiving service that afternoon. Mayor William Duff read the terms of the armistice and Premier Murray's proclamation of a public holiday. That evening, the kaiser was burned in effigy and a band concert and bonfire closed "the most glorious day in the history of Lunenburg."

Bridgewater, too, celebrated the Allied victory "in grand and glorious style." Bells rang and whistles blew for about an hour on November 11, commencing about six in the morning. As if by magic, the *Bulletin* reported on the twelfth, crowds had gathered on King Street and automobiles appeared bedecked with gay streamers and Allied flags. At 9:30 a procession, headed by the band in a motor truck and followed by "seventy-four automobiles filled with merry makers and victory shouters," started from the eastern end of the bridge and ended at the bandstand, where an immense crowd was present, "enthused to the highest degree."

The band "discoursed a fine program of patriotic music of all allied countries, punctuated by cheers for the King, Presidents of the United States and France, the Kings of Italy, Belgium and Serbia, and Marshal Foch, Generals Haig, Currie and Diaz." That afternoon, a thanksgiving service was held at the bandstand, churches still being closed because of the influenza. In the evening, huge bonfires burned and fireworks were set off from a platform on the eastern side of the river. Immense crowds had filled the streets all day and "the perfect weather and bright bunting made a charming spectacle not easily to be forgotten." Commented the *Bulletin*: "Bill Hohenzollern did not size-up the people he went up against."

The *Halifax Herald* had delivered by automobile news of the victory to towns along the South Shore. The paper reported that Chester, too, had rejoiced in the victory, with all the church bells ringing out and the town "immediately beflagged," followed by a "splendid parade of citizens carrying the national colors." The town was "beautifully illuminated at night." Hubbards also fittingly celebrated the day, with a public meeting in the evening in Manchester Hall, the Oddfellows taking a prominent part in arrangements. Petite Riviere, according to the *Progress-Enterprise* of November 20, had celebrated the good war news "in royal style," with flags hoisted everywhere, salutes fired, and schoolchildren parading. Rev. J. S. Coffin's flagpole, with all the flags of the Allies proudly waving in the strong breeze, was thought to be perhaps the best trimmed flagpole in the county.

Armistice Day at Parks Creek School, November 11, 1918.

Reflecting on the ceasing of hostilities at last, the *Bulletin* on the nineteenth welcomed the end of the war. "The Dawn of Peace! Like a brilliant bow of promise arching the thunderstricken eastern horizon comes the news of peace":

> *"Peace!" How glibly we used that word four years ago, how little it meant to most of us then. How much it means to the war-wearied, nerve-shocked and hysterical world today. To us in Canada it means much. It will bring comfort and joy to those whose sons, whose fathers and brothers have borne the battle so long. Peace will not bring back the fallen, neither will it restore the broken bodies of hundreds of heroes who came out of the inferno of battle with shattered remnants of their former selves. Sorrow and suffering will remain with us, and neither this generation nor the next will remove entirely the terrible marks of the world's crucifixion."*

The paper went on to remark that peace had been bought at a tremendous price, but it had been a price worth paying, though the cost here on this continent had been small compared to the brutal tyranny faced by the people of France and Belgium. "Only those captive and heartlessly oppressed and outraged people know to the full what war means and only they can fully realize and appreciate the glad and glorious import of this word which spreads like a golden shaft of light athwart the world—'PEACE!'"

Along with joy that peace had finally arrived was continued rancour toward the enemy. "Let Us Praise God for Our Deliverance from the Hun Beast," ran the banner across the top of the *Bulletin*'s front page. Below was a large photograph of King George v and his message to the Empire. The outbreak of the war "found the whole Empire one." We can now "rejoice to think the end of the struggle finds the Empire still more closely united by common resolve....[T]he hour is one of solemn thanksgiving of gratitude to God."

In the mid-1970s, G. E. Romkey of West Dublin recalled that the greatest event of 1918 was the end of the First World War. In his memoirs, published in the *Progress-Enterprise* in March 1974, he described the boisterous local celebrations, which were decidedly moist, despite prohibition:

> *What a big time we had in West Dublin that day. At 5:30 AM Arch Haughn came to the house yelling like mad that the war was over.... [W]e had the church bells ringing in record time. Arch knew that Sam Hurshman had a bottle of gin so we had Sam out of bed in tails and that bottle of gin dried up making another record. Next we started to organize the village for a real celebration and as we visited house to house it was hard in my capacity for every house a drink was furnished and what a mixture. Under the conditions no one could refuse and to see the old home-made wines with mold on the bottles that was produced in homes that usually were considered strictly temperate folk was a pleasant surprise. Did this stuff have a kick and it was not very long before I was ready to climb the side of a building....Mrs. G. E. had a couple of bottles of brandy hid but when she produced it to the men it just lasted one round. With the church choirs, horns, tin pans and everything that would make a noise we started the parade at 1:30 and it was well worth the effort. Down near James Publicover's the noise stopped and a hymn was sung in memory of Fred, who did not come home. The parade took in the whole village and near Crescent Beach I can still see Mrs. Eli Publicover, a very old woman, ringing a bell....More organization was started for a bonfire on Bushens Hill and a public meeting in the hall, followed by a dance. Everything went in good order and without question it was the biggest and best celebration that West Dublin had to that date.*

On November 22, 1918, the *Halifax Herald* informed its readers that "returning boys" must be welcomed "with a glad and loud acclaim." The "ban is off, so let bands play and cheers ring out" when the great Cunard liner, the *Aquitania*, arrives on Monday. Returning soldiers could now be given a proper reception, for there were no longer any restraints on the press or on citizens. The next day, however, the paper had to explain why the public could not be "permitted to go on the pier promiscuously," for with the band playing the officers would not be able to give instructions, and the docks would be piled with luggage. But on the twenty-ninth, the paper reported that four thousand men had arrived back on the *Aquitania*, "joyous and happy to be home again...with the band sounding out martial airs and hundreds of citizens cheering themselves hoarse in welcome." According to the *Progress-Enterprise* of December 4, several Lunenburg County men had been on board, from Lunenburg, Bridgewater, Chester, Branch LaHave, Barss Corner, Gold River, Blandford, and the LaHave Islands.

The commander of the *Aquitania*, Captain Sir James Charles, was "one of those salts who so nobly help to maintain Britain as mistress of the seas," claimed the *Herald*. The other great wartime captain, the *Olympic*'s Bertram Fox "Bertie" Hayes, had won the Distinguished Service Order for ramming and sinking a U-boat in the English Channel off Portsmouth in May 1918. The *Olympic* had a "matchless war record," according to the *Morning Chronicle* on November 18, carrying nearly 300,000 troops without the loss of a single man.

Home Coming of the Canadian Soldiers of the King.
"*The Ocean Greyhound 'Olympic' Returning to the Land of the Maple Leaf with over 5000 Troops Aboard.*"

"Germany was firmly set on 'bagging' the *Olympic*," declared the *Herald* on November 19, and it was largely due to the superb seamanship of her commander that "the giant transport is afloat today and ready to engage in the joyous work of bringing home the boys."

In the first half of 1919, there were many joyous celebrations as soldiers finally returned home. The men of Lunenburg County who had "taken a valiant part in defeating the foe" should be given a hearty welcome, advised the *Bulletin* on December 3. Indeed, citizens and the local band were usually at the station in Bridgewater to meet trains coming down from Halifax "to give the boys a cheer." A "welcome home" arch was erected on the bridge over the LaHave River; painted pure white and covered with appropriate mottos and flags, it was brilliantly illuminated at night. The *Progress-Enterprise* of January 15 commented, on welcoming home some wounded soldiers to Lunenburg, that the town's citizens greatly appreciated "the efforts of the boys who went 'out there' to defend their homes from the iron hand of the war-mad Prussian race."

Soldiers trickled home to smaller communities as well. On New Year's Eve, a large gathering had assembled in the Foresters Hall at Conquerall Bank, summoned by the local branch of the Red Cross, to welcome home William Heckman and Edson Berrigan, who had been wounded. There was a program of songs, duets, choruses, dialogues, and "tableauxs," and the men were presented with handsome signet rings in token of appreciation of their brave service. The LaHave Islands welcomed home Private James B. Baker. According to the *Progress-Enterprise* of February 12, Baker had been gassed at Vimy Ridge and was eventually taken to a hospital in England, suffering severely from a bruise. His wife and sister died within a few weeks of each other shortly before his return, and his brother Robert, who went overseas with him, had been left behind in Flanders. At the reception, at the home of Mrs. Lillas Richard, Baker was given a handsome sum of money. The evening included refreshments, songs, recitations and various games, and selections on the Graphophone and organ. Baker replied briefly and modestly to the speech of welcome, and would leave shortly for Halifax for further medical treatment.

The *Bulletin* reported on June 3 that about forty friends of Sergeant Karl Marshall, at Falkland Ridge, far inland, had gladly welcomed him home after three years overseas. The lawn and driveway of Marshall's house were decorated with flags, along with a green hemlock arch and banners of welcome. A huge bonfire was kindled in the evening. And in West Dublin, announced the *Progress-Enterprise* on June 18, Councillor A. H. Sperry had remarked in ringing tones that "nothing is too good for the soldier boys who put Lunenburg Co., Nova Scotia, Canada, on the pages of history where it will ever remain."

A typical homecoming was described in the *Bulletin* on April 8, 1919. A presentation took place at the home of Mr. and Mrs. Alvin Eisnor of Wileville, where forty friends gathered to welcome home their son Ambrose and Private Stephen Wamboldt. Ambrose was given a set of gold cufflinks and tie clip, and Stephen a gold signet ring. There was music, singing, and games. A "dainty" luncheon was served. Mrs. William Emeno recited "Lads Who Don't Come Back." Happy reunions after years of separation and anxiety, she read, made for "a very beautiful and touching scene" as troop trains "bearing their precious load of browned veterans" arrived at local stations. But "Who has a cheer for the little widow, the wearied white-haired mother and the fatherless children, dependants of some hero who paid the supreme sacrifice in Flanders fields?" In the excitement and happiness of the homecoming and the elaborate welcomes, the next of kin of dead heroes, "whose heritage is a wooden cross," were liable to be forgotten.

Dominion Day in Mahone Bay, on July 1, 1919, was said to be a red-letter day. Not only were the residents welcoming returning soldiers but they were also celebrating their recent incorporation as a town. There were patriotic speeches, and a parade including returned soldiers, field sports, a tightrope walk, a tub race, men's and ladies' rowing, and a greased pole. The *Bulletin* of July 8 reported that the Masonic Order had catered, feeding three thousand hungry mouths on the picnic grounds.

One returned hero had had an unusual adventure. Captain Rufus Sprague's ship, the ss *Pontiac*, had been torpedoed in the Mediterranean off the coast of Marsa Susa in Libya on April 28, 1917. The steamer, built in Glasgow in 1903, at the time of the loss was owned by J. W. Carmichael of New Glasgow, Nova Scotia, and she was on her way to Port Said with a cargo from Karachi. Captain Sprague, from Bridgewater, was held prisoner on the submarine for six days, then landed at Cattaro, Austria (now Kotor in Montenegro), after which he travelled by train for twelve days to a prisoner-of-war camp in Germany. The *Bulletin* of January 28, 1919, noted that he had been fairly well treated and well supplied with food by the British Red Cross during his nineteen months in captivity. After the signing of the armistice, he was able to leave Germany and arrived in England on December 10, on his way home.

The returning soldiers sometimes embarrassed those waiting to welcome them. The editor of the *Bulletin* on December 3 grumbled, "All our people are eager and glad to give soldiers who are returning from the front a hearty welcome which their heroic sacrifices have earned, but even their great services on the battle field do not give them licence to riot and disgrace themselves and their uniform when they return to their homes. Thankfully, these instances are very few." A couple of returned soldiers had been drunk on King Street, used profane language, and committed acts of vandalism. "True, it was not altogether the soldiers' fault, for the miscreant who gave them the vile liquor was more to blame than the soldiers....There was much evidence of indiscriminate liquor drinking in town that day," concluded the paper primly.

There had been even more serious trouble in Halifax, when in the spring of 1918, troops had rioted and threatened to burn the city hall. A year later, on February 20, 1919, the *Herald* reported that "soldier hoodlums" had wrecked nine stores, windows were broken and furniture smashed. Civilians were also involved, but the leaders were wearing equipment only issued overseas. Several Chinese restaurants had been wrecked and "some of the victims were 'Hebrew' and one was Assyrian," but the attack on the shoe store of Mrs. Joanna Patton, "a respected resident of the North End," seemed to be evidence that the mob was "actuated by no desire save to smash, break and destroy." Bootleggers, with their vile concoctions, were responsible for the outbreaks, claimed the *Herald*. On the twenty-first, the *Morning Chronicle* concluded that "Bolshevism in Halifax" was now "purely passive," confining itself to small groups on street corners because of the effective co-operation of the civil, military, and naval authorities, aided by the Great War Veterans' Association. By midnight the streets of the city were practically deserted and "the period of mob rule was over."

Given the large number of troops returning, it is perhaps not surprising that there was some trouble. The *Bulletin* remarked on May 13 that railway workers were putting in long strenuous days "in these times of demobilization" to get the fighting men back to their homes across the country with the least possible delay. Probably never again would Haligonians see "such a procession of great ships loaded with soldiers in that magnificent harbour." On June 10, the paper noted that forty thousand troops had passed through Halifax during the month of May. The 25th Battalion had embarked for Canada on the *Olympic* on

Canadian troops returning on the Olympic, *Halifax, 1919.*

May 10, and when the troops returned home and mustered out on the Common in Halifax, according to the battalion's historians, only forty-eight of "the originals" answered their names.[1] The *Progress-Enterprise* on June 4 announced that the men of the 85th Battalion, "the last of our noble sons who will come in a body," were expected to arrive on the sixth, on the *Adriatic*.

The Great War had officially ended with the signing of the Treaty of Versailles on June 28, 1919, exactly five years after Archduke Franz Ferdinand had been assassinated in Sarajevo. On July 19, a Peace Day was held in London, with as many as five million people reportedly turning out for the London Victory Parade. A rather smaller, but equally enthusiastic, event had taken place in Lunenburg two days earlier. July 17 had been declared Peace Day in Lunenburg. The celebration began at eight o'clock in the morning with a royal salute, and an hour later all the bells in the town were rung. A united thanksgiving service was held on the bandstand at ten o'clock with hymns and scripture readings, music furnished by a large orchestra, and all the ministers in the town participating. A male quartet was followed by the principal address by Rev. F. C. Ward-Whate. That evening, according to the account in the *Progress-Enterprise* on July 23, there was a large bonfire on Blockhouse Hill and a concert given by the newly reorganized band under the efficient leadership of J. T. Arenburg, accompanied by a brilliant display of fireworks.

In the afternoon, Lunenburg had been defeated 11 to 6 in a baseball match with returned soldiers from Liverpool. During the game, the Lunenburg shortstop, Joseph Boliver, had had a small bone in his ankle fractured. Private Boliver, a grocery clerk before the war, was a small man, at 160 cm and 58 kg when he enlisted, age twenty-one, in November 1914. He was to have a long war, returning to Canada on the *Olympic* only in May 1919. A story that went around town after the war claimed that Boliver was at Vimy Ridge when the cry went up, "Over the top and God Save the King." "The hell with the King," hollered Bolliver, "God save little Joey!"

The ending of the war naturally led to changes at home. The *Bulletin* reported on November 18, only a week after the armistice, that the American naval base in Shelburne was closing, and Halifax was rejoicing over a return to the usage of lights, with the streets now crowded at nights by throngs of people not having to grope their way in the gloom. Closer to home, the *Progress-Enterprise* noted that there were large congregations at the churches, which meant the ban on account of the influenza epidemic had been lifted—temporarily, as it happened. Thanks could now be offered "before the different altars for the glorious victory that is ours." If the Allies had not won, nothing else would have mattered, for "Canada's turn to be laid waste would have come sooner or later, for that is the German way....[I]ron rule would have been executed."

The *Bulletin* announced on the twenty-sixth that restrictions on travel had been lifted and men of military age no longer needed a passport to go to the United States or other foreign countries. Most interned enemy aliens, in particular political prisoners with no criminal charges against them, were to get their liberty, and conscripts not yet overseas were released from service shortly after the end of hostilities. However, Patrick Dennis points out in *Reluctant Warriors* that the armistice did not end the authorities' pursuit of thousands of men who had ignored the call to report, that is, the defaulters. The Governor General did not finally sign an Order in Council proclaiming a general amnesty for all those who had committed offences under the Military Service Act until December 20, 1919. Earlier in the year, on January 15, the *Progress-Enterprise* had suggested, "Now that the war in Europe is over it should end at home as well as abroad." There was a "tendency among certain of the powers that be to wage war in Canada against defaulters, etc., under the MSA. The people are sick and tired of militarism. Let us be done with it."

There was uneasiness as well over the fact that Canada's neighbours to the south seemed to be claiming all the glory. In an item titled "Smug Americans" on January 14, 1919, the editor of the *Bulletin* remarked on the considerable comment in Nova Scotia about the supposed "great part" the United States had taken in the war, "particularly to the fulsome praise meted out to that country by the prejudiced press, some of which go so far as to award the entire credit of winning the war to the Yankees." Had it not been for that "safeguard of the world's peace," the British navy, Germany would soon have made "mincemeat" of the Americans as she did of Belgium and France. As the editor complained on May 13, "The majority of writers on the other side of the line seldom recognize any other nation as having been in the scrap." Fortunately, the fair-minded *New-York Tribune* "gave the meed of praise to Great Britain."

There can be no doubt that America's entry into the war gave a tremendous psychological boost to the Allies, and the size of their army would eventually have made a significant difference had the war continued; however, they were late entering the conflict and not that well prepared when they did. As Tim Cook points out in *Vimy*, the Americans did not contribute much to battlefield success until the late fall of 1918. Canada's battlefield role was much longer and greater, even in the Hundred Days Offensive at the end of the war when both countries were involved in the fighting. Canadians had often resented American neutrality, and it had been a common sentiment during the war that "America counted her profits while Canada buried her dead."[2]

Now that the war was finally over, many wartime activities on the home front also came to an end. The *Progress-Enterprise* on November 20, 1918, noted that patriotic societies such as the Red Cross and the Boscawen Chapter of the IODE were wondering what to do now. They could supply clothing for repatriated refugees of devastated countries, or perhaps money to buy clothing would be as useful. It was reported in the *Bulletin* of April 22, 1919, that the LaHave Chapter of the IODE had given "a very enjoyable bridge and dancing party at the Fairview Hotel in aid of the hospital fund, "a brilliant function largely attended." The local Red Cross Society had given up working as a body, the Lunenburg paper noted on February 12. Stalwart Mary Zinck had received a purse of gold ($117) on behalf of the women of the Red Cross and the citizens of the town for her hard work, and Ada Powers was thanked for the use of her room during the four years of war. The YMCA was raising money for a returned soldier's fund, and the Salvation Army launched a "Million Dollar Fund" for their Soldiers Home Coming Campaign—"God loveth a cheerful giver," hinted their ad.

It is difficult to gauge how much women's roles had changed because of their extraordinary efforts during the war. Certainly, many of the jobs they had held temporarily were taken back by men returning from the front. Some historians have concluded there is little evidence to suggest that the war had any significant impact on attitudes about the place of women in Maritime society. In Canada as a whole, historian Joan Sangster has argued that although middle-class, professional, and politically astute women used their roles as volunteers, fundraisers, recruiters, and allies of the federal government to stake out a claim for enhanced respect, the lives of working-class women were hardly transformed at all by the conflict. In fact, though their contributions to the war effort brought more liberalized attitudes to their proper role in society, no truly radical demands were made by Canadian women, and the general feeling was that the role of women as mothers and protectors of family should be preserved. As Desmond Morton asserts, some women did well out of the war, but others had "little to show for years of loneliness, anxiety, and struggle but a semi-stranger with bad habits and painful memories, trying to resume his place at the head of the family."[3]

Women in Nova Scotia had achieved the right to vote provincially during the war. In the 1917 federal election, women who were relatives of men overseas had, for the first time, been allowed to vote in a national election. As Catherine L. Cleverdon points out in *The Woman Suffrage Movement in Canada*, Prime Minster Borden in March 1918 personally sponsored "a real woman franchise measure": "I do not even base it on the wonderful and conspicuous service and sacrifice which women have rendered to the national cause in the war. Apart from all these, I conceive that women are entitled to the franchise on their merits." The bill received royal assent on May 24, 1918, to go into effect on January 1, 1919.

The *Progress-Enterprise* on the fifteenth pondered the possibility that with the entrance of women voters the political situation would be "revolutionized." On the twenty-ninth, the paper reported that a large and representative audience of women had filled the Red Cross room at a meeting held under the auspices of the WCTU for the purpose of having the names of women voters placed on the voters' lists. Ada Powers presided at the meeting and "explained many points in regard to women voting not fully understood by the majority." The women of Lunenburg, "who have done such magnificent patriotic work during the past four years, who were ever ready to respond to any call for money or work," the paper predicted, would "fully sustain their reputation for cleverness, industry and intelligence when it comes to the matter of having a voice in public life."

There was one matter on which having the vote would make little difference. The *Progress-Enterprise* on October 2, 1918, noted that recent reports from London claimed Canadian soldiers were marrying English women at the rate of a thousand a month. The ability of English girls to select good husbands was thus demonstrated, concluded the paper, but this was rather gloomy news for the girls of Canada.

Many women had worked long and hard for the cause of temperance, and their great success was province-wide prohibition, even before they got the vote. As Tim Cook explains in "Wet Canteens and Worrying Mothers," most soldiers viewed the instigation of temperance legislation as unwanted interference: "these citizen-soldiers had fought for freedom and were now to return home to a country that denied them one of the few pleasures they had found overseas." Certainly, soldiers and other men resisted the law. The *Bulletin* on March 18, 1919, told of the capture of "a liquor still of good capacity" in New Ross by military service officers, who had found about a hundred gallons of manufactured rum, apparently ready to go to market, as well as a couple of deserters. Earlier, a notable liquor case had occurred in Lunenburg, not long after the war ended. J. W. King, a prominent hotel-keeper in the town, had been successfully prosecuted by the WCTU after eight or ten witnesses had given evidence. "Many of them could not define the kind of liquor they got or that it was intoxicating," claimed the *Bulletin* on December 10, "but some were frank in stating it was rum." King was sentenced to four months in prison.

The hunting down of drunks and prosecutions for the illegal use of intoxicating beverages would go on in Nova Scotia until 1929, when the people voted for the government control and sale of liquor. Premier Edgar Rhodes had alleged in August 1927: "Prohibition by statute in my judgement is on all fours with the attitude of the Russian Soviets who believe in rule by force rather than rule by reason."

Liquor would play an important role as well in the economic life of Nova Scotia after the war. The prohibition era of the 1920s was a period of regional depression, according to historian E. R. Forbes, and "it was rum more than the fisheries that became the true 'employer of last resort'....[A]t the primary level of distribution rum-running emerged less as a new industry than as a redeployment of the resources of the fisheries."[4] Indeed, the *Maritime Merchant* in May 1924 claimed that there were seventy-five schooners in Lunenburg engaged as rum runners, as many vessels as in the fishing fleet itself.

Times were indeed hard. As Brian Douglas Tennyson remarks in *Nova Scotia at War*, "postwar prices for agricultural products, fish and lumber all declined, unemployment rose, and wages fell at the very time when thousands of veterans were trying to settle back into civilian society." He continues, the "situation was so serious that when the Great Depression struck in 1930 many people in Nova Scotia claimed that they didn't notice any difference."

The sniping between the county's two feisty newspapers continued after the war, and long after, with each editor supporting the paper's favoured political party. Although J. W. Margeson continued to shine brightly in the pages of the Conservative *Bridgewater Bulletin*, the Liberal *Progress-Enterprise* of Lunenburg, on June 25, 1919, dared to refer to the major as "that gallant soldier who never smelled powder." The *Bulletin* on July 1 suggested that this was "a ticklish reference for those responsible for this statement," one of them being William Duff, MP, who had "used every means in his power to discourage enlistment in this county and who was called to account for interference with the MSA." The other offender was J. J. Kinley, MPP, who, "while within the age limit and an officer of the 75th regiment, had steered clear of enlistment and the MSA and only 'smelled powder' on the plains of Aldershot when blank cartridges were exploded." A "pretty pair to cast aspersions" on Major Margeson, "who DID 'smell powder' on several battlefields in France" and was vice-president of the Great War Veterans' Association of Canada. Margeson could "wipe the floor" with either Duff or Kinley, charged the *Bulletin*.

Major Margeson had returned from overseas in 1917, became head of the Pay and Allowance Board of the Department of Militia and Defence in Ottawa, and was promoted to lieutenant colonel in 1918. In a letter to the editor of the *Bulletin*, published on January 5, 1919, Margeson declared that the bitterness of the past should be forgotten and there should be a united effort to build up the country and its institutions on a stronger and firmer basis than ever. Despite these noble thoughts, he went on to complain that "it must be a source of shame and regret to all of us to recall that certain young, single men within our County, who had worn the King's uniform in times of peace, did not rise to their duty or to their promise of allegiance when in 1914 war rushed down on the whole world." He had not been wrong to support the Union government in 1917 (he had lost to Duff in that election), and conscription had been the only honourable course possible to strengthen the hands of the men who had been sent overseas. Margeson concluded: "Our County is almost unique in its war history. It is one of the few points in Canada visited by German submarines. Let us be thankful they did no more harm."

In May 1919, a heated exchange took place in the House of Commons in Ottawa between Lunenburg MP William Duff and Charles Colquhoun Ballantyne, the minister of naval service. Duff had charged the department with inefficiency and blundering and had cast ridicule upon it, charging that the government had wasted money on the purchase of a lot of utterly useless small boats. Ballantyne, mightily offended, replied that "the men of our patrol service served on small trawlers and drifters in all kinds of weather and deserve as much commendation as our gallant soldiers who fought in the trenches in France." Duff also claimed that "at the time the oil-tanker *Luz Blanca* was sunk several miles from the gas buoy off Halifax the naval officials at Halifax were holding a pink tea and playing bridge whist." This was "unfair and inaccurate," retorted Ballantyne, hoping that Duff was "not taking anything stronger than pink tea"; it was fog that had prevented the patrol vessels getting to the *Luz Blanca*. There may have been a fog in Ottawa, countered Duff, and if so it was around the naval department, but he would "wager $1,000 there was none off Halifax that day."

He also alleged that while a submarine was off the coast, the *Lady Evelyn*, one of the RCN's patrol boats, had been sent to the Magdalen Islands with six lead pencils. And he maintained the *Mont Blanc* should never have been allowed to come up into Halifax Harbour. In response to sneers about his knowledge of marine affairs, Duff, who had come into this world in Carbonear, Newfoundland, and had lived most of his life in Lunenburg—the principal banks fishing port on Canada's east coast—insisted that he knew more about the sea than a gentleman born in Montreal. "I was born with the smell of salt spray in my nostrils and have been familiar with the sea ever since I could toddle."[5]

Lunenburg County, in the riding of Queens–Lunenburg, finally elected a Conservative in September 1926: W. G. Ernst, "a young, able representative in favour of Maritime Rights," according to the *Bulletin* on the twenty-first, and his election "wipes out the stigma which has attached to Lunenburg County since the 6th of December 1917." Duff had never been a popular candidate, insisted the paper; he was the party's choice back in 1915 when no one else would accept the nomination, but when the election came in 1917 the exigencies of war made the MSA a necessity, and its unpopularity in Lunenburg gave Duff an easy victory. Now, at last, the county was lined up with the rest of the province.

Sadly for the Conservatives, however, Mackenzie King's Liberals won the 1926 election. Although defeated, Duff was still high in the councils of the party in power, claimed the *Progress-Enterprise* on the twenty-second, and having the patronage of the riding he would continue to direct affairs from a federal standpoint. And he would "no doubt receive recognition by being appointed to some honorable and useful sphere of service." Duff would go on to represent the riding of Antigonish-Guysborough from 1927 to 1936, and thereafter he spent his final years in politics in the comfort of the Senate. During his time there, he arranged to have Lunenburg sauerkraut featured on the menu in the parliamentary restaurant. Years later, two Lunenburg mariners were overheard reminiscing about the sauerkraut they had packed and shipped off to Duff in Ottawa. Carefully concealed in the middle of each barrel was a keg of black rum.[6]

A curious event of a political nature took place in the town of Lunenburg on March 14, 1937, a day "unique in the history of the town...when sons of Lunenburg, Nova Scotia, entertained sons of Lunenburg, Germany." Having been born in the German town and believing that the ancestors of the Lunenburg Germans came from the same district, Captain Thilo von Seebach of the German cadet training ship *Schlesien*, while at anchor in Halifax Harbour, expressed a desire to see the Nova Scotia town of the same name. Thus he, eleven of his officers, and the acting German consul general were invited to Lunenburg by the town council. On their arrival, along with Mayor Arthur W. Schwartz and town clerk L.W. Geldert who had gone to Halifax to accompany them down, the "honored visitors" were given a civic welcome at the town hall. Leaving the courthouse, they viewed the soldiers' monument, where Captain Seebach recognized familiar names. "Germans Give Nazi Salute to Lunenburg Cenotaph," read one of the headlines in the *Progress-Enterprise*. After a banquet given by the town council at the Hotel Ich Dien, there was a public reception when many citizens took advantage of the affair to extend a welcome to the party. The visitors were then taken on a tour of the town's main sights, including the *Bluenose*, and gifts were exchanged.

When the Second World War began almost two and a half years later, Mayor Schwartz was upset that he still had the German flag he had been given on that occasion and he feared, according to his grand-nephew Eugene Schwartz,[7] that German infiltrators would attempt to brainwash him to fight for the Reich. He went out one night in his back yard with his neighbour, Theophilus "Offie" Nauss, and together they burned the flag in an oil drum while singing "O Canada."

A letter in the *Progress-Enterprise* on October 9, 1946, from Herman Rhode, clerk of the law court in Lüneburg, Germany, to the mayor of Lunenburg, provides a sad postscript to this story. Rhode had found in the city library a copy of *History of the County of Lunenburg*, with the dedication: "To the Mayor of the City of Lunenburg with the Compliments of A. W. Schwartz, Mayor, Town of Lunenburg, Nova Scotia, November 20, 1937." Evidently, Rhode realized, there had been connections between the two towns ten years previously. So he had the idea to write this letter. Given the distress of Germany following the war and the dire privation his officials and their families were living under, he wondered if the officials in Lunenburg's "court" would be prepared to take care of his court until the worst was over. "To ask," he wrote, "is harder than to give."

The war had lasted four long years, and during that time many men from Lunenburg County had given their lives in the struggle. Although each one of them deserves to have his story told, we have been able to meet only a few of them in these pages. But it was now time for those at home to honour the memory of those who had made the ultimate sacrifice. At a special meeting of the town council in Lunenburg on July 11, 1919, it was decided that the best way to honour the fallen soldiers would be to endeavour to build a memorial hospital, provided sufficient funds could be subscribed and collected. Such a building would be a lasting memorial, and the names of all the men who had enlisted would be suitably engraved in the building. The Fishermen's Memorial Hospital did eventually come to pass, and it was officially opened in July 1952.

On December 26, 1919, a "Banquet and Presentation" at the Oddfellows' Hall was "Tendered to Our Returned Soldiers by the Citizens of Luneburg." Each of the two hundred men present received a pair of cufflinks from the Boscawen Chapter of the IODE and a certificate of "Public Recognition" from the town, signed by Mayor Duff, expressing "the gratitude and thanks of the Citizens of Lunenburg... in recognition of your Patriotic Spirit and Noble Sacrifice in voluntarily serving your Country...for the preservation of honour amongst nations, the rights of humanity and the freedom of the World." And in November 1920 a memorial tablet, the gift of the local IODE, was unveiled in the assembly hall of the Lunenburg Academy in memory of the twenty "Lunenburg School Boys who gave their lives in the Great War."

In June 1921, the 168th anniversary of the landing of the first settlers, the Lunenburg war memorial was unveiled on a commanding site on Bunker Hill, between the courthouse and the bandstand. The day began with an 8:00 AM firing of a general salute from the Lunenburg Foundry's yards. The ceremony commenced at 3:30 PM with Mayor Duff's opening address, followed by the singing of "Onward Christian Soldiers." After scriptural readings and prayers, Captain Rev. A. J. MacDonald of Bridgewater, formerly of Lunenburg and chaplain of the 85th Battalion, was the speaker of the day, and he "spoke feelingly of the heroic conduct of the boys who fought, bled and died, so that the principles of civilization, righteousness, and truth should reign instead of might is right." Veterans Charles Hebb and Ivan Schnare unveiled the monument. Soldiers then presented arms and fired a *feu de joie*, and the "Last Post" was sounded by Fred Rodenhizer. The band played "God Be with You Till We Meet Again." Wreaths were laid at the base of the monument and hundreds of schoolchildren marched around the memorial, each depositing a bouquet of flowers. The *Progress-Enterprise* of June 8 estimated there were at least 2,500 people present for the occasion. During an open-air concert in the evening, the Women's Institute sold ice cream for the benefit of the band.

The central figure in the monument is an infantry soldier, looking toward the east and the comrades who were left behind. Three sides portray the names of thirty-seven men who died in the war, and on the fourth side are the first nine lines of "In Flanders Fields." The inscription on the base declares that the monument was erected by the citizens of the town to "the Honoured Memory of the Heroes named Hereon Who Gave their Lives for King and Country and in Honour of the Gallant Soldiers from This Town and Vicinity Who Served So Valiantly in the Great War, 1914–1918." The names of four prominent battles in which local soldiers lost their lives—Ypres 1915, Somme 1916, Vimy 1917, and Passchendaele 1918—are inscribed at the bottoms of the four sides. Finally, there are the Latin words: "*Dulce et Decorum est pro Patria Mori*," from Horace ("It is sweet and proper to die for one's country").

On the war memorial in Chester there are fifty-four names, twenty each from Chester and New Ross, and the rest from Blandford, Mill Cove, Chester Basin, and Gold River. At the brief ceremony on August 4, 1922, the statue in the form of a Nova Scotia Highland soldier was unveiled by two returned soldiers, Ralph E. Hennigar

The war memorial in Chester.

and Karl Mills, "both of whom bore on their bodies, honourable scars, inflicted in battle." The memorial was "more than mere stone and bronze, but a symbol of the sacrifice made that their kinfolk might retain their liberty." A panoramic photograph in the Royal Canadian Legion in Chester reveals the huge crowd in attendance, along with many of the splendid automobiles of the time.

The "stone of remembrance" in Mahone Bay, topped by a Celtic cross, was unveiled by Lieutenant Governor MacCallum Grant on May 24, 1923, and was erected in loving memory of the brave men who laid down their lives in the Great War for "Truth Justice Liberty." Its "massive rough-hewn base," it was said, "reminds us of the strong and hardy character of Nova Scotia's sons."[8] In *Death So Noble*, Jonathan Vance notes that the inscriptions Canadian communities chose for their monuments and war memorials frequently affirmed that the war had been fought "for civilization, humanity, or ideals like Liberty, Truth, Justice, Honour, Mercy or Freedom."

According to an article by Robert Hirtle in Lunenburg County's *Progress Bulletin* of November 19, 2014, the cenotaph at New Ross is believed to be the oldest in Nova Scotia and possibly in Canada. Erected in 1917 to commemorate the centennial of the settling of the community, a year before the cessation of hostilities, the memorial lists the names of the volunteers for overseas.

Unveiling the Chester war memorial, August 4, 1922.

On April 19, 1919, William E. Marshall spoke at a memorial service for Bridgewater soldiers, according to Vance in *Death So Noble*: "Who are we that we should pretend to stand before these saviours? Verily, these whom we reverence, our soldier-dead, are greater than us.... They had suddenly become as gods....[At] calvary places in France, Flanders and England, [they] gave us their mortal lives, and are among the great saviours of mankind." Bridgewater's cenotaph on Victoria Road was officially unveiled on a fine day before a large crowd at Brookside Cemetery on September 6, 1926. It was dedicated to "the honour and memory of the brave men and nurses from Bridgewater and New Dublin Township who paid the supreme sacrifice in the Great War. Their Name Liveth for Evermore." There are sixty-six soldiers listed on the sides of the tall shaft of white granite, plus two nurses, Nursing Sisters Adruenna Tupper and Rebecca MacIntosh.

The Liverpool band, reported the *Bulletin*, led a squad of returned soldiers to the grounds. Mrs. Carrie Dauphinee unveiled the monument and Captain W. G. Ernst read the names of the dead. The Hon. (Captain) J. F. Cahan, himself a wounded soldier, gave the address, "a masterpiece of oratory, deeply sympathetic, couched in beautiful sentiment and pathos which brought tears to the eyes of many present." The *Bulletin* on September 7 reported that there was apparently some controversy surrounding the monument: "While many of the citizens

of this town are not in favour of the location of the memorial and not satisfied with the form the memorial has taken, nevertheless the matter is settled and we must all bow to the inevitable and make the best of it."

A grand event occurred in France ten years later, when, on July 26, 1936, King Edward VIII, soon to abdicate, dedicated Canada's national war memorial at Vimy Ridge. "Enfolding flags released at the touch of a king's hand," related the *Progress-Enterprise* on the twenty-ninth, "disclosed to the world...the white stone symbol of Canada's sorrow and honor and remembrance. On this battle-pocked ridge of Vimy— its scars healed now by the immortality of grass—King Edward VIII stood in the presence of rapt Canadian veterans...to dedicate the stately monument to those other thousands who sleep in the encircling plains." The paper went on to describe the thousands "who stood with faces upturned to the sun toward...the woman who is Canada, brooding over dead sons who lie in a foreign field." A hundred thousand people apparently blackened the crest of Vimy Ridge at the dedication of Walter Allward's magnificent sculpture: thousands of veterans and French soldiers and citizens, and high dignitaries, including King Edward and the president of France Albert Lebrun, as well as Ernest Lapointe representing the Canadian government, and C. G. "Chubby" Power, who read a message from Prime Minister William Lyon Mackenzie King.

It was "a spectacle whose magnitude was without precedent," wrote Lunenburg County's John J. E. Risser of Riverport, who took part in the Vimy Memorial Pilgrimage Tour and published a long account of his trip in the *Bridgewater Bulletin* in September 1936.[9] Veterans' organizations had begun to spring up during the war, the largest being the Great War Veterans' Association founded in 1917. The Canadian Legion was formed in Winnipeg in 1925 by a merger of the GWVA with some other groups. The Bridgewater branch was formed in 1927, Lunenburg the following year, with other branches of the legion scattered around the county, including in Mahone Bay, Chester, Chester Basin, and New Ross. Apart from erecting legion halls across the country, perhaps one of the grandest accomplishments of the legion was the organization of the Vimy pilgrimage tour. Over six thousand pilgrims departed from Montreal on July 16, 1936, sailing across the Atlantic in a convoy of boats as the troops had done a couple of decades earlier. The *Gazette* of Montreal described the crossing as "the greatest peacetime sailing mission in the history of Canada."

John Risser, who travelled over on the CPR transatlantic liner *Montrose*, does not say all that much about the dedication ceremony itself, but he described his travels around Britain and France in great detail, the highlights being the "monster" garden party at Buckingham Palace, given on the grounds by the Duke and Duchess of Gloucester, and a grand luncheon at the Hôtel des Invalides in Paris, presided over by Marshal Pétain. At the other end of the scale was an encounter one evening in London, after spending a short time in the reading room of the YMCA, with "some Mrs. Simpson" (presumably not *that* Mrs. Simpson). The lady had asked, "Will you give me a drink tonight?" and she was apparently "some surprised" when Risser replied that he was too busy. Always the innocent abroad, he wondered if it had been a case of mistaken identity.

Ian McKay and Jamie Swift in *The Vimy Trap* suggest that the Vimy memorial underwent a transformation, becoming not Walter Allward's "sermon against war" or the peace monument many thought it was in 1936, but a war memorial paying tribute to Canada's soldiers, "a cathedral-like monument to Canadian valour."

On December 26, 1923, a fishing schooner sailed out of Lunenburg harbour. The *Keno*, recently built at the John McLean & Sons shipyard in Mahone Bay, was bound for Louisbourg, Cape Breton, and then on to Bay of Islands in Newfoundland to load frozen herring for bait. The captain, Albert Himmelman, had had the vessel built to compete against Captain Angus Walters and the *Bluenose*. In his schooner *Independence*, Captain Himmelman had raced against *Bluenose* in 1921, hoping to be the Canadian entry in the international fishermen's races.

The *Bluenose* won and had gone up against the American contender *Elsie* out of Gloucester that year. Himmelman supported Angus and sailed with him against the *Henry Ford* in 1922 and the *Columbia* a year later, but he was planning a faster schooner of his own. The *Keno* fished during the 1923 season to be eligible to enter the international contest the following year.

Captain Himmelman, age fifty-one, a widower and father of seven grown-up children, lived in Lunenburg. A rather overblown account in the *Lunenburg Argus* of January 31, 1924, paints a portrait of the captain as a paragon.[10] He was a "fine, big hearted, big handed specimen of a fisherman, six foot something in his socks, weighing close on two hundred, and without an ounce of superfluous flesh." He was "as light and active as the nimblest member of the fore gafftopsail shift in the racing schooner." Wearing a checked mackinaw of green-and-black cardigan, "always the most conspicuous object in a turbulent seascape," he was "essentially picturesque." He reportedly had only one inspiring expletive, "Hell's flames." A better sail-dragger than "Long Albert" Himmelman "never pulled on seaboots.... They had a proverb on the Banks: 'When Albert Himmelman turns back the gulls hide under the water.'"

Keno's passage from Lunenburg to Louisbourg was said to be "the fastest ever made by such a vessel in the memory of living man." But there was no word of her after leaving Louisbourg on December 31. Neither schooner nor crew was ever heard from again.

Apart from Captain Himmelman, the crew consisted of the mate John Wilcox, a native of Newfoundland who had married a daughter of Lunenburger Charles Oxner; the cook Gabriel Lohnes, who left behind a large family; and seamen Gabriel Demone from First Peninsula; Raymond Zinck from Blandford; and Heber Miller, Wesley Whynacht, and Aubrey J. Knickle from Stonehurst. "Halt the 'Humph!' if you feel one coming, at this list of names," cautioned the writer in the *Argus*. "These good Canadians are as British as the British Royal Family," he insisted, reacting to comments that had come out of Gloucester during the controversial races in 1923. "The Himmelmans and other original Hanoverians have been in Nova Scotia since 1753.

They were in the Great War three years before that nation which was too proud to fight. Americans need not be proud of having falsely called Albert Himmelman and the Lunenburg heroes 'squareheads' in the heat of the *Bluenose–Columbia* controversy. Canadians will not fall into the same error."

Once again, then, even after the war, the point was made that the Germans of Lunenburg County had as much right to be considered good British subjects as the king himself. The two men who so vociferously protested at the time of the war that the people, despite their origins, were loyal British subjects and not in any way connected to the Germany of the day, were themselves not directly descended from the county's founders. Judge S. A. Chesley and William Duff, born in New Brunswick and Newfoundland respectively, in their potted and sometimes less than accurate histories of the county, were not necessarily speaking for the whole community, but at the same time they likely did reflect widely held sentiments.

One man of German extraction who died during the war was Henry Klinkworth, who had arrived a century after the founders landed on the shores of the bay in 1753. Born in Schleswig-Holstein in December 1828, he settled at Upper LaHave in 1856 and took part in the gold rush at the Ovens on Lunenburg Bay in 1861. He died during the war, on May 10, 1917, and is buried at Rhodes Corner in the Silver Cemetery, located in a cow pasture on the road between Lunenburg and Bridgewater. Perhaps sensitive to his origins in a world at war, on his tombstone it proudly states: "He Was a Loyal Citizen of Canada for over 60 Yrs."

A more tragic story concerns a man who had long been closely connected with the commercial, civic, and political life of the town of Lunenburg. Augustus J. Wolff, born in 1844 on the island of Rügen, off the coast of Pomerania in Prussia, took to the sea as a young man. He turned up in Lunenburg County in 1869 as first mate aboard the barque *Mary*. In Bridgewater he worked with several prominent businessmen building vessels to be used in freighting, and after moving to Lunenburg in 1881 he acted as broker for several insurance companies, including the Lunenburg Marine Insurance Company. For many years he sailed his favourite barque, the *St. Kilda*, built for him in 1879. He married a local woman from West Dublin. On the town's incorporation in 1888 he became Lunenburg's first mayor and served for several terms thereafter before the war. He was "an ardent adherent to all the tenets of Free Masonry," filling the office of master of Unity Lodge No. 4 of Lunenburg, and was elected grand master of the Grand Lodge of Nova Scotia in 1911.

On December 10, 1918, the *Bulletin* announced the "shocking news" that Captain A. J. Wolff of Lunenburg, the day before, had committed suicide. He had been ill for some time, the paper explained, and no doubt the act was committed while he was insane. Captain Wolff

Augustus Wolff in his lodge regalia.

was a "good citizen and a genial, kindly man who was respected and cordially liked by a very large circle of friends," according to the *Progress-Enterprise* on December 11. For the last four years, said the *Bulletin* on the twenty-fourth, he had assisted with the Patriotic Fund, the Red Cross, and all other organizations that were helping the soldiers at the front.

There is no factual account of what happened, just stories around town. According to Ralph Getson, former curator at the Fisheries Museum of the Atlantic, Wolff apparently died in his oak-rimmed, copper bathtub in his house on the corner of King and Lincoln Streets in Lunenburg. Throughout the war he had felt harassed, rumoured to be a German sympathizer. He had given so much and was hurt by the smear campaign. He was a clever man, and the stress of being of Prussian origin during the war "just worked on him." Early in the war, in February 1915, as we have seen, Wolff had "emphatically" declared himself, though born in Prussia, to be a true British subject. Since he felt so strongly, he would not have taken lightly any aspersions about his loyalty.

Both of these men were immigrants from Germany, and their loyalty to their new country is obvious, then and now. It was different, however, to be a descendant of Germans who had arrived in Lunenburg County a century and a half earlier. Few still spoke German, and over the generations they had married people of different ethnic origins. Gertrud Waseem, long-time professor of German at Acadia University, in her book *Germans* comments that the war "broke the last tenuous hold of their particular German dialect, although this survived, in a few cases, in some small villages and isolated farms."

Ralph Getson, descended from original settlers on both sides of his family, thinks that the Lunenburg Germans at the time had no particular feelings for, or ties to, the fatherland. Germany was not a unified country when they left, and they had never gone back. In the beginning they did not want people at home to know how poorly off they were, and later, when they prospered, they did not want others to come. The German scholar Heinz Lehmann, who in the 1930s studied the Germans in Canada, believed that the Lunenburg people "could no longer be characterized ethnically as a German community," though they gave their origin as German in the census. Like some other historians, he suggested that the number of people claiming German origin in Lunenburg County and elsewhere in the 1921 census had apparently declined since the previous pre-war census.[11] He put this down to their anglicization and the "English war propaganda" that made them "ashamed of their German descent."

It says much about the nature of the community during the war that on September 25, 1918, the *Progress-Enterprise* asked why German was being taught in the Lunenburg high school. A query often put, apparently. The prevailing attitude seemed to be that it would be more useful to teach English to the Germans in Germany. Teaching young people to speak their own language fluently and correctly, declared the Lunenburg paper, was "far more to the point than a smattering of German which can figure little in any practical way in their future lives."

In later years, some would no doubt come to see the war as a senseless slaughter, "a conflict of pointless carnage," or as a divisive event that had fractured Canadian society "along linguistic, regional, class, ethnic, and cultural lines."[12] But the people of German descent in Lunenburg County may have supported the war effort because at the time it was generally considered to be a just cause. In the words of Prime Minister Borden, "We went to war to ensure the integrity and maintain the honour of our Empire." Patriotism, a sense of duty, doing one's bit for king and country, was a powerful force.

The people of Lunenburg County likely reacted to the war very much like other Canadians, by making what contributions they could to the cause, and fearing for their men at the front. A man living near Bridgewater, interviewed by Laurie Lacey for his 1982 study of the community, claimed that people in the county had "as much disdain for the Germans as people anywhere had....[M]y heritage is German on both sides of the family and I'm proud of it, but my ancestors came over here a long time ago—my loyalty is with my own country."

Perhaps it's reasonable to suppose that most Lunenburgers of German descent by the time of the First World War simply thought of themselves as Canadian, which can be seen as a positive development, but not at all a rejection of their German heritage.

ACKNOWLEDGEMENTS

It will be obvious to all that my main sources for this book have been the two splendidly cantankerous and rival Lunenburg County newspapers, the *Bridgewater Bulletin* and the *Progress-Enterprise* of Lunenburg. Their words have been harvested frequently, for it is hard to improve on their colourful language. Newspapers do not always get the facts straight, for they are produced as events unfold, in the heat of the moment, but they do capture the flavour and the spirit of the times. In the period covered here, they reflect the popular obsession with the war and shed light on many of the concerns and attitudes of the people on the home front. These newspapers, and the *Canadian Fisherman*, were read on microfilm at the Fisheries Museum of the Atlantic in Lunenburg.

Above all, I must thank my friend Ralph Getson of Upper LaHave, who has been with me from the beginning of this project, helping in so many ways, by pointing me to sources, by finding useful images, and by reading and commenting on the chapters as they emerged. As former curator of education at the Fisheries Museum of the Atlantic, Ralph is generously willing to share his incredible knowledge of the history of Lunenburg County. He is a natural, and first-rate, storyteller, and he provided me with many entertaining "stories around town."

Stephen Ernst, former sergeant-at-arms at the Royal Canadian Legion Branch no. 23 in Lunenburg, also kindly read the manuscript. He provided invaluable and expert help with the images, as one would expect from the proprietor of S. A. Ernst Photography. As well, Libby Oughton of Windsor, Nova Scotia, read the manuscript with her practiced publisher's eye and made many thoughtful comments. Thank you to Jennifer James of Rose Bay, who provided me with the photo of, and stories about, her great-grandmother, Ada Louise Powers. Lyne Allain, manager and curator of the Mahone Bay Museum, made me welcome, as did Donna Massey at the Royal Canadian Legion in Bridgewater, and others at the legions in Chester and Mahone Bay.

Once again, as for my previous book, *The August Gales*, Lunenburg artist Jay Langford has created a spectacular painting to adorn the cover. No one paints water like Jay does!

At the Lunenburg branch of the South Shore Public Libraries, I would like to thank Barbara Himmelman and her colleagues, who acquired many of the books I needed through interlibrary loans. In Halifax, many books were read at the Killam Memorial Library at Dalhousie University and the Halifax newspapers were read on microfilm at the Nova Scotia Archives. The book is primarily about the county on the home front, but the personnel records of the soldiers at Library and Archives Canada provided details about many of the men from Lunenburg County who served overseas.

At Nimbus, I have enjoyed working with managing editor Whitney Moran and with non-fiction editor Angela Mombourquette. Paula Sarson improved the manuscript with her fine editing, and it was a pleasure to work with her once again. Any shortcoming or errors that remain are of course my responsibility.

Last, but never least, Michael Browne. He said I'd write this book. I only wish he was still here to read it.

NOTES

*   Thanks to Ralph Getson, Upper LaHave, for the story of Mr. and
Mrs. Jacob Zinck.

†   The "Lunenburg Song," also given to me by Ralph Getson, was
written by William T. Lindsay (1863–1939) sometime before the
war. Lindsay lived on a farm on the outskirts of town. Though born
in Lunenburg, he was of Scottish descent (his father was born in
Castle Douglas). He was apparently Lunenburg's first town clerk
in 1888 and was secretary and manager of the Lunenburg Iron
Company in 1891.

Natalie Corkum of Lunenburg, who died in January 2017 at
the grand age of 101, related to Stephen Ernst that, when she
was about four years old and living near the Lindsay farm, the
Spanish influenza struck Lunenburg. The ground in that winter of
1918–1919 was too cold to dig graves, and so bodies were stored
in Lindsay's barn until they could be buried with the spring thaw.
Thereafter, Lindsay tore down the barn and built a new one.

There are echoes in the Lunenburg song of the well-known
1910 toast at the Holy Cross College alumni dinner to "good old
Boston": "The home of the bean and the cod. / Where the Lowells
talk only to Cabots, / And the Cabots talk only to God."

CHAPTER 1. "THE GREAT BROIL ACROSS THE SEA"

1   Romkey Memoirs, *Progress-Enterprise*, February 27, 1974, in the Fisheries Museum of the Atlantic files.

2   Granatstein and Hitsman, *Broken Promises*. Cook in *Clio's Warriors* points out that more than 70 per cent of the men in the First Contingent were British born, though many had been living in Canada for decades. By the end of the war, only a little more than 50 per cent of the force was Canadian born.

3   Tennyson in *Nova Scotia at War* notes that such ads, using military and patriotic terms, were clever but they reflected the naïve innocence of August 1914; later they would be regarded as tasteless. Prince, in his PhD dissertation "The Mythology of War," observes that military metaphors permeated the text of advertisements. For example, the human body was "often metaphorically depicted as a battlefield in ads for products which claimed to promote better health."

4   Sangster, "Mobilizing Women for War."

5   George II was indeed the elector of Hanover, and duke of Braunschweig-Lunëburg, but according to Winthrop Pickard Bell in *The "Foreign Protestants" and the Settlement of Nova Scotia*, few if any of the original settlers of Lunenburg came from that area. Rather, they mainly came from southwestern Germany, Württemberg, and the Palatinate.

CHAPTER 2. MANLY MEN AND FORMIDABLE WOMEN

1   In Ontario, rural recruiting leagues used voters' lists and asked schoolteachers to supply the names, addresses, and ages of all men residing in the school section. Wilson, *Ontario and the First World War*.

2   Granatstein and Hitsman, *Broken Promises*.

3   Mackenzie, "Eastern Approaches," from *Weekly Courier*, Digby, September 8, 1916.

4   Davis, "I'll Drink to That"; McKay, "The 1910s."

5   Bliss, "The Methodist Church and World War 1."

CHAPTER 3. SERVING AT HOME AND OVERSEAS

1   Brown, *Robert Laird Borden*, vol. 2.

2   Shaw, "Expanding the Narrative."

3   Epperly in *The Fragrance of Sweet-Grass* contends that *Rilla of Ingleside* "is an authentic war novel, Canada's only contemporary fictionalized woman's account of the First World War."

4   Rubio and Waterston, eds., *The Selected Journals of L.M. Montgomery.*

5   Mann, ed., *The War Diary of Clare Gass.*

6   Linda J. Quiney, "Gendering Patriotism."

7   MacDonald, "Hidden Costs, Hidden Labour."

8   Cleverdon, *Woman Suffrage Movement.*

9   Warsh, "John Barleycorn Must Die" in Warsh, ed., *Drink in Canada.*

10   MacDonald, "Mary Russell Chesley"; and MacDonald, "Hidden Costs, Hidden Labour."

11   Canada. House of Commons, *Debates,* February 28, 1916.

12   Brown, *Robert Laird Borden,* vol. 2.

13   Rubio and Waterston, eds. *The Selected Journals of L.M. Montgomery.*

14   Brown and Cook, *Canada, 1896–1921;* and MacMillan, *The War That Ended the Peace.*

15   Written by R. W. Lillard and published in the *New York Evening Post,* printed in the *Halifax Herald,* August 8, 1918, and in the *Progress-Enterprise,* November 20, 1918.

16   Armstrong, *Halifax Explosion and the Royal Canadian Navy.*

17   The *Kölnische Zeitung* quotation also appeared in the *Halifax Herald,* in early January 1918. See Kitz, *Shattered City.*

18   The name was spelled in the records and in the press variably as both Cossman and, the more usual spelling, Cossmann. Originally on the attestation paper, before correction, the name was even spelled Crossman. There are many soldiers with the spelling Cosman in the records, but no Charles or C. A. Cosman. Cossmann is buried in the Chester Farm Cemetery in Belgium.

CHAPTER 4. "HOW WOULD THE KAISER VOTE?"

1   Wilson, *Ontario and the First World War.*

2   Granatstein and Hitsman, *Broken Promises.*

3   Brown and Loveridge, "Unrequited Faith"; and Brown, *Robert Laird Borden,* vol. 2.

4   Morton and Granatstein, *Marching to Armageddon;* and Shaw, *Crisis of Conscience.*

5   Beck is also quoted in the Mackenzie article. Nationally, according to Brown and Cook in *Canada, 1896–1921,* Liberals won 62 in Quebec; 10 of 28 in the Maritimes; 8 of 82 in Ontario; and 2 of 57 in the west. The Unionists won 153 constituencies nationwide, only 3 seats in Quebec. The country was politically divided along cultural lines. But, as McKay and Swift point out in *The Vimy Trap,* the debate over conscription was

"not reducible to a squabble between English and French Canadians." Civilians in Prince Edward Island, Nova Scotia, Quebec, and the Yukon voted against the Union government, and countrywide the conscriptionist majority was not that large. The soldiers' vote, however, was overwhelmingly in favour of the government.

6   Mainville, *Till the Boys Come Home.*

7   McKay, "The 1910s."

8   Tennyson points out in *Canada's Great War* that the opposition to conscription among those likely to be conscripted was almost as great in English Canada as it was in Quebec; after going through the appeals process, the exemption rate in Quebec was 9 per cent but in Ontario—so vociferous in proclaiming its loyalty and denouncing the French—the rate was 8.2 per cent, not a significant difference.

CHAPTER 5. A "NEAR RIOT," SUBMARINES, AND SPIES

1   At least a dozen of the fishermen in the Lunenburg fleet who had been conscripted under the MSA perished when their vessels sank during the fierce storms of the mid-1920s. For an account of their fate, see Hallowell, *The August Gales.*

2   As to why the police had been sent to Lunenburg looking for defaulters, Tennyson speculates in *Nova Scotia at War*: "Whether this was motivated by the fact that the community had a high default rate, or because most people there were of German ancestry, or because they had elected an anti-conscription Member of Parliament in the recent election, is unknown."

3   Morton and Granatstein, *Marching to Armageddon.*

4   Davis, "Of War and Remembrance."

5   Granatstein, *Greatest Victory;* and Cook, *Shock Troops.*

6   Hadley, *U-Boats against Canada.*

7   An opera based on the story of the fourteen nursing sisters who perished on the *Llandovery Castle* premiered at the Calvin Presbyterian Church in Toronto on June 26, 2018; produced in conjunction with the Bicycle Opera Project, music was by Stephanie Martin, libretto by Paul Ciufo.

8   Hadley, *U-Boats against Canada.* Earlier, on July 21, U-156 had fired on the town of Orleans on Cape Cod, the only military attack on American soil during the First World War. Commander Tony German in *The Sea Is at Our Gates* claims that twenty-eight vessels were sunk in Canadian waters in a little over a month, nineteen of them by U-156. He goes on to say, "But twenty-three were fishing vessels"; only the *Luz Blanca* was significant "in the scheme of the war." He does not give details of these losses.

9   According to Captain Matthew Mitchell in 1998. The *Progress-Enterprise* of October 16, 1941, writing at the time of Captain Mack's death, said that he was born in Leba, Germany, now a town in Pomerania, Poland. He became a British subject in 1899, and that year also became master of his first vessel, a square-rigger. He sailed vessels for W. C. Smith & Company for twenty-two years before retiring in 1934.

10   Armstrong, *Halifax Explosion and the Royal Canadian Navy.*

11   Hadley and Sarty, *Tin-Pots and Pirate Ships.*

12   In various sources, the name of the captain of *Elsie Porter* was given as Richard Eisenhauer, Irvin Eisenhauer, Edward Eisenhaur, Irving Isnor, Dickey Eisener, Captain Eisnor, and Capt. Isoner!

13   Wilson, *Ontario and the First World War.*

14   Gimblett, *Naval Service of Canada.*

15   The Navy League of Bridgewater, according to the *Bulletin* of December 24, 1918, had just sent to Halifax a very suitable Christmas gift for the sailors calling at that port: "26 kit bags, 10 x 12 inches, made of navy blue duck, and containing a pair of socks, muffler, briar pipe, box of matches, handkerchief, book, housewife, steel mirror, writing pad, package of envelopes, pencil, puzzle or cards, Santa Claus, two packages of tobacco and two boxes of chocolate." The work had been carried out by "a very efficient committee of young lady members of the League," which collected the funds, made the bags, and filled them, and the "Young Ladies' Reading Club very generously contributed all the socks."

CHAPTER 6. "WITH VICTORY SO NEAR"

1   Morton, "Supporting Soldiers' Families"; and Morton, *Fight or Pay.*

2   Morton, "Supporting Soldiers' Wives and Families in the Great War"; and Bowker, *A Time Such as There Never Was Before.*

3   Morton, *Fight or Pay.*

4   Janigan, "Treason to Their Memory."

5   Dr. Marble, chair of the Medical History Society of Nova Scotia, provided me with these statistics from the *Journal of the Nova Scotia House of Assembly,* 1920, Appendix 25.

6   Jennifer Hoegg, "Historic Pandemic: Nova Scotia and the 1918 flu," *Valley Journal Advertiser,* October 27, 2009 (Press Reader online); Dr Marble was addressing the Wolfville Historical Society.

7   Wartime Heritage Association, Yarmouth.

CHAPTER 7. "THE DAWN OF PEACE"

1   MacDonald and Gardiner, *Twenty-Fifth Battalion.*

2   Bowker, *A Time Such as There Never Was Before.*

3   Mackenzie, *Canada and the First World War*, Sangster "Divided on the Home Front"; and Morton, "Supporting Soldiers' Families."

4   Forbes, "The East-Coast Rum-Running Economy."

5   House of Commons, *Debates*, May 26, 1919.

6   Story told to the author by Ralph Getson, January 2019.

7   As told to Ralph Getson, October 23, 2002.

8   Descriptions of the Mahone Bay and Chester memorials are from "'We Will Remember': War Memorials in Canada." See also Vance, "Remembering Armageddon."

9   Risser, "Scrapbook Notes on Vimy Memorial Pilgrimage Tour, by a Member of the Party," *Bulletin*, September 3, 1936, and various issues thereafter. Nova Scotia Archives, MG1.791.

10 The same item appears in the *Progress-Enterprise* of January 30, 1924, with the name "C. H. J. Snider, Toronto Telegram," within parentheses, which suggests that Snider wrote it.

11 See also McLaughlin, *Germans in Canada*, who maintains that the German population in Nova Scotia after the war suddenly decreased by ten thousand, or more than 30 per cent. The 1921 census in fact presents a problem: the column under the heading "Race or Tribal Origin" is largely unreadable for most of the Lunenburg County Germans, especially in Lunenburg town and neighbouring areas. To me, it appears that "English" was written in first and then that word was stroked out and "German" written over it. Who made these changes, when, and why? Whoever digitized the census claimed all these people to be "English." Some people obviously of German origin, notably in Maders Cove, claimed to be "Dutch," but at least in Mahone Bay the people with Lunenburg County German names were clearly identified as of German descent. Given the state of the census, I believe it is impossible, even with closer study, to determine how many people changed their ethnic origin from German to English, or not.

12 Cook, "Battles of the Imagined Past."

BIBLIOGRAPHY

Armstrong, John Griffith. *The Halifax Explosion and the Royal Canadian Navy: Inquiry and Intrigue.* Vancouver: UBC Press, 2002.

Bell, Winthrop Pickard. *The "Foreign Protestants" and the Settlement of Nova Scotia.* Toronto: University of Toronto Press, 1961.

Betts, Amanda, ed. *In Flanders Fields: 100 Years.* Toronto: Alfred A. Knopf Canada, 2015.

Bird, Michael J. *The Town That Died.* Toronto: McGraw-Hill Ryerson, 1962.

Bird, Will R. *And We Go On: A Memoir of the Great War.* Introduction and afterword by David Williams. 1930. Montreal and Kingston: McGill-Queen's University Press, 2014.

Bird, Will R. *Ghosts Have Warm Hands.* Toronto: Clarke, Irwin, 1968.

Bliss, J. M. "The Methodist Church and World War I." In *Conscription 1917.* Toronto: University of Toronto Press, n.d.

Bowker, Alan. *A Time Such as There Never Was Before: Canada after the Great War.* Toronto: Dundurn, 2014.

Boyden. Joseph. *Three Day Road.* Toronto: Penguin Canada, 2005.

Bray, R. Matthew. "'Fighting as an Ally': The English-Canadian Patriotic Response to the Great War." *Canadian Historical Review* vol. 61, no. 2 (1980).

Brown, Robert Craig. *Robert Laird Borden: A Biography,* vol. 2, *1914–1937.* Toronto: Macmillan of Canada, 1980.

Brown, Robert Craig, and Donald Loveridge. "Unrequited Faith: Recruiting the CEF 1914–1918." *Revue Internationale d'Histoire Militaire* no. 54, Edition Canadienne (1982).

Brown, Robert Craig, and Ramsay Cook. *Canada, 1896–1921: A Nation Transformed.* Toronto: McClelland and Stewart, 1974.

Clements, Captain Robert N. *Merry Hell: The Story of the 25th Battalion (Nova Scotia Regiment), Canadian Expeditionary Force, 1914–1919.* Edited by Brian Douglas Tennyson. Toronto: University of Toronto Press, 2013.

Cleverdon, Catherine L. *The Woman Suffrage Movement in Canada.* 1950. Toronto: University of Toronto Press, 1974.

Cook, Tim. *At the Sharp End: Canadians Fighting the Great War, 1914–1916,* vol. 1. 2007; Toronto: Penguin Canada, 2009.

———. "Battles of the Imagined Past: Canada's Great War and Memory." *Canadian Historical Review* vol. 95, no. 3 (September 2014).

———. *Clio's Warriors: Canadian Historians and the Writing of the World Wars.* Vancouver: UBC Press, 2006.

———. "'More a medicine than a beverage': 'Demon Rum' and the Canadian Trench Soldier of the First World War." *Canadian Military History* vol. 9, no. 1 (Winter 2000).

———. *The Secret History of Soldiers: How Canadians Survived the Great War.* Toronto: Allen Lane, 2018.

———. *Shock Troops: Canadians Fighting the Great War, 1917–1918,* vol. 2. 2008. Toronto: Penguin Canada, 2009.

———. *Vimy: The Battle and the Legend.* Toronto: Allen Lane, 2017.

———. "Wet Canteens and Worrying Mothers: Alcohol, Soldiers and Temperance Groups in the Great War." *Histoire Sociale/Social History* vol. 35, no. 70 (November 2002).

Craig, Grace Morris. *But This Is Our War.* Toronto: University of Toronto Press, 1981.

Davies, Adriana A., and Jeff Keshen, eds. *The Frontier of Patriotism: Alberta and the First World War.* Calgary: University of Calgary Press, 2016.

Davis, C. Mark. "I'll Drink to That: The Rise and Fall of Prohibition in the Maritime Provinces, 1900–1930" (PhD dissertation, Department of History, McMaster University, 1990).

Davis, Wade. "Of War and Remembrance." In *In Flanders Fields: 100 Years.* Edited by Amanda Betts. Toronto: Alfred A. Knopf Canada, 2015.

———. *Into the Silence: The Great War, Mallory, and the Conquest of Everest.* Toronto: Vintage Canada Edition, 2012.

Dennis, Patrick M. *Reluctant Warriors: Canadian Conscripts and the Great War.* Vancouver: UBC Press, 2017.

Eksteins, Modris. *Rites of Spring: The Great War and the Birth of the Modern Age*. Toronto: Lester & Orpen Dennys, 1989.

Epperly, Elizabeth Rollins. *The Fragrance of Sweet-Grass: L. M. Montgomery's Heroines and the Pursuit of Romance*. Toronto: University of Toronto Press, 1992.

Fisher, Susan R. *Boys and Girls in No Man's Land: English-Canadian Children and the First World War*. Toronto: University of Toronto Press, 2011.

Forbes, Ernest R. *Challenging the Regional Stereotype: Essays on the 20th Century Maritimes*. Fredericton: Acadiensis Press, 1989.

———. "The East-Coast Rum-Running Economy." In *Drink in Canada: Historical Essays*. Edited by Cheryl Krasnick Warsh. Montreal and Kingston: McGill-Queen's University Press, 1993.

———. "Prohibition and the Social Gospel in Nova Scotia," *Acadiensis* vol. 1, no. 1 (Autumn 1971).

Forbes, E. R., and D. A. Muise, eds. *The Atlantic Provinces in Confederation*. Toronto: University of Toronto Press, and Fredericton: Acadiensis Press, 1993.

Gates, Michael. *From the Klondike to Berlin: The Yukon in World War I*. Madeira Park, BC: Lost Moose, 2017.

Geller, Gloria. "The War-time Elections Act of 1917 and the Canadian Women's Movement." *Atlantis* vol. 2, no. 1 (Fall 1976).

German, Commander Tony. *The Sea Is at Our Gates: The History of the Canadian Navy*. Toronto: McClelland & Stewart, 1991.

Gibson, Charles Dana, "Victim or Participant? Allied Fishing Fleets and U-Boat Attacks in World Wars I and II." *Northern Mariner* vol. 1, no. 4 (October 1991).

Gimblett, Richard H., ed. *The Naval Service of Canada, 1910–2010: The Centennial Story*. Toronto: Dundurn, 2009.

Glassford, Sarah, and Amy Shaw, eds. *A Sisterhood of Suffering and Service: Women and Girls of Canada and Newfoundland during the First World War*. Vancouver: UBC Press, 2012.

Granatstein, J. L. *The Greatest Victory: Canada's One Hundred Days, 1918*. Don Mills: Oxford University Press, 2014.

———. *Hell's Corner: An Illustrated History of Canada's Great War, 1914–1918*. Vancouver: Douglas & McIntyre, 2004.

Granatstein, J. L., and J. M. Hitsman. *Broken Promises: A History of Conscription in Canada*. Toronto: Oxford University Press, 1977.

Granatstein, J. L., and Dean F. Oliver. *The Oxford Companion to Canadian Military History*. Don Mills: Oxford University Press, 2011.

Hadley, Michael L., and Roger Sarty. *Tin-Pots and Pirate Ships: Canadian Naval Forces and German Sea Raiders, 1880–1918*. Montreal and Kingston: McGill-Queen's University Press, 1991.

Hadley, Michael L. *U-Boats against Canada: German Submarines in Canadian Waters*. Montreal and Kingston: McGill-Queen's University Press, 1985.

Hallowell, Gerald. *The August Gales: The Tragic Loss of Fishing Schooners in the North Atlantic, 1926 and 1927*. Halifax: Nimbus, 2013.

Harrison, Charles Yale. *Generals Die in Bed*. 1930. Hamilton: Potlatch Publications, 1975.

Hebb, Ross, ed. *Letters Home: Maritimers and the Great War, 1914–1918*. Halifax: Nimbus, 2014.

Heron, Craig. *Booze: A Distilled History*. Toronto: Between the Lines, 2003.

Humphries, Mark Osborne. "The Horror at Home: The Canadian Military and the 'Great' Influenza Pandemic of 1918." *Journal of the Canadian Historical Association* New Series, vol. 16 (2005).

———. *The Last Plague: Spanish Influenza and the Politics of Public Health in Canada*. Toronto: University of Toronto Press, 2013.

Hunt, M. S., ed. *Nova Scotia's Part in the Great War*. Halifax: Nova Scotia Veteran Publishing, 1920.

Itani, Frances. *Tell*. Toronto: HarperCollins, 2014.

Janigan, Mary. "Treason to Their Memory." In *In Flanders Fields: 100 Years*. Edited by Amanda Betts. Toronto: Alfred A. Knopf Canada, 2015.

Keshen, Jeffrey A. *Propaganda and Censorship during Canada's Great War*. Edmonton: University of Alberta Press, 1996.

Kitchen, Martin. "The German Invasion of Canada in the First World War." *International History Review* vol. 7, no. 2 (May 1985).

Kitz, Janet F. *Shattered City: The Halifax Explosion and the Road to Recovery*. Halifax: Nimbus, 1989.

Lacey, Laurie. *Ethnicity and the German Descendants of Lunenburg County, Nova Scotia*. Halifax: Ethnic Heritage Series, International Education Centre, Saint Mary's University, 1982.

Lackenbauer, P. Whitney. "Soldiers Behaving Badly: CEF Soldier 'Rioting' in Canada during the First World War." In *The Apathetic and the Defiant: Case Studies of Canadian Mutiny and Disobedience, 1812–1919*. Edited by Craig Leslie Mantle. Kingston: Canadian Defence Academy Press and Toronto: Dundurn, 2007.

Lehmann, Heinz. *The German Canadians, 1750–1937: Immigration, Settlement and Culture*. Translated, edited, and introduced by Gerhard P. Bassler (published in German in March 1939). St. John's: Jesperson Press, 1986.

Litt, Paul. "Canada Invaded! The Great War, Mass Culture, and Canadian Cultural Nationalism." In *Canada and the First World War: Essays in Honour of Robert Craig Brown*. Edited by David Mackenzie. Toronto: University of Toronto Press, 2005.

MacDonald, F. B., and John J. Gardiner, *The Twenty-Fifth Battalion, Canadian Expeditionary Force: Nova Scotia's Famous Regiment in World War One.* Sydney: J. A. Chadwick, 1983.

MacDonald, Sharon M. H. "Hidden Costs, Hidden Labour: Women in Nova Scotia during Two World Wars" (master's thesis, Atlantic Canada Studies, Saint Mary's University, 1999).

———. "Mary Russell Chesley." *Women Suffrage and Beyond: Confronting the Democratic Deficit.* June 20, 2012, http://womensuffrage.org/?p=1164.

Mackenzie, David, ed. *Canada and the First World War: Essays in Honour of Robert Craig Brown.* Toronto: University of Toronto Press, 2005.

Mackenzie, David. "Eastern Approaches: Maritime Canada and Newfoundland," In *Canada and the First World War: Essays in Honour of Robert Craig Brown.* Edited by David Mackenzie. Toronto: University of Toronto Press, 2005.

MacMillan, Margaret. *The War That Ended the Peace: The Road to 1914.* Toronto: Penguin Canada, 2013.

McKay, Ian. "The 1910s: The Stillborn Triumph of Progressive Reform." In *The Atlantic Provinces in Confederation.* Edited by E. R. Forbes and D. A. Muise. Toronto: University of Toronto Press, 1993.

McKay, Ian, and Jamie Swift. *The Vimy Trap: Or, How We Learned to Stop Worrying and Love the Great War.* Toronto: Between the Lines, 2016.

McLaughlin, K. M. *The Germans in Canada,* Canadian Historical Association booklet no. 11, Canada's Ethnic Groups, Ottawa, 1985.

Mainville, Curtis. *Till the Boys Come Home: Life on the Home Front, Queens County, NB, 1914–1918.* Fredericton: Goose Lane, 2015.

Mann, Susan, ed. *The War Diary of Clare Gass, 1915–1918.* Montreal and Kingston: McGill-Queen's University Press, 2000.

Marshall, Debbie. *Firing Lines: Three Canadian Women Write the First World War.* Toronto: Dundurn, 2017.

Mennel, Robert M. *Testimonies and Secrets: The Story of a Nova Scotia Family, 1844–1977.* Toronto: University of Toronto Press, 2013.

Milner, Marc. *Canada's Navy: The First Century.* Toronto: University of Toronto Press, 1999.

Montgomery, L. M. *Rilla of Ingleside.* 1920. Toronto: Penguin, 2010.

Morton, Desmond, *A Military History of Canada,* 5th ed. Toronto: McClelland & Stewart, 2007.

———. *Fight or Pay: Soldiers' Families in the Great War.* Vancouver: UBC Press, 2004.

———. "Supporting Soldiers' Families: Separation Allowance, Assigned Pay, and the Unexpected." In *Canada and the First World War: Essays in Honour*

of Robert Craig Brown. Edited by David Mackenzie. Toronto: University of
Toronto Press, 2005.

———. "Supporting Soldiers' Wives and Families in the Great War: What
Was Transformed?." In *A Sisterhood of Suffering and Service: Women and
Girls of Canada and Newfoundland during the First World War.* Edited by
Sarah Glassford and Amy Shaw. Vancouver: UBC Press, 2012.

———. *When Your Number's Up: The Canadian Soldier in the First World War.*
Toronto: Random House Canada, 1993.

Morton, Desmond, and J. L. Granatstein. *Marching to Armageddon: Canadians
and the Great War, 1914–1919.* Toronto: Lester & Orpen Dennys, 1989.

Morton, Desmond, and Glenn Wright. *Winning the Second Battle: Canadian
Veterans and the Return to Civilian Life, 1915–1930.* Toronto: University of
Toronto Press, 1987.

Mossman, David. *Going Over: A Nova Scotian Soldier in World War I.*
Lawrencetown Beach, Nova Scotia: Pottersfield Press, 2014.

Pettigrew, Eileen. *The Silent Enemy: Canada and the Deadly Flu of 1918.*
Saskatoon: Western Producer Prairie Books, 1983.

Prince, Robert S. "The Mythology of War: How the Canadian Daily
Newspaper Depicted the Great War" (PhD dissertation, Department of
History, University of Toronto, 1998).

Quiney, Linda J. "Gendering Patriotism: Canadian Volunteer Nurses as the
Female 'Soldiers' of the Great War." In *A Sisterhood of Suffering and Service:
Women and Girls of Canada and Newfoundland during the First World War.*
Edited by Sarah Glassford and Amy Shaw. Vancouver: UBC Press, 2012.

Quinn, Shawna M. *Agnes Warner and the Nursing Sisters of the Great War.*
Fredericton: Goose Lane, 2010.

Reid, Mark Collin, ed. *Canada's Great War Album: Our Memories of the First
World War.* Toronto: HarperCollins, 2014.

Remarque, Erich Maria. *All Quiet on the Western Front.* 1929. London:
Mayflower Paperbacks, 1968.

Rubio, Mary, and Elizabeth Waterston, eds. *The Selected Journals of L. M.
Montgomery,* vol. 2: 1910–1921. Toronto: Oxford University Press, 1987.

Rutherdale, Robert. *Hometown Horizons: Local Reponses to Canada's Great War.*
Vancouver: UBC Press, 2004.

Sangster "Divided on the Home Front." In *Canada's Great War Album: Our
Memories of the First World War.* Edited by Mark Collin Reid. Toronto:
HarperCollins, 2014.

———. "Mobilizing Women for War." In *Canada and the First World War:
Essays in Honour of Robert Craig Brown.* Edited by David Mackenzie.
Toronto: University of Toronto Press, 2005.

Shaw, Amy J. *Crisis of Conscience: Conscientious Objection in Canada during the First World War.* Vancouver: UBC Press, 2009.

———. "Expanding the Narrative: A First World War with Women, Children, and Grief." *Canadian Historical Review* vol. 95, no. 3 (September 2014).

Silliker, Gary. *A Deadly Drive: The Miramichi Experience during the Great War.* Victoria: Friesen Press, 2014.

Tennyson, Brian Douglas. *Canada's Great War, 1914–1918: How Canada Helped Save the British Empire and Became a North American Nation.* Lanham, Maryland: Rowman & Littlefield, 2015.

———. *Nova Scotia at War, 1914–1919.* Halifax: Nimbus, 2017.

Vance, Jonathan F. *A Township at War.* Waterloo: Wilfrid Laurier University Press, n.d.

———. *Death So Noble: Memory, Meaning, and the First World War.* Vancouver: UBC Press, 1997.

———. *Maple Leaf Empire: Canada, Britain, and Two World Wars.* Don Mills: Oxford University Press, 2012.

———. "Remembering Armageddon." In *Canada and the First World War: Essays in Honour of Robert Craig Brown.* Edited by David Mackenzie. Toronto: University of Toronto Press, 2005.

Wallace, Frederick William. *Roving Fisherman: An Autobiography.* Gardenvale, QC: Canadian Fisherman, 1955.

Warsh, Cheryl Krasnick, ed. *Drink in Canada: Historical Essays.* Montreal and Kingston: McGill-Queen's University Press, 1993.

Waseem, Gertrud. *Germans.* Halifax: Nimbus, 2000.

Wilson, Barbara M., ed. *Ontario and the First World War, 1914-1918: A Collection of Documents.* Toronto: Champlain Society, University of Toronto Press, 1977.

"'We Will Remember': War Memorials in Canada." Centre for Distance Learning and Innovation, Newfoundland and Labrador. cdli.ca/monuments/index.htm.

IMAGE CREDITS

Mahone Bay Museum, Accession # 2018.1.6 (page 6)

Nova Scotia Archives (pages 49, 92, 112, 137, 147, 174)

Library and Archives Canada, 3635703 (page 20), 3394817 (page 104),
3667222 (page 159), 3261367 (page 195)

Courtesy of the Nova Scotia Museum, Fisheries Museum of the Atlantic,
F2010.17.21 (page 46), F93.1288.3 (page 57), F93.1288.9 (page 126)

Royal Canadian Legion, Branch no. 24, Bridgewater (page 60)

Royal Canadian Legion, Branch no. 44, Chester, courtesy of Marion Fryday-
Cook (pages 208-9)

Royal Canadian Legion, Branch no. 23, Lunenburg (pages 41, 120, 183)

Royal Canadian Legion, Branch no. 49, Mahone Bay (page 191)

Courtesy of Hugh Corkum (page 59)

Courtesy of Stephen Ernst (pages 169)

Courtesy of Ralph Getson (pages 29, 188, 214)

Courtesy of Jennifer James (page 45)

Courtesy of Regan Murphy, Yarmouth (page 108)

Courtesy of Barbara Spindler (page 143)

Author's photo (page 207)

Progress-Enterprise, Lunenburg, June 7, 1916 (page 7)

Bridgewater Bulletin, August 13, 1918 (page 140), August 6, 1918 (page 164)

Canadian Fisherman, September 1917. Women's Auxiliary, Organization of Resources Committee, in Co-operation with The Hon. W.J. Hanna, Food Controller (page 161)

INDEX